MW00510930

NeNa's Garden

Recipes
from the Heart

Kathy Boyd

Faith Publishing
Hartsville, South Carolina

ISBN 0-9711664-0-4

Library of Congress Control Number: 2001134130

First Printing   March 2002   3,000 copies
Second Printing   November 2002   3,000 copies

Faith Publishing
154 Erwin Road
Hartsville, SC 29550

WIMMER
COOKBOOKS

ConsolidatedGraphics
1-800-548-2537

Dedication

Beth Cox Brown
This book is dedicated to
my mother who taught me that
love is unselfish.

And now that these three remain:
faith, hope, love. But the greatest of
these is love.

1 Corinthians 13:13

Introduction

My younger brother, Alex, was diagnosed with colorectal cancer in August 1999 at the age of forty-three. I helplessly watched as he underwent chemotherapy, radiation and a colostomy. Almost a year after his initial treatment, the doctors have found that the cancer has spread to his lungs. As I again watch him struggle with his cancer and chemotherapy treatments, I feel so terribly helpless.

The idea of NeNa's Garden has been thought of out of love for my brother and my need to reach out and try to make a difference in the fight against colorectal cancer. Big sisters should be able to fix things for their little brothers and little brothers should not get cancer. You think it will never happen. Trying to raise public awareness about colorectal cancer and the importance of screening and early detection is one way I feel I can make a difference. If just **ONE** person reads the information in this book and gets screened, it may save a life. The knowledge that **ONE** person learns will be passed on to others. The small beginning can develop into lives being saved because of early detection and also spare families the heartache of a loved one fighting this disease.

During the process of compiling NeNa's Garden, I started praying the Prayer of Jabez:

Oh, that You would bless me indeed,
and enlarge my territory
that Your hand would be with me,
and that You would keep me from evil.

God has truly blessed me and my territory has been enlarged. Doors have opened for me and things have happened only because God has had His hand on me. Through Him NeNa's Garden blossomed and became a reality.

I don't think any of us are really aware that what we do in our lives touches other people's lives. God has a master plan for us. He moves people in and out of our lives and we each leave a mark on the other. I have met people and made new friends because of Nena's Garden and each one has added love to my life. We all have stories to tell and the way we live does affect other people. We all have a bond with each other through our life experiences. We all have life lessons to learn and some are so difficult but through them we need to remember that loving and caring for people will be one of the most important things we do in our lifetime. Our happiness, contentment, peace and joy flow out of love.

It is my sincere hope that NeNa's Garden will touch many people and will help research find a cure for colorectal cancer and my brother. I have big dreams for this battle and my brother.

Kathy Boyd

Acknowledgments

NeNa's Garden is a collection of recipes from family, friends and community. Without all the support I received, this project would not have been possible.

First, I want to thank God for giving me the faith to believe that I could accomplish this task. Special thanks to my daddy, Howard Brown, my aunts Judy Brown and Anne Dawkins, my brothers Bo and Alex, sister-in-laws Lucy and Debbie for their love and support.

Thanks to the many friends who gave their time to help; Cecelia Alford, Diane Ollis, Beth Rush, Joan Coker, Trey and Nita at Jiffy Print, Jane Truett, Mary Jane McDonald, Jackie Segars, Margaret Reaves, Gail Mobley, Jim Stanton, Sylvia Avant and Kyle Segars. A big thank you to Sharon Needham for her many unselfish hours of work and guidance on this book.

I thank my husband, Edwin, for his input, support and also his many hours of typing. Last but not least, my children, Benton and Weldon, for their patience during this process. They can finally have their computer back.

Cover Art Design

The cover art was designed by Mary Grayson Segars. It is an oil painting of a flower garden at my family's farm. The garden is in memory of my mother, Beth Cox Brown, who was known as NeNa to her five grand-children, D, Lauren, Alex, Benton and Weldon. It is NeNa's Garden.

Mary is basically a self-taught artist, having graduated with a biology degree from the College of William and Mary. From the age of nine, drawing has been an ever-present hobby for her, leading to years of dabbling in pencil sketching, pastels and scratchboard. Three years ago, Mary decided it was time to take her lifelong art obsession seriously. She enrolled in a few workshops and began a course of self-study and practice that has opened the doors to a new passion for oil painting. Mary lives with her family in Beaufort, South Carolina, where she is represented by Art' n Soul Gallery and the Art Market Gallery.

National Colorectal Cancer Research Alliance

The National Colorectal Cancer Research Alliance (NCCRA) was cofounded by NBC Today show co-anchor Katie Couric, nationally known fund raiser Lilly Tartikoff, and the Entertainment Industry (EIF), a California-based 501(c)3 nonprofit organization.

The NCCRA proposes to combine basic, clinical, and epidemiological research, conducted by the nation's leading scientists, to study the risk factors associated with colorectal cancer and identify potential preventive treatment therapies and ultimately a treatment.

The NCCRA's researchers will also be searching for better, non-invasive tests to help detect colorectal cancer in its early, easy to treat stages.

The NCCRA will strive to raise public awareness about the nation's second leading cancer killer, as the disease is more than 90% curable if caught early and if potentially cancerous colorectal polyps are removed. Even though the disease is highly preventable, fewer than half of all Americans over the age of 50 have ever been tested for the disease, according to the Centers for Disease Control.

NCCRA's Funding Promise

Every penny raised by the National Colorectal Cancer Research Alliance is spent on public education efforts and in support of the best and most advanced research, looking for better tests, treatments, and cures for colorectal cancer.

NCCRA's goal is to raise not only money, but awareness. Colorectal cancer is curable - if caught early. And, since the disease takes between 5 and 15 years to develope, there's plenty of time for people to be tested and treated - preventing millions of surgical procedures or chemotherapy treatments.

Get tested. This one can be cured.

Nobody is immune to cancer, However, it can be beaten when you discover it early. Today, cancer of the colon has become one of the worst killers in our country, largely because of our discomfort in dealing with it. Don't be afraid. Don't kid yourself that it couldn't happen to you. Regardless of your sex, age, race, or general state of health, you may be at risk. Just get tested. Do it for yourself and the ones you love.

# Colorectal Cancer ... What is it?

Colorectal cancer, or cancer of the colon or rectum, often begins as a polyp, a tiny growth inside the colon or rectum which later becomes cancer. While colorectal cancer is the second-leading cause of cancer deaths in the United States, it often goes untested, even though it is also one of the most easily detected and treatable cancers. More Americans die each year from colorectal cancer than from breast cancer or AIDS.

★ It is estimated 156,000 Americans were diagnosed with colorectal cancer in 1999, and approximately 57,000 died from the disease.

★ Up to two-thirds of those deaths are preventable with simple screening and prevention methods.

★ Most colon cancers begin as benign polyps, and cancer can be prevented by their removal.

★ Men and women are equally at risk for colorectal cancer.

★ The older you are, the higher your risk; nevertheless, 13,000 cases will still be diagnosed in people under the age of 50.

★ For most Americans, standard screening with a sigmoidoscopy and checking the stool for blood should begin at 50.

★ Those with family history of colorectal cancer, or polyps, or a personal history of inflammatory bowel disease are at a higher risk.

★ Colorectal cancer is most curable when found before it causes symptoms. More than 90% of colorectal cancers can be cured when caught in their earliest stages.

★ When symptoms are present, the cancer may still be curable if not ignored. Symptoms include any blood from the rectum, change in bowel habits, persistent abdominal cramps, weight loss, anemia and/or unusual fatigue.

★ Regular exercise and folic acid supplements may help to prevent colorectal cancer, but are no substitute for regular screening.

Know your Risks★★★

There are simple steps anyone can take to greatly reduce their risk of this preventable, yet deadly, cancer.

Know your family: If an immediate family member has had colon polyps, colon, rectal, uterine, breast, prostate, or testicular cancer, then you should be tested when you are 10 years younger than they were diagnosed.

Exercise: Even a small amount each day can work towards reducing colon polyp growth.

Hormone Replacement Therapy: If you are a woman, and past the age of menopause, ask your doctor about studies which have shown a potentially promising link between hormone replacement therapy and reduced colorectal polyp growth.

Folic Acid, Aspirin or Cox-2 pain relievers: Recent research has found that daily folic acid supplements, taken over a long period of time, may reduce your chances of developing colorectal cancer. Taking an aspirin a day also has been shown to potentially reduce pre-cancerous colon polyp growth. Preliminary studies have shown reductions for newer, similar prescription pain medicine.

RISK FACTORS

★ Both men and women are at equal risk for colorectal cancer

★ The older you are, the higher the risk; nevertheless, 13,000 cases will still be diagnosed in people under 50

★ African Americans have higher colorectal cancer rates than men and women of other racial and ethnic groups.

★ Other unhealthy habits like smoking and being overweight increase your risk of colorectal cancer.

★ A big risk factor is having family history or personal history of colorectal cancer, inflammatory bowel disease, colon polyps, cancer of the breast, or uterus.

Colorectal Cancer★★★

It's One Cancer You Can Easily Avoid.

Colorectal cancer usually develops with few - if any - symptoms, until it's too late. However, if caught in the early stages, the disease has a **greater than 90% cure rate**. Screening is by far the most important thing you can do to fight colorectal cancer. With regular screenings and early polyp or growth removal, the chances are even better you can avoid the silent killer.

Choices you make:

★ Exercise at least a small amount daily.

★ Don't smoke.

★ Keep your weight in check.

★ Limit your alcohol intake.

Actions you take:

★ Regular preventive testing, such as a FOBT (Fecal Occult Blood Test), Sigmoidoscopy, Colonoscopy, or Double Barium Enema.

★ Talk to your doctor about risk factors.

★ Talk to your family to see if anyone has had polyps, cancer of the colon, rectum, uterus or breast.

Other Ways to Reduce Your Risk:

★ Talk to your physician about taking an aspirin daily.

★ Talk with your doctor about taking a multivitamin containing folic acid every day

★ Talk to you physician about hormone replacement therapy, if you are a post-menopausal woman.

Tests Which Can Save Your Life

You should discuss your potential risk factors with your doctor to determine if you should begin screening before the age of 50 and which tests to use.

Fecal Blood Occult Test

Taken in the privacy of your own home, and mailed to a lab for testing, this test examines a smear sample of your stool (feces) for hidden blood - a sign of possible colorectal cancer. It should be done once a year.

Sigmoidoscopy

A 10-minute outpatient procedure every 5 years to examine the lower third of the colon, where 50% of cancers and polyps occur.

Double Contrast Barium Enema

A radiological procedure recommended every 5-10 years to detect the presence of large polyps and cancers in the entire colon and rectum. If abnormal, a colonoscopy will be required.

Colonoscopy

The best and most comprehensive weapon against colorectal cancer, this procedure both detects and prevents the disease, through removal of pre-cancerous colon polyps. Recommended every 10 years on an outpatient basis, it takes less than an hour and can replace fecal blood testing, sigmoidoscopy, and barium enema.

You Can Do This

Please pass on the information you read about on colorectal cancer to your family, friends and loved ones. Call your doctor and get tested. It may one of the most important things you do. It may save your life.

★Contents★

Bear with each other and forgive whatever grievances you may have against one another. Forgive as the Lord forgave you. And over all these virtures put on love, which binds them all together in perfect unity.

Colossians 4:10

★Shining Star★

Walter Alexander Brown
My little brother

A silver star is the national symbol for colorectal cancer and these celebrities are stars for taking the time and caring enough to respond to my request for a recipe. I am so touched by their kindness. Their giving has made such an impact on my family.

My brother, Alex, has been such an inspiration to me over the past two years. His outlook, attitude and faith are unwavering. He, like my mother, has taught me that love is unselfish. My little brother is truly a shining silver star.

And do not forget to do good
and to share with others,
for with such sacrifices, God is pleased.

Hebrews 13:16

Southwestern Cheese Spread

Mark and Alicia O'Meara

Pro Golfer

1	(12-ounce) package cream cheese	1	(71/2-ounce) jar pesto
2	tablespoons butter	1/2	cup sun-dried tomatoes packed in oil, chopped and drained
3	cloves garlic, minced		Basil leaves
	Pinch of black pepper		
1/2	pound provolone cheese, thinly sliced		

In a medium bowl, mix cream cheese, butter, garlic, and pepper. Set aside. Line an 8-inch round bowl with plastic wrap, leaving an overhang. Overlap about two-thirds of the provolone cheese to cover bottom and sides of the bowl. Layer cream cheese mixture, pesto, and tomatoes. Repeat layers. End with remaining provolone. Fold plastic wrap over loaf. Press gently to compact. Chill at least two hours. Fold plastic back. Invert onto serving platter. Garnish with basil leaves. Serve with crackers or thinly sliced French bread and Italian salami. Yield: 15 to 25 servings.

Cold Avocado Soup

Linda Evans

Crystal on Dynasty

1	avocado	1	teaspoon curry powder
2	cups chicken broth	1/2	teaspoon salt
1	cup sour cream		Juice of 1/2 lemon

Put all ingredients in a blender. Blend until smooth. Add more chicken broth if too thick. Chill 2 hours. Yield: 2 servings.

Cottage Cheese Salad

Vanna White

Wheel Of Fortune

1   *(32-ounce) container plain cottage cheese*
1   *(3-ounce) package lime jello*
1   *(8-ounce) can crushed pineapple, in own juice*

1   *(8-ounce) container Cool Whip*
    Chopped walnuts or pecans (optional)

Place cottage cheese in a large bowl and pour dry jello mix on top. Mix well. Drain pineapple and add to mixture. Fold in whipped topping. Add nuts if desired. Refrigerate until ready to serve. Yield: 6 to 8 servings.

Melon Mold
Troy Aikman
Dallas Cowboy Quarterback, Retired

2 (3-ounce) packages orange
   jello
4 tablespoons sugar
2 cups boiling water
2 cups lemon-lime soda

2 cups cantaloupe or honey
   dew melon balls
2 (3-ounce) packages cream
   cheese, softened

In a large bowl, dissolve jello and sugar in boiling water; add soda. Chill two and one-half cups of jello until syrupy thick. Let remaining jello sit at room temperature. Add melon balls to thickened jello and chill in a 2-quart mold or dish until set but not firm. Blend reserved jello into cream cheese. Chill until very thick. When thickened, beat cream cheese mixture until very fluffy and spoon over fruit layer. Chill until set. Yield: 12 servings.

Helping kids. . .one dream at a time.

THE
Troy Aikman
FOUNDATION

Mississippi Medley

Leeza Gibbons

TV Talk Show Host

2   cups chopped fresh spinach
1   large tomato, chopped and
    drained
1   small onion, chopped
1   (15 1/2-ounce) can black-eyed
    peas, drained

1/4   cup olive oil
3   teaspoons balsamic vinegar
      Salt to taste
      Black pepper to taste

In a large bowl, combine all ingredients and mix well. Chill and serve. Yield: 4 to 6 servings.

Kathy —
I'm not much of
a grand chef...
hope this helps.
Good luck with your
project.   Leeza

Shrimp Salad

Cale and Betty Jo Yarborough

Nascar Racing Legend

1	cup rice	1 lemon, sliced
3	pounds fresh shrimp	1 1/2 cups chopped celery

Sauce

1 cup sour cream	Paprika
1 cup Miracle Whip salad dressing	Salt and pepper to taste
1 onion, grated	

Cook rice according to package directions. Let cool. Boil shrimp with lemon in a large pot of water. Cool. Peel and devein. In a large bowl, combine all sauce ingredients. Mix well. Stir in rice, shrimp, and celery. Chill 1 hour. Yield: 5 to 6 servings.

Tomato and Onion Salad

Arnold Palmer

Pro Golfer

Sliced Beefsteak tomatoes	Bleu cheese crumbles
Sliced Vidalia onions (or Bermuda if Vidilia not in season)	Vinaigrette dressing
	Salt and pepper to taste

Layer tomatoes and onions on a salad plate. Sprinkle with bleu cheese crumbles. Pour desired amount of dressing over top.

Focaccia

Rooster's Gourmet Market and Gifts

Greensboro, North Carolina

5 1/4 cups bread flour
2 tablespoons yeast
1 tablespoon salt
2 1/4 cups water

1/2 cup olive oil or flavored oil
Sarah's Mediterranean Sea
salt or herbs of choice

Preheat oven to 400 degrees. In a large mixing bowl, combine flour, yeast, and salt. Add water and oil. Stir with a fork to combine. Turn out onto counter and knead until smooth and springs back to touch. Place in bowl and coat with a small amount of oil. Cover and let rise until double...about 1 hour. Remove and punch down. Shape into desired shape and let rise 20-30 minutes in a warm place. Make depressions in dough using fingertips. Place on a greased baking sheet. Drizzle with garlic oil and sprinkle with sea salt. Bake at 400 degrees for 15 minutes or until browned.

Kugle

Steve and Candace Garvey

Former 1st Baseman Los Angeles Dodgers

2 (12-ounce) packages medium egg noodles
1 stick unsalted butter, melted
1 (16-ounce) container sour cream
3/4 (16-ounce) container lowfat cottage cheese

3 eggs
1 teaspoon vanilla
3/4 cup raisins (optional)
1 tablespoon cinnamon
1 2/3 cups sugar

Preheat oven to 325 degrees. In a large saucepan, cook noodles according to package directions. Grease a 9x13-inch glass casserole dish. In a large bowl, combine butter and next four ingredients. Add raisins if desired. Add noodles and carefully mix with hands. Place noodle mixture in prepared dish one handful at the time. Mix cinnamon and sugar together. Sprinkle on top of noodles. Bake at 325 degrees for 1 hour and 30 minutes. Yield: 6 to 8 servings.

Mouth Watering Bread Pudding

Bill Cosby

**Actor, Author, Comedian, Creator of "Fat Albert"
and the "Little Bill" Series**

1	*pint of half-and-half*	2	*teaspoons vanilla extract*
1	*stick butter*	1	*egg, beaten*
1/2	*pint heavy cream*	6-7	*slices stale bread*
1/2	*cup honey*		*Fresh grapes (yes, that's*
	Dash of ground nutmeg		*correct)*

Preheat oven to 450 degrees. In a medium saucepan, combine half and half, butter, cream, and honey. Slowly heat until warm. Stir in nutmeg, vanilla, and egg. Grease the inside of a covered glass casserole dish. Tear bread into bite-sized pieces. In prepared dish, layer bread and grapes. End with layer of bread. Pour half and half mixture on top of bread and grapes. It should wet all of the bread, if not, add a little milk. Cover the dish and place in a pan of water. Bake at 450 degrees for 10 minutes. Lower heat to 350 degrees and cook 35 to 40 minutes.

Note: Not for dieters! Great hot or cold.

Poplar Muffins

Max and Denalyn Lucado

**Author Of Many Best-Selling Books Including The Applause of Heaven,
When God Whispers Your Name, God Came Near**

1/4	*cup sugar*	1	*egg*
2	*cups flour*	1	*cup milk*
3	*teaspoons baking soda*	1/4	*cup oil*
1	*teaspoon salt*		

In a medium bowl combine sugar, flour, baking soda, and salt. Add egg, milk, and oil. Stir well. Batter will be lumpy. Spoon batter into a greased muffin tin or paper liners, filling two-thirds full. Bake at 400 degrees for 20 minutes. Yield: 12 muffins.

Note: You always have the ingredients for these.

Grandma's Spoon Bread

Genevieve Peterkin

SC Author- Heaven is a Beautiful Place

1	quart milk	3	tablespoons Crisco
1	cup cornmeal	3	eggs, separated
1	teaspoon salt		

In a medium saucepan, heat milk to boiling point. Stir in cornmeal and salt. Add Crisco. Stir constantly 5 minutes. Do not boil. Cool mixture. Add well beaten egg yolks. Beat egg whites until a thick froth and fold into mixture. Pour batter into a greased 2-quart casserole. Bake at 350 degrees for 40 minutes. Serve immediately.

Gin Fizz Pie

Pat Sajak

Host of Wheel of Fortune

6	strips thick bacon, 1-inch pieces	6	slices Jack or American cheese
1	onion, diced	1	dozen eggs
1	(28-ounce) can peeled tomatoes	1/2	cup cream
10	fresh mushrooms, sliced		Parmesan cheese
2	cans Vienna sausages, 1/4-inch slices		Pimento strips
			Sour cream
			A shaker of gin fizzes

In a large skillet, fry bacon pieces until crisp. Pour off most of grease. Brown onion in remaining bacon grease. Mix in tomatoes, mushrooms, and sausage. Let simmer 15 minutes. During last few minutes stir in cheese slices. Gently beat eggs with cream. Stir into mixture. Bake at 350 degrees for 30 minutes or until eggs have cooked to nice golden brown crust. For last five minutes of baking sprinkle cheese over crust. Serve in pie slices. Garnish with thin strips of pimento on each slice and a bowl of sour cream for those who desire this final touch.

Note: Mix a shaker of gin fizzes on entry of pan into oven, and enjoy until eggs are done.

Alaska King Crab Legs
Bobby Allison
Retired Nascar Great

Alaska crab legs   *Melted butter*

Place melted butter and crab legs in a large zip lock bag. Steam in microwave 2 minutes. Yield: 2 servings.

Blackened Redfish
Barbara Bush
Former First Lady

1	tablespoon paprika	3/4	teaspoon black pepper
2 1/2	teaspoons salt	1/2	teaspoon dried thyme
1	teaspoon onion powder	1/2	teaspoon dried oregano
1	teaspoon cayenne pepper	3	pounds redfish, filleted
1	teaspoon garlic powder		Melted butter or margarine
3/4	teaspoon white pepper		

In a medium bowl, mix all dry ingredients together. Dip fish in the melted butter or margarine and then in mixture of seasonings. Cook in a cast iron skillet, preheated until very hot. Cook 2 minutes on one side, turn, and cook another minute. This dish is very smoky to prepare. It cooks well outside on a grill or campstove.

Note: One of the family's most popular recipes.

Crab Quiche

John Travolta

**Actor: Civil Action, Grease, Michael,
Pulp Fiction, Broken Arrow, Swordfish**

Pie Crust

1/2 cup chilled butter

3 tablespoons vegetable shortening

2 cups all-purpose flour

5-6 tablespoons cold water

1/2 teaspoon salt

Custard

11/2 cups heavy cream

3 eggs plus 1 yolk

Salt and pepper to taste

Filling

1 cup grated Jack cheese, divided

11/2 cups grated Gruyère cheese, divided

1 pound fresh jumbo lump cleaned crabmeat

2 tablespoons chopped fresh tarragon

2 tablespoons chopped fresh basil

1 tablespoon chopped fresh chervil

Preheat oven to 350 degrees. For pie crust, put chilled butter and shortening in a mixer with flour and salt. Use the paddle attachment. Mix on medium speed until blended 3 to 4 minutes.(It will look like cornmeal) Then add water. As soon as dough comes together, turn mixer off. This should only take about 10 seconds. Do not over mix. Take out of machine and chill in refrigerator about 1 hour.

For custard, in a medium bowl, mix all ingredients together.

To assemble, roll out dough to a 1/4-inch thickness. Line the bottom of a 9-inch pie plate. Sprinkle one half of each cheese on bottom. Add crabmeat. Sprinkle on herbs. Sprinkle with remaining cheese. Pour custard over all ingredients almost to the top of the pie plate. Bake at 350 degrees for 1 hour and 15 minutes. Let stand 30 minutes before serving. Yield: 8 servings.

Dinner Party Crab Casseroles

Pat and Sandra Conroy

**South Carolina Author - The Lords Of Discipline,
The Prince Of Tides, Beach Music**

1	pound white crabmeat	1	tablespoon Worcestershire
2	eggs, hard boiled and		sauce
	chopped	2	raw eggs, beaten
1	small onion, finely chopped	1/2	cup Hellmann's mayonnaise
1	bell pepper, chopped		Buttered breadcrumbs
	Juice of 1 lemon		

Preheat oven to 350 degrees. In a large mixing bowl, combine all ingredients except breadcrumbs. Mix well. Spoon crabmeat mixture into individual mini-casserole dishes or shell-shaped baking dishes. Top with breadcrumbs. Bake at 350 degrees for 30 minutes or until casseroles are set and breadcrumbs are golden brown.

Herb Pasta with Seafood

Rooster's Gourmet Market and Gifts

Greensboro, North Carolina

1	(1-pound) package strozzapreti pasta	1/3	cup fresh basil (or 1 tablespoon dried)
1/2	cup extra virgin olive oil	1/2	cup fresh parsley, chopped
2-3	cloves garlic, minced	11/2	cups kalamatas and oil
2/3	cup feta cheese, crumbled		cured olives
2/3	cup Reggiano Parmesan, freshly grated	3/4	cup red onion, chopped
1/2-3/4	cup fresh oregano (or 1 tablespoon plus 1 teaspoon dried)	1/2-1	pound cooked scallops (grilled, poached or sautéed)
			Salt
			Freshly ground black pepper

Cook pasta according to package directions. Drain, rinse and drain again. In a large bowl, toss with olive oil. Add remaining ingredients one at the time. Gently toss together. Season with salt and pepper. To serve line a serving bowl with romaine leaves, heap on pasta and garnish with fresh herbs... oregano, basil, chive blossoms, etc. Yield: 8 to 10 servings.

Gingered Shrimp

Chef Bruce A. Sacino, CEC

Executive Chef South Carolina Governor's Mansion

1 1/2	pounds shrimp, peeled and deveined	3/4	teaspoon sugar
			Pinch kosher salt
3	tablespoons grated gingerroot	3	tablespoons lime juice
1/4	cup chopped scallions	3/4	vegetable oil, heated

Bring a large pot of salted and seasoned water to full boil. Add shrimp and cook 2 to 3 minutes until just pink and firm. Shock with ice water and immediately drain well. In a large stainless steel bowl, combine the gingerroot, scallions, sugar, salt, lime juice, and heated vegetable oil and toss with shrimp. Marinate in refrigerator several hours. Stir occasionally. Yield: 4 servings.

Lime Coconut Rice

Chef Bruce A. Sacino, CEC

Executive Chef South Carolina Governor's Mansion

1	cup Wehani rice or long grain and wild rice	1/2	cup golden raisins
		1/2	cup currants or raisins
1/2	tablespoon butter	1/2	cup chives
1	teaspoon yellow mustard seeds	1	tablespoon chopped parsley
		1	cup shredded coconut
2/3	cup cashew nuts or slivered almonds	1/2	cup lime juice
			Zest of 1 lime
1	teaspoon ground coriander	3	tablespoons olive oil
1/2	teaspoon ground ginger		

Cook rice until tender yet firm. Empty into a colander. Rinse with cold water and drain well. Heat butter in a skillet. Add mustard seeds. Cook, stirring constantly about 5 minutes until they start to pop. Add almonds and sauté gently until lightly browned, but do not let burn. Add the coriander, ginger, and rice. Remove from heat and stir to combine. Transfer to a stainless steel mixing bowl. Place currants and golden raisins in a small saucepan with water to cover. Bring to a boil and simmer a few minutes until softened. Drain and add to rice with remaining ingredients. Season with salt to taste. Serve at room temperature with a little marinade over it. Yield: 8 servings.

Shrimp Casserole

Genevieve Peterkin

South Carolina Author - Heaven Is A Beautiful Place

1/2 cup chopped onion	1 (8-ounce) jar Cheese Whiz
1 cup chopped celery	4 cups cooked rice
Butter	4-6 cups cooked shrimp, peeled
2 (103/4-ounce) cans cream of	and deveined
chicken soup	Pepper to taste
1 large bunch broccoli, slightly	Buttered breadcrumbs
cooked, chopped	

Preheat oven to 350 degrees. In a medium saucepan sauté onion and celery in butter. Transfer to a large mixing bowl and add soup, broccoli, and cheese. Fold in cooked rice and shrimp. Add pepper. Put in a casserole dish and top with breadcrumbs. Bake at 350 degrees until edges bubble. Yield: 8 to 10 servings.

Note: Freezes well so bake extra.

Shrimp Sardi

Sardi's

Famed Time Square Restaurant and Bar
Been Toast of Broadway for 78 years

1 small carrot, chopped	*1 1/2 cups fish stock or chicken*
1/2 garlic, finely chop 4	*stock*
cloves	*1 branch thyme*
1 rib celery, chopped	*1/2 bay leaf*
1 white onion, chopped	*3 stems parsley*
1 large tomato, cubed	*3 stems tarragon*
2 pounds shrimp (16/20),	*1 soup spoon tomato purée*
peeled and save shells	*6 tablespoons butter*
1 cup white wine	*1 1/2 ounces olive oil*

Sauce

In a medium pot put a few drops of olive oil. Add all chopped vegetables except tomato. Cook until colored lightly. Add the shrimp shells (color will change to a reddish color) add wine and let reduce by one-half. Then add stock, herbs, tomato, and purée. Simmer 20 minutes on very low heat. Strain. Keep the juice on the stove until it has a very strong shrimp flavor. Remove from heat and whisk in butter. Season to taste. To make spicy add ground cayenne pepper.

Shrimp

Season shrimp lightly with salt and pepper. In a very hot frying pan add olive oil. When oil hot, add shrimp. Sauté over low heat. Do not overcook. Shrimp will turn pinkish-red color. One minute prior to removing from heat add 1 teaspoon finely chopped garlic. Then add sauce. Do not boil.

Presentation

In the center of a plate place 2 croutons made from French or Italian baguettes. Place shrimp around the croutons. Pour the sauce to cover all the food. Sprinkle with chopped tarragon or chives. Serve with rice. Yield: 4 servings.

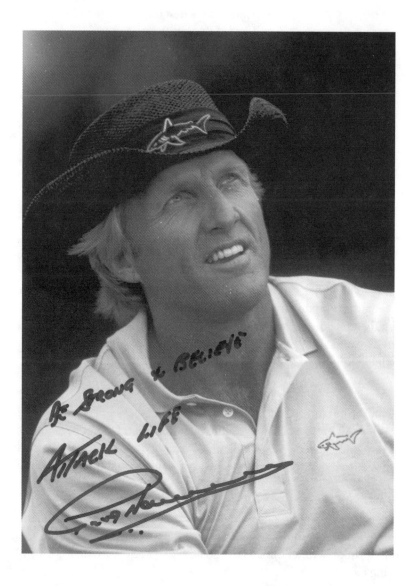

Australian Meat Pie

Greg Norman

"The Shark"
Pro Golfer

1 ounce butter or margarine	2 tablespoons Worcestershire
2 small onions, finely chopped	sauce
2 pounds chopped sirloin	1/4 cup chopped parsley
2 tablespoons all-purpose flour	Pinch nutmeg
2 1/2 cups beef bouillon or stock	Pastry for two (9-inch) pie
Salt and pepper to taste	crust
1 teaspoon dried thyme	1 egg, slightly beaten

Preheat oven to 400 degrees. Melt butter in a large saucepan. Add onions and fry over moderate heat until onions soften. Add beef and fry pressing down with fork until beef is browned. Drain. Sprinkle flour over beef. Stir and continue cooking 2 more minutes. Remove pan from heat. Gradually add stock. Return pan to heat and stir constantly until mixture boils and thickens. Add salt and pepper and the next four ingredients. Cover pan and simmer over low heat 30 minutes. Line a (9-inch) pie plate with pastry. Prick the base several times with a fork. Using a sharp knife, trim off excess pastry. Spoon in filling. Brush around edges with beaten egg. Top with pastry pressing edges together. Cut a hole in the center of pie. Brush with remaining egg. Cook at 400 degrees for 25 minutes or until crust is golden brown. Yield: 4 to 5 servings.

Al's Chili
Al Roker
NBC Weatherman

2 pounds chuck steak, cubed in
   bite-sized pieces
1 pound hot Italian sausage
   removed from casings
2 large onions, diced
12 cloves garlic, diced
1 tablespoon cumin
1 tablespoon paprika
1 tablespoon pure chili powder
1 (32-ounce) can crushed
   tomatoes

1 (16-ounce) can pinto beans
1 (16-ounce) can Northern
   beans
1 (16-ounce) can dark red
   kidney beans
   Chopped scallions
   Sour cream
   Shredded Cheddar cheese

In large Dutch oven, brown the beef and sausage. Remove the meat and reserve. Drain off fat, reserving about 2 tablespoons. Sauté the onions and garlic about 7 to 8 minutes until translucent. Add the cumin, paprika, and chili powder. Add the tomatoes and beef mixture. Stir and simmer 1 hour and 30 minutes. Add all of the beans. Simmer 30 more minutes. Serve with dishes of scallions, sour cream, and cheese.

Mexican Casserole
Tommy Bowden
Head Football Coach Clemson University

1 (10-ounce) can Rotel
1 (16-ounce) package Velvetta
   cheese
1 pound ground beef
1 (1 1/4-ounce) package taco
   seasoning

1 (10-ounce) package yellow
   rice, cooked
1 (3 1/2-ounce) bag Nacho
   Cheese Doritos, crushed

Preheat oven to 350 degrees. In a saucepan, combine Rotel and cheese. Cook on low heat until cheese melts. In a large skillet, brown beef; drain. Add taco seasoning, rice, and cheese mixture. Pour mixture into a 9x13-inch casserole dish. Cover mixture with Doritos. Bake at 350 degrees for 20 minutes.

Lamb Shanks
Janet Leigh
**Best Known Role In The Original Psycho Movie
Mother Of Jamie Lee Curtis**

	Lamb shank	*1*	*teaspoon ground ginger*
1	*onion, sliced*		*Dash of Worcestershire sauce*
2	*whole cloves*	*1/2*	*cup red wine*
2	*tablespoons brown sugar*	*1*	*(10 3/4-ounce) can cream of*
2	*tablespoons vinegar*		*mushroom soup*
	Salt	*1*	*(10 3/4-ounce) can of celery*
	Black pepper		*soup*
	Celery seed or salt	*3*	*tablespoons water*
	Chopped garlic to taste	*3*	*tablespoons flour*

In a skillet, brown meat. Place in a roasting pan with all ingredients except water and flour. Stew about 6 or 7 hours on low heat. If thicker gravy is desired, make a smooth paste of water and flour, and cook another 30 minutes.

Lou Holtz Chili
Carolina Football
Lou Holtz
Head Football Coach University of South Carolina

2	*cloves garlic*	*1*	*(12-ounce) can tomato paste*
	Olive oil	*1*	*(12-ounce) can water*
1 1/4	*pounds ground sirloin*	*1*	*(15 1/2-ounce) can dark red*
3	*tablespoons chili powder*		*kidney beans*
1	*(46-ounce) can spicy*		*Shredded Cheddar cheese*
	vegetable juice		*Chopped onions*
1	*(28-ounce) can crushed*		
	tomatoes		

In a large Dutch oven, brown garlic lightly in olive oil. Remove garlic and set aside. Brown sirloin in garlic flavored oil. Once meat is browned, return garlic to meat. Add all the remaining ingredients except kidney beans. Simmer to desired thickness (about 1 hour and 30 minutes). Add kidney beans during the last 30 minutes of cooking. Lou likes a small amount of cooked elbow macaroni at bottom of bowl with chili over top. If desired, sprinkle with cheese and/or onions.

Troy's Favorite Meatloaf

Troy Aikman

Dallas Cowboy Quarterback, Retired.

3/4 cup equal portions of barbecue sauce and milk to moisten crumbs
1 cup seasoned bread crumbs (from a stuffing mix)
1 1/2 pounds ground beef
1 egg, slightly beaten
2 tablespoons chopped bell pepper

1 small onion, chopped
1 tablespoon basil
Seasoned salt and pepper to taste
1/2 cup shredded Cheddar cheese
1/2 cup shredded Monterey Jack cheese

Preheat oven to 350 degrees. In a small bowl, pour barbeque sauce and milk mixture over crumbs to moisten; set aside. In a separate bowl, mix beef, egg, bell pepper, and next three ingredients. Add bread mixture. Adjust more or less crumbs to your own preference and add more barbecue sauce, if needed, to keep meatloaf moist. Pat meat into a 1/2-inch thick rectangle on a square of tin foil or waxed paper. Sprinkle cheeses over meat, to within one inch of edges. Roll up jelly roll fashion and pinch all around to seal. Put seam-side down in a baking pan. Bake at 350 degrees about 1 hour and 30 minutes, or until done. During last half of baking, spread occasionally with more barbecue sauce.

Helping kids. . .one dream at a time.

THE **Troy Aikman** FOUNDATION

Smooth Talking Dolmathes

Bob Costas

NBC Sports Announcer

1 pound ground sirloin	1/4 cup ice water
5 eggs, beaten, divided (can	Salt and pepper to taste
use egg substitute)	1 (32-ounce) can chicken broth
1 medium onion, chopped	Fresh grape leaves or 1 jar/
1/2 cup uncooked rice	can in brine sauce
1/4 cup chopped parsley	3 lemons
1 tablespoon fresh mint leaves	Hot broth from Dolmathes

In a large bowl, mix sirloin, two eggs, and next six ingredients. Set aside. If using fresh grapes leaves, soak them in hot water 5 minutes to soften. If using jar or can, rinse in warm water. Remove hard stem ends, and place leaves shiny side down. Put small amount of meat mixture in center of each leaf, roll, then fold inside to seal ends. Place plate over top to hold firmly in place. Layer stuffed leaves in saucepan. Pour chicken broth over leaves, cover, and cook 45 minutes to 1 hour. While grape leaves are cooking, beat remaining 3 three eggs. Add the juice of lemons. Slowly add hot broth, beating constantly. Sauce should be fluffy and foamy. Add to Dolmathes. Yield: 6 to 8 servings.

My Personal Favorite Recipe

Bob Costas

NBC Sports Announcer

1)   Identify your town's best pizzeria.
2)   Call to order delivery of savory thick crust pie with extra cheese.
3)   Wait 20-30 minutes.
4)   Answer doorbell.
5)   Pay tab with generous tip.
6)   Pour beverage.
7)   Consume and enjoy!

Note: I have never cooked a meal in my life (the honest truth). Hence, this is my favorite recipe!

Bob Costas

Stuffed Green Peppers

Lynda Petty

Wife of Richard Petty
7 Time Nascar Winston Cup Winner

6	bell peppers, cut in half and cleaned	2	eggs
1 1/2	pounds ground beef	1	cup ketchup
1	medium onion, finely chopped	1	cup corn flakes
1	tablespoon chili powder		Salt and pepper to taste

Sauce

2 1/2	cups ketchup and tomato paste (use more ketchup than paste)	2	tablespoons brown sugar
		2	tablespoons ground mustard
		1	tablespoon vinegar

Preheat oven to 375 degrees. In a large saucepan, boil peppers 5 minutes. In a medium bowl, mix other ingredients together. Stuff peppers with mixture and arrange in bottom of 9x13-inch casserole dish. In a small bowl, mix sauce ingredients together and pour over peppers. Bake at 375 degrees for 30 to 40 minutes. Yield: 6 servings.

Chinese Barbecued Chicken

Chevy and Jayni Chase

Actor- National Lampoon's Vacation movies; Spies Like Us

4	tablespoons peanut oil	1/3	cup soy sauce
2	tablespoons fresh chopped gingerroot	1	tablespoon sugar
		1	tablespoon sesame oil
1/4	cup chopped scallions	17	chicken thighs, or 3 pounds
2	cloves garlic, chopped		chicken parts

In a small skillet or saucepan, heat peanut oil until hot. Add ginger, scallions, and garlic and stir-fry 1 minute. Add soy sauce and sugar and bring to a boil. Turn off heat and add sesame oil. Marinate the chicken in this mixture 1 to 2 hours. Remove chicken from marinade and barbecue or broil until golden brown. Baste with marinade, turn pieces over, and cook until done. Skin should be crispy.

Chevy Chase

Blue Cheese Encrusted Chicken

Rosie O'Donnell

TV Talk Show Host; Actress

Boneless/skinless chicken
breasts
Balsamic vinegar
Olive oil
Minced garlic

Sun-dried tomatoes
Capers
Chopped green onions
Crumbled blue cheese

Marinate the chicken in balsamic vinegar and a little olive oil for a few hours prior to cooking. In a skillet, sauté garlic, sun-dried tomatoes, capers, and green onions in olive oil until all items are soft. In a separate skillet, add a small amount of olive oil and cook the chicken breasts on medium-high heat until browned on each side. During the chicken cooking process, add small amounts of the balsamic vinegar. After the chicken is cooked, transfer the breasts to a baking dish. Spoon the sun-dried tomato mixture on top of the chicken breasts. Sprinkle blue cheese on top of the mixture. Put in the oven to broil until the blue cheese begins to turn brown. Serve hot.

Bar-B-Que Chicken

Cale Yarborough

Nascar Racing Legend

1	chicken, cut in half	1	pint vinegar
	Cooking oil to rub chicken on	1/2	cup hot sauce
	both sides	1/8	cup cayenne pepper

Wash chicken and cut in half. Rub oil on both sides of chicken and grill, covered, on an outside grill for 30 minutes at 350 degrees. While the chicken is grilling, simmer the vinegar, hot sauce, and pepper in a saucepan. Start dipping the chicken into the saucepan with sauce and placing back on the grill. Cook for 45 minutes or until done. Yield: 2 hungry or 4 with other fixings.

Note: This is hot, but good! Enjoy

Chicken and Wild Rice Casserole

Jim and Margaret Harrison

South Carolina Artist

3-4 boneless chicken breasts
1 (6-ounce) box Uncle Ben's
Wild Rice, original recipe only
1 rib celery
1/2 medium onion
Butter or margarine

1 (10³/4-ounce) can cream of
celery soup
1 cup grated medium Cheddar
cheese, divided
Grill Creations chicken
seasoning (optional)

Preheat oven to 350 degrees. Cook chicken in a pot of water. Remove chicken from broth and set broth aside. Cool. Cut chicken into bite-sized pieces. Prepare rice according to package directions. While rice is cooking, chop the celery and onion. In a saucepan, sauté the celery and onion in butter slowly so it does not burn. Pour rice into a 2-quart casserole dish. Add celery soup, onion, celery, and one-third of the cheese. Add seasoning if desired. Fold all this together adding chicken and a spoonful of the chicken broth if necessary. Sprinkle the remaining cheese on top and dot with butter. Bake at 350 degrees for 1 hour. Yield: 6 to 8 servings.

Spicy Chicken

Elizabeth Taylor

Actress; National Velvet, Cleopatra, Who's Afraid of Virginia Wolfe?

2 teaspoons curry powder	1 onion, chopped
1 teaspoon cumin	1 teaspoon fresh grated ginger
1/2 teaspoon ground ginger	1 medium chicken, cut into
1/2 teaspoon tumeric	serving pieces and skinned
1/2 clove garlic, crushed	

In a bowl, combine dry ingredients with garlic, onion, and ginger. Coat chicken with mixture and refrigerate 2 hours, preferably longer. Place on a moderately hot grill or broil in oven about 30 minutes or until done, turning once. Yield: 4 servings.

Jay Leno's Uncle Louie's Chicken Wings Marinara

Jay Leno

Tonight Show Host

2-3 dozen chicken wings	1 (28-ounce) can Italian plum
Safflower or peanut oil	tomatoes
Olive oil	Chopped parsley
Crushed garlic or garlic	Salt
powder	Durkee's hot sauce

Cook chicken wings by broiling, or lightly flour them and deep fry in oil. While they are cooking, prepare the sauce. Heat one-eight inch of olive oil in a pan, add garlic powder or crushed garlic to taste. Mash tomatoes through a sieve and cook in the olive oil. Add a few teaspoons of chopped parsley and salt to taste. Cook about 20 minutes. At the end of this cooking time, add hot sauce (put in a little or a lot, depending on how hot or mild your taste), but put in at least 2 tablespoons or the sauce won't be as tasty. Add a little garlic powder and cook another 3 to 4 minutes. In a bowl, toss the chicken wings with one-half cup of the sauce and serve with the remaining sauce on the side to dip the wings into.

Katie's Lemon Chicken
Katie Couric
Anchor-NBC Today Show; Co-founder NCCRA

4 boneless, skinless chicken breasts	3 tablespoons flour
Flour, for dredging	Juice of 2 lemons
2 tablespoons butter	3 cups chicken broth
2 tablespoons olive oil	Salt to taste
	Ground white pepper to taste

Pound chicken breasts with meat pounder to a uniform thickness. Dredge lightly in flour, shaking off excess. In a large sauté pan over medium-high heat, melt the butter and oil until it sizzles. Add the chicken breasts and sauté, turning once or twice until cooked through and juices run clear. Remove chicken and set aside. Whisk in flour and cook 1 minute until the mixture boils. Add lemon juice to the chicken stock and whisk into sauté pan. Reduce heat to a simmer. Return chicken to pan to heat through, thickening sauce to desired consistency. Season to taste with salt and ground white pepper. Serve the chicken on a bed of Bastami rice, and spoon the sauce over the chicken. Garnish with chopped parsley and lemon slices. Yield: 4 servings.

Oriental Chicken Rolls

Mrs. Billy Graham

Wife of Evangelist Preacher Billy Graham

3/4	cup light red Russian dressing or light sweet and spicy dressing
1	tablespoon soy sauce (more if you like)
1	(8-ounce) can sliced water chestnuts, drained

1/3	cup sliced mushrooms
1/4	cup chopped green onions
2	whole chicken breasts (about 1 pound each) split, boned, skinned, and pounded flat
1	tablespoon sesame seed
2	cups hot cooked rice

Preheat oven to 350 degrees. In a cup, mix dressing with soy sauce and set aside. In a small bowl, combine water chestnuts, mushrooms, onions, and 2 tablespoons dressing mixture. Divide vegetables equally and put on top of chicken. Roll up, secure with toothpicks. Place chicken in a 11/2-quart oblong baking dish. Add remaining dressing mixtures. Sprinkle with sesame seed. Bake, covered, at 350 degrees for 35 minutes or until tender. Serve over cooked rice. Garnish with additional green onions. Yield: 4 servings.

Y.A. Tittle's Tamale Pie

Y.A. Tittle

One Of The All-Time Great Quarterbacks In Professional Football

1	whole fryer
1	package corn tortillas
2	jalapeño peppers Sharp Cheddar cheese, shredded

1	(103/4-ounce) can cream of mushroom soup
1	(103/4-ounce) can cream of chicken soup

Preheat oven to 350 degrees. Boil chicken until tender. Let cool. Remove chicken from bones and cut into small pieces. Tear tortillas into small pieces and spread along bottom of a 9x13-inch casserole dish. Spread some of the chicken over the tortillas. Remove seeds from jalapeño peppers and cut into small pieces. Spread over the chicken. Sprinkle cheese over the top. Repeat layers until casserole is nearly full. In a separate bowl, add the mushroom soup, chicken soup and 1 soup can of milk. Stir until smooth. Pour over the casserole. Sprinkle cheese over the top. Bake at 350 degrees for 45 minutes.

Brussels Sprouts with Maple-Orange-Walnut Butter

Matt Lauer

Host of NBC Today Show

1	pound brussels sprouts	1/4	cup toasted chopped walnuts
2	sticks butter		Salt and pepper
1/4	cup pure maple syrup		Zest of 1 lemon
	Grated rind of 2 oranges		

Clean brussels sprouts and score them by cutting a small x into each stem. Add to a pot of boiling salted water and cook on high 8 to 10 minutes, or until soft. In a medium bowl, cream butter and add remaining ingredients, mixing well. Strain brussels sprouts and toss with flavored butter. Garnish with lemon zest. Yield: 4 to 6 servings.

Cornbread Casserole

Tom and Hillary Watson

Senior PGA Golfer

2	eggs	1/4	cup butter
1	cup whole kernel corn	1	(8 1/2-ounce) box Jiffy
1	(14 3/4-ounce) can cream style		cornbread mix
	corn	1/4	cup grated Cheddar cheese
1	cup sour cream		

Preheat oven to 350 degrees. In a medium bowl, beat eggs with kernel corn, cream corn, sour cream and butter. Add cornbread mix. Mix well. Sprinkle cheese on top. Pour into a 9x13-inch pan, Bake at 350 degrees for 50 minutes. Yield: 4 to 6 servings.

Dave's Favorite Pasta

Dave Thomas

Founder Of Wendy's

14 Roma tomatoes, chopped
4 cloves garlic, chopped
2 tablespoons chopped fresh
   basil
2 tablespoons olive oil
2 tablespoons of wine vinegar
1 (16-ounce) package angel
   hair pasta

1 tablespoon fat-free chicken
   broth
Mushrooms
Black pepper
Parmesan cheese, fat-free
Olive oil cooking spray

Combine tomatoes, garlic, basil, olive oil, and vinegar in a wooden bowl. Let sit at room temperature at least 2 hours. Tomato mixture should be warm (room temperature). If not warm, microwave 1 minute but DO NOT COOK. In a saucepan, boil pasta in water and 1 tablespoon chicken broth (to prevent sticking) until done. Slice fresh mushrooms and place on a baking sheet, spray lightly with olive oil nonstick cooking spray and broil a few moments. Turn mushrooms, spray with spray and broil again. Drain pasta. Return to dish and toss immediately with tomato mixture. Spoon sliced mushrooms on top. Sprinkle with pepper and cheese. Yield: 8 servings.

Note: You may also add sliced red peppers and onion to mixture if you wish.

Delicious Squash

У. А. Tittle

Inducted Into The Professional Football Hall Of Fame In 1971

5   *(141/2-ounce) cans yellow squash, drained*
2   *(103/4-ounce) cans cream of chicken soup*
1   *(2-ounce) jar pimento, drained*
2   *sticks margarine, melted*
1   *(8-ounce) container regular sour cream*

1   *(8-ounce) container light sour cream*
2   *carrots, grated*
1   *small medium onion, chopped*
1   *(6-ounce) package Kraft Stove Top Cornbread Stuffing mix*

Preheat oven to 350 degrees. Lightly mash squash in a large bowl. Add all remaining ingredients and mix well. Pour into a 9x13-inch greased casserole dish. Bake, uncovered, at 350 degrees for 45 minutes or until hot and bubbly. Yield: 8 servings.

Farmer's Market

Laura Bush

First Lady

1 1/4 cups pinto beans, soaked overnight and drained
1 teaspoon salt
1 bay leaf
1 teaspoon dried oregano
1 pound tomatoes, fresh or canned, peeled, seeded, and chopped; juice reserved
2 ancho chilies
1 pound mixed summer squash
4 ears corn (about 2 cups kernels)
1 teaspoon ground cumin
1/2 teaspoon ground coriander

2 tablespoons corn or vegetable oil
2 yellow onions, 1/4-inch squares
2 cloves garlic, finely chopped
2 tablespoons red chili powder, or more to taste
8 ounces green beans, 1-inch lengths
4 ounces Jack or Muenster cheese, grated
1/2 bunch cilatro leaves roughly chopped
Whole cilatro leaves

Cook the pre-soaked beans about 1 hour and 30 minutes to 2 hours in plenty of water with salt, bay leaf, and oregano. Remove them from the heat when they are soft but not mushy, as they will continue to cook in the stew. Drain the beans, and save the broth. Prepare the tomatoes. Open the chili pods and remove the seeds and veins; then cut the chilies into narrow strips. Cut the squash into large pieces. Shave the kernels from the corn. Heat the oil in a large skillet, and sauté the onions over high heat 1 to 2 minutes. Lower the heat, add the garlic, chili powder, cumin, and coriander and stir everything together. Add a little bean broth, so the chili doesn't scorch or burn. Cook until the onions begin to soften, about 4 minutes, then add the tomatoes and stew 5 minutes. Stir in the squash, corn, green beans, and chili strips along with the cooked beans and enough broth to make a fairly wet stew. Cook slowly until vegetables are done, about 15 to 20 minutes. Taste the stew and adjust the seasoning. Stir in the cheese and chopped cilantro, and garnish with whole leaves of cilantro. Serve with cornbread or tortillas. Yield: 6 servings.

Note: A great one-dish meal if you have a garden or have just visited the Farmer's Market. THE WHITE HOUSE
WASHINGTON

Seared Portobello and Wilted Chard Over Barley Pilaf

Martha Stewart Living

2	onions	2	teaspoons chopped rosemary
3/4	cup barley	1/8	teaspoon freshly ground pepper
1	teaspoon salt		
4	large portobello mushrooms, stems trimmed	8	ounces (about 1/2 bunch) green Swiss chard leaves, cleaned and roughly chopped
1/4	cup plus 2 tablespoons Marsala wine	1	tablespoon unsalted butter Olive oil cooking spray
2	cups homemade or low-sodium canned vegetable stock		

Place a medium saucepan over medium-high heat. When hot, spray with cooking spray. Add onions; stir, cover, and cook 1 minute. Add barley; cook, stirring frequently, until barley is lightly toasted, about 8 minutes. Add salt and 1 1/2 cups water. Cover, and bring water to a boil. Simmer until water has been absorbed, about 20 minutes. Remove saucepan from heat, and keep covered. Heat a large nonstick skillet over medium-high heat. When hot, spray with cooking spray. Add mushrooms, tops up; cover, and cook 8 minutes. Turn mushrooms over; cook 5 minutes more. Transfer to a plate. Add Marsala to skillet; cook 10 seconds. Increase heat to high; add vegetable stock, rosemary, and pepper. Cook until liquid has reduced by three-fourths and has slightly thickened, about 12 minutes. Add Swiss chard; cook, stirring once or twice, until chard has slightly wilted, 1 to 2 minutes. Transfer chard to a plate. Add butter to pan; swirl until combined. Remove the sauce from the heat. Cut the mushrooms thinly on bias. Divide barley among four plates. Top each with chard, mushrooms, and sauce. Yield: 4 servings.

Tony's 30 Minute Pomidoro Sauce

Tony Danza

Actor; Taxi, Who's the Boss, Family Law

2 (28-ounce) cans of plum   Basil
   tomatoes with basil   Wine
   Black pepper   Garlic
   Salt   1/4 cup olive oil
   Parmesan cheese   1 (6-ounce) can of tomato paste

Strain tomatoes through colander and toss pulp. Place tomatoes in a medium saucepan. Add pepper (a lot), salt (very little), parmesan cheese (good stuff, a lot), basil (a lot and fresh), and wine (I like a lot). Set aside. In a saucepan, brown garlic in olive oil (maybe 10 cloves, cut into pieces). Add tomato paste and cook until soft. It will soak up oil and garlic. Add to tomatoes and other ingredients. Simmer at low heat 20 minutes. Yield: 4 to 6 servings.

Note: Voilla!

Ice Cream Dessert

Arnold Palmer

Pro Golfer

Vanilla ice cream	*Whipped cream*
Godiva Chocolate liqueur	*Cherry*

In an individual serving bowl, pour desired amount of liqueur over ice cream. Top with whipped cream and a cherry!

Popcorn Cake

Joanne Woodward

Actress - Wife of Paul Newman

3/4 cup popcorn	1/2 cup sugar
1 (12-ounce) can unsalted peanuts	1 teaspoon cream of tartar
1 (16-ounce) bag M and M's	3 tablespoons of butter
1 cup white Karo syrup	1 teaspoon baking soda

Grease a 10-inch tube pan. Pop the popcorn and remove unpopped kernels. Mix popped corn with peanuts and M and M's. Set aside. In a 3-quart saucepan, mix together the Karo syrup, sugar, and cream of tartar. Bring to a boil and boil 1 minute without stirring. Remove from heat and stir in butter and baking soda. Pour this mixture over popcorn mixture, coating all ingredients. Pack into prepared pan and refrigerate. Yield: 16 to 20 servings.

Fresh Apple Cake

Mrs. Billy Graham

Wife of Evangelist Preacher Billy Graham

Cake

1 cup cooking oil	3 cups all-purpose flour
2 cups sugar (or perhaps	1/2 teaspoon salt
1 1/2 cups)	1 teaspoon soda
2 eggs, well beaten	3 cups fresh apples, chopped
2 teaspoons vanilla	1 cup chopped nuts

Glaze

1/2 cup margarine	1/4 cup evaporated milk
1 cup brown sugar	1 teaspoon vanilla

Preheat oven to 300 degrees. In a large mixing bowl, combine oil, sugar and eggs. Add vanilla. Measure and sift flour, salt, and soda. Add to first mixture. Stir in apples and nuts; mix well. Mixture will be very stiff. Pour into a 9x13-inch greased pan. Bake at 300 degrees for 1 hour.

For glaze, place margarine and sugar in double boiler, allow to melt. Add milk. Bring to full boil. Cool. Add vanilla. Pour over cake. Yield: 12 to 16 servings.

Angel Food Cake

Lynda Petty

Wife of Richard Petty
7 Time Nascar Winston Cup Winner

1 1/2 cups egg whites (10-12 eggs)	1 cup sifted flour (sift 4 more times)
1 teaspoon cream of tartar	
1 1/2 cups sugar	1/4 teaspoon salt
1 teaspoon vanilla	

Preheat oven to 325 degrees. In a medium bowl, beat egg whites until foamy. Add cream of tartar and beat until stiff, but not dry. Gradually beat in sugar. Add vanilla; then fold in flour and salt as gently as possible. Pour into a ungreased (10-inch) tube pan. Bake at 325 degrees for 1 hour and 15 minutes or until top is nicely browned. Yield: 16 to 20 servings.

Heavenly Hash

Jeff Varner

Survivor- Kucha Tribe

Cake

2 sticks butter	1 1/2 cups self-rising flour
4 tablespoons cocoa	1 teaspoon vanilla
4 eggs	2 cups pecans, chopped
2 cups sugar	1 (16-ounce) bag marshmallows

Icing

4 tablespoons cocoa	Dash of salt
4 tablespoons butter	1 teaspoon vanilla
1 (16-ounce) box powdered sugar	Milk

Preheat oven to 310 degrees. Grease and flour a 9x13-inch baking dish. In a saucepan, melt butter and cocoa. In a small bowl, beat together eggs and sugar. Add to cocoa mixture. Add flour and mix well. Stir in vanilla and nuts. Pour in prepared pan. Bake at 310 degrees for 30 minutes. While cake is hot, spread marshmallows on top of cake. With a fork, softly mash marshmallows a little to help melt but don't let them melt all away.

For icing, mix cocoa and butter in medium saucepan. Add sugar, salt, and vanilla. Add a little milk to make the mixture easy to spread. Dribble over marshmallows. Yield: 12 to 16 servings.

Rum Cake
James E. Clyburn
6th District SC Member of Congress

Cake

1	*(1 pound, 2-ounce) box yellow cake mix*
1/2	*cup cooking oil*
1/2	*cup water*
1/2	*cup rum*

1	*(3.4-ounce) box vanilla instant pudding mix*
4	*eggs*
1/2	*cup chopped nuts*

Topping

1	*stick butter*
1	*cup sugar*

1/2	*cup water*

Preheat oven to 325 degrees. Grease and flour a Bundt pan. In a mixing bowl, beat all of the ingredients together 2 minutes at medium speed with an electric mixer. Pour into prepared pan. Bake at 325 degrees for 1 hour.

For topping, in a saucepan, boil butter, sugar and water one minute. Pour over cake in pan and let stand for several hours. Loosen edges with a butter knife and turn onto cake plate. Yield: 16 to 20 servings.

Congress of the United States
House of Representatives
Washington, DC 20515–4006

Paul's Favorite Cake

Paul Azinger

Pro Golfer

1/3-1/2 cups powdered sugar   *1/2 teaspoons vanilla*
1 1/2 pints heavy cream

Bake your favorite chocolate cake in two round 9-inch pans. Cool. Cut layers in half to make 4 layers. In a medium bowl, mix sugar with heavy cream. Put in refrigerator and leave at least 1 hour. Add vanilla. Beat together about 5 minutes until stiff. Fill layers and top. Yield: 16 to 20 servings.

Wonderful Sugar Cookies

Charlie Daniels

The Charlie Daniels Band

1 1/2 cups powdered sugar	1 1/2 teaspoons vanilla
1 cup butter	1 teaspoon baking soda
1 egg	1 teaspoon cream of tartar

In a large bowl, mix all ingredients together. Refrigerate for 3 hours. Divide dough in half and roll out one half at the time. Roll thin-1/8 to 1/4 inch. Use seasonal cookie cutters. Sprinkle with granulated sugar, either white or colored sugar if desired. Bake at 375 degrees for 7 to 8 minutes.

Note: This is a recipe that we've made at Christmas time with our son, every year for 30 years. A real family tradition! Of course you can make them at any holiday and use the appropriate cookie cutters for the occasion.

Pecan Roll Cookies

Elizabeth Dole

Politician

2 sticks margarine, softened	1 teaspoon vanilla extract
1/4 cup powdered sugar	2 cups pecan pieces
2 cups flour	Powdered sugar
1 tablespoon cold water	

Preheat oven to 275 degrees. In a medium bowl, beat the margarine and sugar until creamy. Add flour, water and vanilla. Mix well. Stir in pecans. Shape with floured hands into date-like shapes. Arrange on a greased baking sheet; crease lengthwise with a knife. Bake at 275 degrees for 1 hour. Roll the warm cookies in powdered sugar. Yield: 50 cookies

Oatmeal Raisin Cookies

Chonda Pierce

Christian Comedienne

1 cup margarine	*1 teaspoon vanilla*
1 cup brown sugar	*1 1/2 cups self-rising flour*
1 cup white sugar	*3 cups quick cooking oats*
2 eggs	*1 cup raisins*

In a mixing bowl, cream shortening. Add sugars and beat well. Add the eggs and vanilla and stir to blend. Add flour; mix well. Stir in the oatmeal and raisins. Drop by spoonfuls on ungreased baking sheet. Bake at 325 degrees for 10 minutes. Yield: 5 dozen

Note: Oatmeal raisin cookies are a friendship ritual of Chonda Pierce and her best friend Allison Evans. "We always have them when we get together, whether we are at one another's homes or if we are meeting up while Chonda is traveling" states Allison. "And we like them with a couple of diet Pepsi's! You can get a lot of catching-up and problem-solving done that way!"

Summer Day Fruit Cobbler

Sally Field

Actress; Flying Nun, Steel Magnolia, Forrest Gump

1	*stick of margarine or butter*	*3/4*	*cup milk*
3/4	*cup flour*	*2*	*cups sweetened fruit*
1	*cup sugar*		*(peaches, berries, cherries,*
2	*teaspoons baking powder*		*etc.)*
	Pinch salt		

Put stick of butter in a 2 1/2-quart baking dish and place in oven. Set oven at 350 degrees and let it melt. In a large bowl, mix all other ingredients, except fruit, and pour into dish with melted butter. On top of this put the sweetened fruit. Do not stir. Bake at 350 degrees until crusty. Yield: 6 servings.

Banana Pudding

Dot Jernigan

SC Author- Joy and Sorrow, But Most Of All, Love

1 scant cup sugar	Vanilla wafers
2 1/2 cups milk, divided	Bananas
3 tablespoons cornstarch	1 teaspoon vanilla
3 eggs, separated	

In a saucepan, heat sugar with two cups of milk. Set aside. In a separate saucepan, combine remaining milk with cornstarch. Pour over egg yolks, stirring constantly. Pour egg mixture into saucepan with sugar and milk. Stir constantly and cook until thickened. Cool. Layer wafers and bananas in a bowl. Before pouring pudding over bananas, add vanilla. Yield: 6 to 8 servings.

Brenda Schwarzkopf's Sour Cream Peach Pie

H. Norman Schwarzkopf

General, USA, Retired

2 pounds fresh peaches or 1 large can sliced peaches, drained	1/2 cup sugar, if using fresh peaches, increase to 3/4 cup
2 tablespoons cornstarch, use with fresh peaches only	1/4 teaspoon salt
	1 cup sour cream
1/4 cup apple juice, use with fresh peaches only	1 (9-inch) deep dish pie crust, unbaked
1/3 cup flour	1 tablespoon of sugar
	1/4 teaspoon cinnamon

Preheat oven to 350 degrees. Peel and slice fresh peaches (10 to 12 slices each). Place in large bowl. If using fresh peaches, mix cornstarch and apple juice until smooth. Pour over peaches. Toss gently to coat. Let stand 10 to 15 minutes. For canned peaches, drain and place in large bowl. In medium bowl, mix flour, sugar, salt and sour cream. Arrange peaches in pie crust. Top with sour cream mixture. Mix sugar and cinnamon together and sprinkle over top. Bake at 350 degrees for 30 to 40 minutes or until crust is lightly browned. Peach slices for garnish. Yield: 10 servings

Paper Bag Apple Pie

Idella Bodie

SC Author- Mystery of the Pirates Treasure, Stranded!, Ghost in the Capitol, Ghost Tales for Retelling.

Pie

1/2 cups sugar	2 tablespoons flour
1/2 teaspoon lemon juice	1 (9-inch) unbaked pie crust
4 large tart apples, peeled and sliced	

Topping

1/2 cup sugar	1/3 cup butter or margarine
1/2 cup flour	

Preheat oven to 425 degrees. In medium bowl, mix sugar and next three ingredients. Place in pie crust. For topping, in medium bowl, mix sugar and flour. Cut in butter. Mixture will be crumbly. Sprinkle over top of pie. Place a large brown paper bag on baking sheet. Slip pie inside and staple or pin shut and at corners to flatten. Bake at 425 degrees for 1 hour and 10 minutes. No peeking. Yield: 6 servings

Note: I double for two pies.

" Nothing evokes treasured family memories more than using recipes remembered fondly - like the smell of warm apple pie with ice cream."

Idella Bodie

Elizabeth Coker's Cucumber Pickles

Penelope Coker Hall

Author- aka Emily Brooks- Riding High

3	pounds cabbage	1	quart white vinegar or rice wine vinegar
3/4	cup salt		
1	pound onions	4	cups sugar
3	green peppers	1 1/2	tablespoons tumeric
3	red peppers	1	heaping teaspoon mustard seed
10	Kirby cucumbers		
3/4	cup flour	1	heaping teaspoon celery seed
4	tablespoons dry mustard		

Quarter and cut cabbage. Cover with salt and let stand for two hours. Squeeze out. Slice vegetables. In a small bowl, combine flour and mustard. Add small amount of cold water to make a paste. Set aside. In a large canning pot, combine vinegar, sugar, tumeric, mustard and celery seed. Add vegetables. When mixture comes to a boil add paste and turn heat down. Boil about 10 minutes. Fill canning jars that have been boiled and are hot. Seal.

★ Appetizers ★
Beverages

Margaret Reaves and Beth Brown
Coffee drinking buddies

Mama and "Miss" Margaret were coffee drinking buddies over 35 years. This was almost a daily ritual, morning and afternoon. I could almost tell time by their drinking schedule! If Mama wasn't home mid-morning or late afternoon, I knew where I could find her. I'm sure over the years and their cups of coffee, they solved many problems, shared laughter and sorrow and most of all built a cherished friendship that lasted many years. The word coffee brings to mind Mama and Margaret. It binds them together.

Of all the gifts
that a wise providence grants us
to make life full and happy,
friendship is the most beautiful.

Epicurus

Cheesy Black-Eyed Pea Dip

Anne Dawkins

1	medium onion, chopped	1	cup sour cream
2	tablespoons butter	1	cup mayonnaise
1	(16-ounce) can black-eyed peas, drained and rinsed	1	(1-ounce) envelope Ranch salad dressing mix
1	(14-ounce) can artichoke hearts, drained and chopped	1	cup shredded mozzarella cheese
2	tablespoons Parmesan cheese		

Preheat oven to 350 degrees. In a skillet, sauté onion in butter. In a medium bowl, combine onion with remaining ingredients and mix well. Spoon into a 8x12-inch baking dish. Bake at 350 degrees for 20 minutes. Serve with crackers or tortilla chips. Yield: 15 servings.

Horsey Cheesy Beef

Anne Dawkins

1	(3-ounce) package cream cheese, softened	1	tablespoon fresh horseradish
4	green olives, chopped	1/2	pound package dried beef

In a medium bowl, blend cheese, olives, and horseradish. Spread on a slice of beef. Roll and fasten with toothpicks. Brush with butter and cut each roll into three pieces. Broil until heated through. Serve immediately. May be chilled Yield: About 20 rolls.

Note: If preferred, rolls may be chilled until firm. Cut into three pieces and serve cold.

Cheese Dip
Tacky Vosburgh

1 (8-ounce) package cream cheese
1 (8-ounce) package grated sharp Cheddar cheese, room temperature

1 red onion, chopped
1/2 cup mayonnaise

Preheat oven to 350 degrees. In a medium bowl, combine all ingredients and mix well. Pour into a quiche dish or similar sized dish. Bake at 350 degrees for 30 minutes. Yield: 8 to 10 servings.

Sausage Cheese Dip
Wendy Folsom

1 pound mild bulk sausage
1 (16-ounce) Velvetta cheese, cubed (Mexican, if available)

1 (16-ounce) jar mild chunky salsa

In a skillet, brown sausage and crumble. Drain on a paper towel. Melt cheese in a heavy saucepan over medium heat, stirring frequently until cheese melts. Stir in sausage and salsa. Transfer to a serving bowl or chafing dish. Serve hot with Frito corn chips. Yield: 10 to 12 servings.

Sausage Dip
Robin Lane

1   pound bulk sausage, mild or   1   (10-ounce) can of Rotel
    hot
1   (8-ounce) package cream
    cheese, softened

In a skillet, brown sausage, crumble and drain. Return sausage to pan and turn on low heat. Stir in cream cheese until well blended. Stir in Rotel mixing well. Transfer to a chafing dish. Serve with Frito scoops. Yield: 10 to 12 servings.

Pizza Dip
Robin Atkins

1   (8-ounce) package cream   3/4   cup pizza sauce
    cheese, softened   1/2   cup chopped pepperoni
1/2 cup sour cream   1/4   cup chopped green onions
1/2 teaspoon dried oregano   1   cup shredded mozzarella
1/4 teaspoon garlic powder   cheese
1/4 teaspoon cayenne pepper   Tortilla chips

Preheat oven to 350 degrees. In a medium bowl, beat the first five ingredients together at medium speed with an electric mixer until blended. Spread in a lightly greased 9-inch pie plate. Spoon pizza sauce over top. Sprinkle with pepperoni and onions. Bake at 350 degrees for 10 minutes. Sprinkle with cheese and bake 10 more minutes until cheese melts. Serve with tortilla chips. Yield: 4 servings.

Taco Bean Dip
Melinda Sansbury

2   (8-ounce) packages cream
     cheese, softened
2   (15-ounce) cans Hormel chili
     with beans

1   large onion, chopped
1   (8-ounce) package taco
     shredded cheese

Preheat oven to 350 degrees. Spread cream cheese in a 9x13-inch glass baking dish. Layer chili with beans over cream cheese and spread onions over top. Sprinkle with cheese. Bake at 350 degrees for 20 to 30 minutes until bubbly. Serve with white corn taco chips. Yield: 10 to 12 servings.

Low Fat Spinach Dip
Meg Easterling

1/2 (16-ounce) bag of frozen
      chopped spinach
1   (12-ounce) can artichoke
      hearts
1   (8-ounce) package low fat
      cream cheese
1   teaspoon black pepper

     Dash of salt
1/2 red onion, chopped
1   cup shredded Gruyère or
      Swiss cheese
1   (16-ounce) round loaf
      Hawaiian bread

In a saucepan, cook spinach and artichoke hearts according to directions on spinach package. Drain water if there is an excess amount. Mix spinach mixture with cream cheese, pepper, salt, onion, and cheese in a large bowl. If cheese is lumpy, melt in the microwave. Hollow out the center of the bread to make a bread bowl. Reserve center of bread to make bread cubes. Fill the hollowed bread bowl with hot dip. Serve with raw vegetables, crackers or bread cubes. Yield: 12 to 15 servings.

Warm Mushroom and Bacon Dip

Lucy Brown

6	slices bacon	1/8	teaspoon black pepper
2	medium cloves garlic, finely chopped	1	(8-ounce) package cream cheese
1/2	pound mushrooms, thinly sliced	1	(8-ounce) container sour cream
1	(1 1/4-ounce) envelope onion soup mix		

In a medium skillet, cook bacon; remove and crumble. Reserve two and one half tablespoons of drippings in skillet and add garlic and mushrooms. Cook over medium heat, stirring occasionally, until mushrooms are tender and liquid is almost evaporated. Add soup mix and pepper. Stir in cream cheese. Simmer, stirring constantly, until cream cheese melts. Stir in sour cream and bacon; heat through. Garnish with bacon crumbles. Serve with crackers or bread. Yield: 2 cups.

Mexican Layered Dip

Hiller Ann Spires

3	medium avocados	1	cup chopped green onions
2	tablespoons lemon juice	2	cups chopped tomatoes
	Salt and pepper to taste	1	(4-ounce) can chopped black olives, drained
1	pint sour cream		
1/2	cup mayonnaise	1	(8-ounce) package Monterey Jack cheese, shredded
1	(2-ounce) package taco seasoning		Large tortilla chips
2	(10 1/2-ounce) cans jalapeño bean dip		

In a small bowl, mash avocados with lemon juice, salt, and pepper. In a separate bowl, mix sour cream, mayonnaise, and taco seasoning. On a 9x13-inch serving platter, layer ingredients in the following order: bean dip, avocado mixture, sour cream mixture, onions, tomato, olives, and cheese. Cover and chill until ready to serve. Serve with large tortilla chips. Yield: 12 to 15 servings.

Shrimp Dip or Sandwich Spread
Ellen Baldwin

1	pound fresh shrimp	2	teaspoons finely grated onion
	Salt	2	teaspoons horseradish
	Vinegar	1/4	teaspoon Texas Pete
	Celery leaves	1/2	teaspoon fresh lime juice
1/2	cup Duke's mayonnaise		Dash salt and pepper

Cook shrimp in a medium saucepan of water, with a little salt, vinegar and celery leaves until pink; drain. Cool. Peel and devein. Finely chop shrimp in blender with remaining ingredients. Yield: 8 to 10 servings.

Cucumber Dip
Patty Holley

2	(8-ounce) packages cream cheese, room temperature	2	cucumbers, grated
1	small onion, grated		Mayonnaise

In a medium bowl, beat cream cheese with an electric mixer until smooth. Add onion and cucumbers. Blend well. Add enough mayonnaise to give a consistency for dipping. Great served with Bugles. Yield: 2 cups.

Dill Dip
Kathy Boyd

1	cup sour cream	1	teaspoon garlic salt
1	cup mayonnaise	1/2	teaspoon dill weed
1	teaspoon seasoned salt	2	drops Texas Pete hot sauce
1	teaspoon dried green onion		

In a medium bowl, combine all ingredients and blend well. Refrigerate at least six hours. Serve with raw vegetables. Yield: 3 cups.

Fruit Dip

Vicky Earle

1   (8-ounce) container Cool Whip
1   (8-ounce) container sour cream
1/2 cup brown sugar

Dash of cinnamon
3-4 drops of red food coloring
    or other colors

Whisk all ingredients together in a medium bowl. Chill and serve. Yield: 2 cups.

Note: May use low-fat Cool Whip and sour cream.

Delicious Fruit Dip

Priscilla Bowers

1   (8-ounce) package cream
    cheese
1   (8-ounce) container plain
    yogurt

14 packages Equal
1   teaspoon vanilla
1   teaspoon lemon zest

In a medium bowl, combine all ingredients and mix well. Decorate plate with any kind of fruits you prefer. Yield: 2 cups.

Caramel Dip

Kathy Boyd

1   (14-ounce) package caramels
1   (14-ounce) can sweetened
    condensed milk

1/2 cup butter or margarine

Melt caramels in microwave or saucepan. Add milk and butter. Serve warm as dip with apple slices. Yield: 3 cups.

Boursin Cheese
Suiter Coxe

*1 (8-ounce) package cream
   cheese room temperature
1/2 stick butter, room temperature
1/2 teaspoon Beau Monde
1 medium or large clove garlic,
   pressed*

*1 teaspoon water
1/4 teaspoon Heavenly Herbes de
   Provence
1 teaspoon chopped fresh
   parsley
   Fresh cracked black pepper*

In a medium bowl, mix all ingredients, except pepper. Shape into a patty and cover with fresh cracked black pepper. Mellow for 12 hours. Serve with crackers. Yield: 1 1/2 cups.

Note: Can be frozen.

Brie En Croute
Anne Dawkins

*1 (8-inch) wheel of Brie cheese
1 frozen Pepperidge Farm puff
   pastry sheet*

*1 egg yolk
1 tablespoon water*

Preheat oven to 375 degrees. Thaw sheet of puff pastry 20 minutes, then unfold. Roll out sheet large enough to cover the top and sides of the Brie. Put pastry over Brie and place in a baking dish. Beat egg yolk and water. Brush top of pastry with the egg mixture. Bake at 375 degrees for 15 to 20 minutes or until golden brown. Serve with crackers. Yield: 20 to 25 servings.

Note: Pepper jelly, preserves, or chutney go well as a topper.

Brown Sugar Brie

Anne Dawkins

1 (2-pound) wheel of Brie cheese	1/2 stick butter
1/4 cup brown sugar	1/2 cup sliced almonds

Place Brie in a 9-inch lightly greased quiche dish. Heat; either on high for 3 minutes in a microwave, or in a 300 degree oven for 15 minutes. In a saucepan, melt butter, add sugar and almonds. Pour over Brie. Broil until top is lightly toasted. Serve with French bread. Yield: 16 servings.

Mary's Brie

Mary Zimmerman

1 1/2 cups apricot preserves	1 (5-inch) wheel of Brie cheese
1/3 cup orange liqueur	Raspberries

In a saucepan, heat together the preserves and liqueur. Pour, while hot, over the Brie. Place raspberries on top. Serve with crackers. Yield: 12 to 14 servings.

Mustard Brie Amandine

Kathy Boyd

4 tablespoons Dijon mustard	1/4 cup sliced almonds, toasted
2 tablespoons orange marmalade	Triscuit wafers or fresh fruit
1 (15-ounce) wheel Brie cheese	

In a small bowl, blend mustard and marmalade. Place Brie on microwavable serving plate, top with mustard mixture. Microwave on high 1 to 3 minutes, rotating the cheese a quarter turn and checking for desired softness every 30 seconds. Sprinkle with almonds. Serve with wafers or fruit. Yield: 8 to 10 servings.

Cheese Spread

Trisha Montgomery

1 pound sharp Cheddar cheese, grated	1/2 onion, chopped
1 (8-ounce) package cream cheese	1 cup pecans, chopped
	1 cup mayonnaise
	Raspberry jelly

Combine cheeses, onion, pecans and mayonnaise. Process in food processor until smooth. Spoon into a mold lined with saran wrap and refrigerate overnight. Unmold and place jelly in center of a ring mold. Serve with wheat crackers. Yield: 15 to 20 servings.

Corn and Olive Spread

Denise Amerson

2 (8-ounce) packages cream cheese	1 (11-ounce) can whole kernel corn, drained
1 (1-ounce) envelope of Ranch salad dressing mix	1 (4-ounce) can chopped green chilies, drained
1 medium red pepper, chopped	
1 (41/2-ounce) can chopped olives, drained	

In a medium bowl, beat cream cheese until smooth. Add dressing mix and stir. Add remaining ingredients and stir to combine. Cover and refrigerate 1 to 2 hours. Serve with crackers. Yield: 15 to 20 servings.

Toasted Almond Party Spread

Jacqueline Segars

1   *(8-ounce) package cream cheese, softened*

6   *ounces shredded Swiss cheese*

/3 *cup Miracle Whip salad dressing*

2   *teaspoons chopped green onions*

1/8 *teaspoon nutmeg*

1/3 *cup sliced almonds, toasted*

Preheat oven to 350 degrees. In a medium bowl, combine all ingredients. Blend well. Spread in a small pie plate or quiche dish. Bake at 350 degrees for 15 minutes. Serve with crackers. Yield: 12 servings or double for 24 servings.

Dried Beef Spread

Stephanie McCullum

1   *(8-ounce) package cream cheese, softened*

3   *tablespoons milk*

1   *tablespoon minced onion*

1/4 *cup chopped green pepper*

1   *(2 1/2-ounce) jar dried beef, finely chopped*

1/2 *cup sour cream*

1/2 *cup pecans, chopped*

Preheat oven to 350 degrees. Combine cream cheese and next five ingredients in a medium bowl. Mix well. Place in a 9-inch pie plate. Top with pecans. Bake at 350 degrees for 20 minutes. Serve hot with crackers. Yield: 8 to 10 servings.

Seafood Spread
Kathy Boyd

1	(8-ounce) package cream cheese	5	green onions, minced
	Juice of 1 lemon		Mayonnaise
1	pound shrimp, boiled and coarsely ground		Hot sauce
			Worcestershire sauce
1	pound crabmeat, flaked		Salt and pepper to taste

In a medium bowl, soften cream cheese with lemon juice. Add shrimp, crabmeat, and onions. Add enough mayonnaise to give a consistency for spreading on crackers. Season with hot sauce, Worcestershire, salt, and pepper. Better if made at least 8 hours ahead. Yield: 15 servings.

Crab Spread
Mary Catherine Stuckey

1	(6-ounce) can crabmeat	Dash horseradish
1	(8-ounce) package cream cheese, softened	Dash Worcestershire sauce
		Dash lemon juice
1	tablespoon chopped bell pepper	Dash of Texas Pete or
1	tablespoon chopped onion	Tabasco sauce

In a medium bowl, combine all ingredients and blend well. Adjust seasonings to your taste. Serve cold with crackers. Yield: About 2 cups.

Alyce's Crab Casserole

Alyce Gandy

4	tablespoons butter	1	cup grated Cheddar cheese
2	tablespoons flour	2	(6-ounce) cans crabmeat
1/2	cup half-and-half	1	small bell pepper, minced
1/4	cup whole milk	3-4	tablespoons sherry
	Dash black pepper	1/2	cup grated New York State
	Salt to taste		cheese
1	teaspoon dry mustard	1	cup buttered breadcrumbs

Preheat oven to 350 degrees. Melt butter in a medium saucepan. Add flour and mix until smooth. Add half-and-half and milk. Cook until thickened over low heat. Add pepper, salt, mustard, and cheese. Stir in crabmeat and bell pepper. Remove from heat; add sherry and mix thoroughly. Put in a glass casserole dish. Top with New York State cheese and breadcrumbs. Bake at 400 degrees until bubbly and lightly browned. Serve hot with sesame crackers. Yield: 10 to 12 servings.

Crab Pâté

Harriette Crouch

1	(10 3/4-ounce) can cream of mushroom soup, undiluted	1	(6-ounce) can crabmeat, drained and flaked
1	(1/4-ounce) envelope unflavored gelatin	1	small onion, grated
3	tablespoons cold water	1	cup finely chopped celery
3/4	cup mayonnaise		Parsley sprigs
1	(8-ounce) package cream cheese, softened		

Heat soup in a medium saucepan over low heat. Remove from heat. Dissolve gelatin in cold water. Add to soup, stirring well. Add next five ingredients, mix well. Spoon into a greased 4-cup mold. Chill until firm. Unmold and garnish with parsley. Serve with assorted crackers. Yield: About 4 cups.

Cream Cheese Oyster Roll
Kathy Boyd

1	(3-ounce) can smoked oysters
1	(8-ounce) package cream cheese, room temperature
2	tablespoons mayonnaise
1/2	teaspoon garlic powder
	Salt and pepper to taste

Milk, as needed for consistency
1/2 cup pecans, chopped fine
Dehydrated or frozen chopped chives
Assorted crackers

Drain oysters, chop finely and set aside. In a medium bowl, combine cheese, mayonnaise, and garlic powder. Add salt and pepper to taste. Add milk if needed for consistency. Spread cheese mixture evenly about 1/8-inch thick in an 8x10-inch rectangle on a sheet of aluminum foil. Put in freezer until very firm. Combine chopped oysters and nuts; mix well. Sprinkle evenly over cheese and roll up jelly roll fashion, peeling foil away as you roll up. Sprinkle chives evenly over a sheet of waxed paper and coat roll. Wrap in waxed paper. Refrigerate overnight or until firm. Serve with assorted crackers. Yield: 30 to 36 servings.

Salmon Log
Margaret Reaves

1 (15-ounce) can red salmon
1 (8-ounce) package cream cheese, softened
1 tablespoon lemon juice
2 teaspoons grated onion

1 teaspoon horseradish
1/4 teaspoon liquid smoke
1/4 teaspoon salt
Chopped nuts
Parsley

In a medium bowl, mix all ingredients together by hand. Shape into a 10-inch log and roll in parsley or chopped nuts or both. Chill several hours. Serve with crackers. Yield: 10-inch log.

Maryland Shrimp Mousse
Kathy Boyd

1	(103/4-ounce) can tomato soup	1/2	cup chopped celery
1	(1/4-ounce) envelope unflavored gelatin softened in 1/4 cup cold water	1/2	cup onion, minced
		5	(41/2-ounce) cans shrimp, drained and chopped
1	cup mayonnaise		Salt to taste
1	(8-ounce) package of cream cheese, softened		Worcestershire sauce to taste
		1/4	cup bell pepper, chopped (optional)

In a saucepan, heat soup. Stir in gelatin. Cool. In a medium bowl, cream mayonnaise with cream cheese. Add remaining ingredients. Blend well. Pour into a 11/2-quart mold or fish mold. Chill. Serve with crackers. Yield: 25 servings.

Note: Fresh or frozen shrimp may be used. Use 2 to 3 cups.

Southwestern Pimento Chili Spread
Ann Marie Pennington

1/2	pound sharp Cheddar cheese, grated	1-2	teaspoons vinegar to taste
1/2	pound Monterey Jack cheese grated	1/2	teaspoon chili powder
		1/2	small onion, grated
1	(4-ounce) can green chilies	2	hard boiled eggs, finely chopped
1	(2-ounce) jar pimentos		Salt and pepper to taste
1/4	cup mayonnaise		

In a medium bowl, combine all ingredients and mix well. Refrigerate. Serve as a dip or spread. Yield: 10 to 12 servings.

Note: Best to prepare in advance, so flavors can develop.

Two Bored Women's Pimento Cheese
Harriett Lemke

1   package sharp Cheddar
    cheese, any size
1   package mild Cheddar cheese,
    same size package as sharp
    cheese

Duke's Mayonnaise, enough
to make mixture creamy
Pimentos, chopped, to taste
Tony's seasoning to taste

Grate cheeses. Combine all ingredients in a food processor. Mix to desired consistency. Garnish with green and red grapes. Serve with a good wheat cracker or use as a sandwich spread.

Note: Enjoy a truly southern favorite! Also good on grilled hamburgers, or as a topper for grits.

Monterey Jack Salsa
Cely Anne Reynolds

1   (4-ounce) can chopped green
    chilies
1   (4-ounce) can chopped black
    olives
4   green onions, chopped
1/4 pound Monterey Jack cheese,
    shredded

1   tomato, chopped
1/2 cup Italian salad dressing
1/4 cup fresh chopped cilantro
    Tortilla chips

Blend all ingredients together in a medium bowl. Chill. Serve with tortilla chips. Yield: 4 to 6 servings.

Chunky Salsa
Anne Braddock

1-2 large tomatoes, chopped
1 (4-ounce) can chopped ripe olives, drained
1 (4 1/2-ounce) can chopped green chilies, drained
1 bunch spring onions, chopped

2/3 cup white vinegar
1/4 cup vegetable oil
1 tablespoon sugar
1 teaspoon black pepper
1 teaspoon garlic powder
Tortilla chips

Combine vegetables and place in a bowl. In a jar with a tight-fitting lid, combine vinegar and next four ingredients. Shake well and pour over vegetables. Refrigerate at least 2 hours but best if refrigerated overnight. Drain before serving. Serve with chips. Yield: 6 to 8 servings.

Cajun Chips
Gail Mobley

1 (20-ounce) bag tortilla chips
1 pound smoked sausage, cut into bite-sized pieces
1 pound small shrimp (or crayfish), cooked and shelled
1 large tomato, diced
1 large red onion, cut in rings

1 (3.8-ounce) can sliced black olives, drained
2 tablespoons of creole seasoning
1 (15-ounce) jar of Cheese Whiz, melted in microwave

Layer ingredients in order listed on an ovenproof platter. Place under broiler in oven 3 minutes or until chips start to brown. Yield: 8 servings.

Mushroom Bacon Bites
Kathy Boyd

24 medium fresh mushrooms
12 bacon strips, halved

1 cup barbecue sauce

Wrap each mushroom with a piece of bacon; secure with a toothpick. Thread onto metal or soaked bamboo skewers; brush with barbecue sauce. Grill, uncovered, over indirect medium heat 10 to 15 minutes or until the bacon is crisp and the mushrooms are tender, turning and basting occasionally with remaining barbecue sauce. Yield: 2 dozen.

Baked Mushrooms

Susie Bennett

1   *pound mushrooms, sliced*   *Parsley flakes*
   Garlic powder   *Salt and pepper to taste*
   Italian breadcrumbs   1   *tablespoon oil*

Preheat oven to 350 degrees. Layer mushrooms in a 9-inch baking dish. Sprinkle with garlic powder, breadcrumbs, parsley, salt, and pepper to lightly cover mushrooms. No specific measurements, just add seasoning to taste. Dot with oil. Bake at 350 degrees for 15 minutes. Serve hot with crackers. Yield: 6 to 8 servings.

Stuffed Mushrooms

Lea Saunders

2   *(16-ounce) packages large*   1   *(12-ounce) package cream*
   fresh mushrooms   *cheese*
1 1/2 *pounds spicy pork sausage*
   Red crushed pepper to taste
   or hot sauce

Preheat oven to 350 degrees. Decap mushrooms. Wipe mushrooms clean with paper towel. Do not use water. In a skillet, cook sausage until brown and crumbly. Drain excess grease from sausage. Add pepper and cream cheese. Cook until bubbly. Stuff mushrooms with mixture. Place in a baking dish. Bake at 350 degrees until bubbly. Yield: 15 servings.

Stuffed Mushrooms

Jennifer Schock

Mushrooms	*Seasoned breadcrumbs*
Onions	*Salt and pepper to taste*
Butter	*Paprika*
Fresh Parmesan cheese	

Preheat oven to 350 degrees. Wipe mushrooms clean with a paper towel. Remove stems from mushrooms and set caps aside. Finely dice stems and onion. In a saucepan, sauté stems and onion in butter. Add enough cheese to see it throughout the mushrooms. Add breadcrumbs to thicken mixture. Add salt and pepper to taste. Stuff mushrooms with breadcrumb mixture. Sprinkle with paprika to add color. Place on a baking sheet. Bake at 350 degrees for 15 to 20 minutes. Yield: 2 mushrooms per person.

Note: This recipe truly is a bit of this, a bit of that. You cannot do anything to mess this up! You can even add white wine to your mixture - YUM!

Marinated Olives

Anne Dawkins

4 *cups assorted olives, kalamata, niçose and green picholine*	2 *cloves garlic, pressed or mashed*
1/4 *cup olive oil*	2 *teaspoons freshly minced rosemary*
1 *teaspoon grated orange or lemon zest and or strips of skin*	2 *dashes cayenne pepper*
	1 *teaspoon fennel seeds (optional)*

Combine all ingredients in a glass bowl and marinate for at least one hour at room temperature or up to one week refrigerated. Yield: 4 cups.

Asparagus Rolls
Wilma Casstevens

20 slices white bread, without
   crust
3 ounces blue cheese
1 (8-ounce) package cream
   cheese, softened

1 egg, beaten
1 (14 1/2-ounce) can asparagus
   spears, drained
2 sticks butter or margarine,
   melted

Use a rolling pin to flatten each slice of bread. Combine blue cheese, cream cheese, and egg in a medium bowl. Mix well. Spread evenly on bread covering to edges. Place one asparagus spear on each slice, roll up and secure with 3 tooth picks. Dip in melted butter. Place on a baking sheet and freeze. Partially thaw and slice each roll into three rounds. Bake at 375 degrees for 15 minutes. Serve hot. Yield: 60 rolls.

Bar-B-Que Grazing Mix
Anne Dawkins

2 tablespoons margarine
2 teaspoons BBQ seasoning

1 (8-ounce) can mixed nuts
1 (3-ounce) can chow mein
   noodles

BBQ seasoning
1 teaspoon seasoned salt or
   celery salt

1 teaspoon chili powder

Melt margarine in a medium saucepan. Add seasoning and stir well. Add nuts and noodles. Stir gently to coat with margarine mixture. Cook, uncovered, on high about 7 minutes or until toasted, stirring frequently. Spread on a baking sheet and let stand until crisp. Yield: 3 cups.

Sugar Coated Peanuts
Paula Bowen

1 cup sugar   2 cups raw peanuts
1/2 cup water

Preheat oven to 300 degrees. In a medium saucepan, melt sugar in water. Stir in peanuts and cook until all syrup is gone and peanuts are sugar coated. Watch closely as water decreases and stir constantly to keep from burning. Pour into a large baking pan. Bake at 300 degrees for 20 minutes. Stir frequently. Yield: 2 cups.

Crunchy Snack Mix
Danielle Hall

4 cups bite-sized pretzels
3 cups honey graham cereal
2 cups crispy wheat cereal squares
1 1/2 cups pecan halves
3/4 cup butter or margarine, melted

1 1/2 tablespoons Worcestershire sauce
2 tablespoons light brown sugar

Preheat oven to 250 degrees. Combine first four ingredients in a 10x15-inch jelly roll pan. In a small bowl, combine butter, Worcestershire sauce, and brown sugar; pour over cereal mixture, stirring to coat. Bake at 250 degrees for 1 hour; stirring every 15 minutes. Remove from oven and cool. Store in airtight container. Yield: 8 cups.

Flour Tortilla Wraps
Trisha Montgomery

2 (8-ounce) packages cream
   cheese, softened
1 (1-ounce) envelope Ranch
   salad dressing mix
2 stems chopped green onions
1/2 cup diced black olives

1/2 cup chopped pimentos
1/2 cup chopped green chilies
   Jalapeños, chopped
   (optional)
1 (20-ounce) package flour
   tortillas

In a medium bowl, combine cream cheese, dressing mix, and onions. Blend well. Drain olives, pimentos, and chilies and place on paper towel to soak up excess moisture. Stir into cream cheese mixture, mixing well. Spread evenly on tortillas and roll up jelly roll style. Individually wrap each tortilla in plastic wrap. Refrigerate overnight. Cut into one-half inch slices just before serving. Yield: 200 pieces.

Hot Bacon Appetizers
Anne Dawkins

1/2 pound of bacon
3/4 cup shredded American
   cheese

1/4 cup margarine, softened
2 teaspoons caraway seeds
50 Melba toast rounds

In a skillet, cook bacon; drain. Cool and crumble. In a medium bowl, combine all the ingredients and spread evenly on the rounds. Broil 2 minutes or until the cheese melts. Serve hot. Yield: 50 bacon appetizers.

Hot Cheese Puffs
Fran Sligh

5	cups grated sharp Cheddar cheese	1 1/2	teaspoons salt
2	sticks butter or margarine, softened	2 1/2	teaspoons paprika
		1	(10-ounce) package dates
2	cups all-purpose flour	1	pound whole pecans

Preheat oven to 400 degrees. In a large bowl, combine cheese and next four ingredients. Mix well. Set aside. Cut dates and pecans in half. Insert pecan into date and wrap dough around the date to form a ball. Place on a baking sheet. Bake at 400 degrees for 10 to 15 minutes. Yield: 100 puffs.

Note: If making for future use, freeze puffs on a baking sheet and store in plastic bags. To bake, place frozen puffs on baking sheet. Do not need to thaw.

Hot Pepper Jelly Turnovers
Anne Dawkins

1	(5-ounce) jar sharp processed cheese spread	1	cup all-purpose flour
1/2	cup butter		Pepper jelly
		1	tablespoon cold water

Preheat oven to 375 degrees. In a mixing bowl, cut cheese spread and butter into flour. Sprinkle water over mixture. Stir only until dry ingredients are moistened. Shape dough into ball and chill about 4 hours. Divide dough in half. Roll dough out to a 1/8-inch thickness. Cut into 3-inch rounds. On each round, place about one-fourth teaspoon of pepper jelly, then fold over and seal. Moisten the edges with water. On a lightly greased baking sheet, bake turnovers at 375 degrees for 10 to 12 minutes. Cool on rack. Yield: 2 dozen.

Cheese Wafers
Lee Hicks

2 sticks salted butter, softened	1 1/2 cups chopped pecans or
2 cups all-purpose flour	1 cup Grapenuts cereal
1/2 teaspoon cayenne pepper	
4 cups grated extra sharp	
Cheddar cheese	

Combine butter and flour in a large bowl. Mix with a wooden spoon. Sprinkle in pepper and begin to mix with hands. Add grated cheese. Continue mixing with hands. Add pecans or grapenuts and thoroughly mix. Divide dough into fourths and roll into four 10-inch rolls. Wrap each roll in waxed paper. Put into refrigerator to chill overnight. Slice 1/4-inch thick and place on a baking sheet lined with parchment paper. Bake at 325 degrees for 8 to 10 minutes or until browned. Yield: About 100 wafers.

Note: Grapenuts make wafers crunchier.

Jill's Cheese Thins
Jill Burdette

1 stick butter, softened	1/2 (1 1/4-ounce) envelope onion
1/2 pound sharp Cheddar cheese,	soup mix
shredded	Cayenne pepper to taste
1 cup all-purpose flour	

Preheat oven to 375 degrees. In a medium bowl, thoroughly mix all ingredients. Roll dough out on floured surface to a 1/8-inch thickness. Cut into small rounds. Place on a baking sheet. Bake at 375 degrees for 10 to 15 minutes. Yield: About 4 dozen.

Rooster's Famous Fire Crackers

Bill Dawkins, Sr.

1 (15-ounce) box Keebler Zesta fat-free saltines	Red pepper flakes or cayenne pepper
2 teaspoons seasoning of choice, Cherchies Lem'n Savory seasoning (spicy blend) or Pueblo Rub (grill ing spice)	1 (10-ounce) log Cracker Barrel extra sharp Cheddar cheese, shredded

Preheat oven to 500 degrees or 450 to 475 degrees if your oven runs hot. Arrange crackers (about 40) in rows on a 10x15-inch jelly roll pan. Make sure the crackers are touching each other. Sprinkle seasoning over crackers, then sprinkle as many pepper flakes as you dare. Top evenly with cheese. Place pan on center shelf of oven. Close door and turn off oven. Leave in oven overnight or at least 4 hours. Break apart and eat or store. Yield: 40 to 50 pieces.

Note: Pepper-hot, crisp, crunchy, cheesy crackers are perfect for party food, a great tailgate snack or a wonderful homemade gift.

Party Ham Biscuits

Mary Jane McDonald

Biscuits, homemade or store bought, prebaked until almost done	Country ham pieces Mayonnaise, enough to hold ham together

Preheat oven to 275 degrees. Place ham pieces on a broiler pan. Bake at 275 degrees for 20 minutes. Remove ham from oven and turn oven up to 400 degrees. Place ham in a food processor and grind. In a medium bowl, mix ham and add enough mayonnaise to hold ham together. Spoon 1 tablespoon of ham mixture into each biscuit. Place on a baking sheet. Bake at 400 degrees for 20 minutes or until golden brown. Yield: 2 biscuits per serving.

Note: Will keep well in freezer.

Tex Mex Chili Cups
Deborah Griggs

1 (12-ounce) package Won Ton wrappers	*2 tablespoons Lawry's chili mix*
1 1/2 pounds chicken, cooked and finely chopped	*2 cups shredded Monterey Jack cheese*
1/4 teaspoon salt	*1 (4-ounce) can green chilies, drained*
1/4 teaspoon black pepper	*1 cup Ranch salad dressing*

Preheat oven to 350 degrees. Push wrappers into mini muffin pans and bake 5 minutes. In a medium bowl, mix all remaining ingredients. Fill wrappers in muffin tins with chicken mixture. Bake at 350 degrees for 10 to 12 minutes. Yield: 3 dozen cups.

Note: These can be kept covered in the refrigerator until ready to cook.

Vegetable Bars
Minnie Bryant

2 (8-ounce) cans refrigerated crescent rolls	*1 cup broccoli, finely chopped*
2 (8-ounce) packages cream cheese	*1 cup carrots, finely chopped*
1 (1-ounce) package Ranch salad dressing mix	*1 cup cauliflower, finely chopped*
1 cup Miracle Whip salad dressing	*2 cups shredded sharp Cheddar cheese*

Preheat oven to 350 degrees. Press crescent rolls into 10x15-inch jelly roll pan. Bake at 275 degrees for 10 minutes. Cool. In a medium bowl, mix cream cheese, dressing mix, and salad dressing. Spread over crust. Sprinkle vegetables over mixture. Top with cheese. Chill several hours. Cut into bars. Bake at 350 degrees for 10 minutes. Yield: 4 dozen bars.

Grouper Fingers

Beth and Jamie Morphis

Grouper filets	1	cup orange marmalade
Buttermilk	1/4	cup yellow mustard
House of Autry seafood mix	2	tablespoons horseradish
Oil		sauce or to taste

Cut filets into 1x3-inch fingers. Place in a medium bowl and soak in buttermilk. Batter fingers in seafood mix. Deep fry until crispy brown. In a small bowl, combine marmalade, mustard, and horseradish. Mix well. Serve fingers with marmalade sauce. Yield: 2 fingers per serving.

Marinated Shrimp

Beth Brown

Submitted by Kathy Boyd

2	pounds of shrimp, cooked, peeled and deveined	1 1/2	teaspoons salt
		2	tablespoons celery seed
1	large onion, sliced and ringed		Dash of hot pepper sauce
2-3	bay leaves	2	teaspoons Worcestershire
2	cups oil		sauce
1 3/4	cups vinegar	2	tablespoons capers

In a large glass bowl, layer shrimp, onion, and bay leaves. In a separate bowl, mix together the remaining ingredients. Pour over shrimp. Stirring gently to coat. Marinate in refrigerator 48 hours. Stir occasionally. Remove bay leaves and serve. Yield: 6 to 8 servings.

Stuffed Shrimp

Becky Brown

24 shrimp, cooked
1/4 cup butter, divided
1 medium onion, finely chopped
1/2 red bell pepper, finely chopped
1/2 bell pepper, finely chopped
2 cloves garlic
1 tablespoon cajun seasoning

1/2 cup fine dry breadcrumbs
1 egg, beaten
1/3 cup mayonnaise
1 pound crabmeat, finely chopped
2 tablespoons lemon juice
2 tablespoons Chablis wine

Preheat oven to 350 degrees. Peel shrimp leaving tails intact. Devein. Cut shrimp down the center, cutting almost but not completely through. Open the two halves flat to resemble a butterfly shape. In a saucepan, melt two tablespoons of butter. Add onion, bell pepper, and garlic. Sauté until vegetables are tender. Add seasoning and breadcrumbs. Set aside. In a separate bowl, combine egg, mayonnaise, and crabmeat. Stir in vegetables and mix well. Stuff each shrimp with crab mixture, dividing evenly. Arrange shrimp on a foil lined pan. Bake at 350 degrees for about 10 minutes. Melt remaining butter in a small saucepan. Add lemon juice and wine. Blend well. Remove shrimp from oven and lower oven to 300 degrees. Drizzle shrimp with butter mixture and return oven long enough to heat butter mixture. Yield: 24 shrimp.

Barbequed Chicken Wings

Catherine Pate

1 egg
1 cup cooking oil
3 tablespoons salt

1 teaspoon black pepper
1 pint apple cider vinegar
3 pounds chicken wings

Preheat oven to 375 degrees. In a medium bowl, beat egg and mix with next four ingredients. Place chicken in a 9x13-inch casserole dish. Pour sauce over top. Bake at 375 degrees for 45 minutes. Remove from oven and pour off most of sauce. Return to oven 15 additional minutes or until browned. Yield: 6 to 10 servings.

Sesame Chicken Appetizers

Anne Dawkins

1/2	cup soy sauce	4	chicken breast halves,
2	teaspoons sesame oil		skinned and boned
1	teaspoon ground ginger	1/2	cup sesame seeds
3	green onions, sliced		Sweet and sour sauce
2	cloves garlic, minced		

Combine first five ingredients in a small bowl. Stir well. Cut each chicken breast half into four strips. Add chicken to marinade. Cover and chill 1 hour. Remove chicken from marinade. Weave 1 chicken strip on each of 16 skewers. If using wooden skewers, soak in water before placing the chicken on them. Coat with sesame seeds. Place on rack in a broiler pan. Broil about 5 inches from heat 3 minutes. Turn skewers. Broil 3 more minutes or until done. Serve with sweet and sour sauce. Yield: 16 servings.

Barbecue Brisket of Beef

Betty Greene
Submitted by Byron Greene

1	(8-pound) choice fresh	1	tablespoon dry mustard
	boneless brisket of beef	1	tablespoon garlic salt
	Unseasoned meat tenderizer	6	dashes of Tabasco sauce
2 2/3	cups ketchup	18	dashes of Worcestershire
1	cup lemon juice		sauce
1 1/2	cups vinegar		Salt and pepper to taste

Preheat oven to 270 degrees. Put brisket in a roasting pan and sprinkle with meat tenderizer. In a small bowl, mix remaining ingredients together. Pour over brisket. Bake at 270 degrees for 1 hour. Increase temperature to 325 degrees and bake 3 to 4 more hours until well-done. Do not overcook. Baste occasionally. Add a little water if sauce becomes too thick. Remove meat from sauce and chill overnight. Slice very thin and return to sauce for heating. Serve in chafing dish with hot rolls. Yield: 40 servings.

Sweet-Sour Beef Balls with Pineapple and Peppers
Betty Greene
Submitted by Byron Greene

Beef Balls

1 pound ground beef	1 teaspoon salt
1 egg	2 tablespoons chopped onion
1 tablespoons cornstarch	Dash black pepper

Sauce

1 tablespoon oil	6 tablespoons water
1 cup pineapple juice	1/2 cup sugar
3 tablespoons cornstarch	4 slices pineapple, cut in pieces
1 tablespoon soy sauce	3 large bell peppers, cut in
3 tablespoons white vinegar	12 to 15 strips lengthwise

For beef balls, in a medium bowl, combine all ingredients. Mix well. Form into tiny balls. Makes about 20 to 24 balls. In a saucepan, brown balls in a small amount of oil; drain. To prepare sauce, combine oil and pineapple juice in a medium saucepan. Cook over low heat a few minutes. Add cornstarch, soy sauce, vinegar, water, and sugar. Cook until thickens, stirring constantly. Add meat balls, pineapple pieces, and bell pepper. Heat thoroughly. Serve hot. Yield: 10 servings.

Lib McGee's Meatballs
Joan Hoffmeyer

1 pound ground chuck	1 teaspoon salt
1 egg, beaten	1/4 teaspoon pepper
1 tablespoon cornstarch	1 (12-ounce) jar chili sauce
1 tablespoon minced onion	1 (8-ounce) jar grape jam

Combine ground chuck and next five ingredients. Form into balls using one teaspoon of meat per ball. In a saucepan, combine chili sauce, and jam. Bring to a boil. Drop meatballs into sauce and cook 7 minutes. Serve in a chafing dish. Yield: 50 meatballs.

Hot Mocha Mix

Kathy Boyd

1 cup unsweetened cocoa	2 cups dry nonfat milk powder
2 1/2 cups sugar	1/2 cup instant coffee
2 cups dry nondairy coffee creamer	1 vanilla bean, cut in quarters

Combine all ingredients in a large dry bowl. Stir until well blended. Pack into jars, making sure a piece of vanilla bean is in each jar. Seal and label. Store in refrigerator at least a week before using to allow vanilla flavor to be absorbed into the mix. Yield: 8 cups mocha mix.

Note: Use 3 tablespoons mocha mix for every 3/4 cup boiling water. Top with a marshmallow or whipped cream.

Hot Spicy Cider

Jean Beasley

1 gallon apple cider	1 (16-ounce) can frozen orange juice concentrate
1/2 cup brown sugar	
1/2 teaspoon ground nutmeg	1/2 cup lemon juice
1 teaspoon ground cloves	Cinnamon sticks (optional)
2 teaspoons ground cinnamon	

Combine apple cider, sugar, and spices in a large saucepan. Bring to a boil, cover, reduce heat and simmer 10 minutes. Add orange juice concentrate and lemon juice. Stir until thoroughly heated. Serve hot with cinnamon stick, if desired. Yield: 30 servings.

Festive Wassail
Bertha Thompson

2	quarts apple cider	4	cups orange juice
1/2	cup brown sugar	2	cups pineapple juice
4	sticks cinnamon	3-4	thick orange slices, halved
24	whole cloves		

In a 3-quart saucepan, combine cider, sugar, cinnamon and clove. Bring to a boil over medium heat. Reduce to low and simmer 5 minutes. Add orange and pineapple juice. Heat through but do not boil. Push additional cloves through rind of orange slices and set aside. To serve, pour cider mixture through a sieve into a warm pitcher or slow cooker. Float orange slices in wassail. Yield: 25 servings.

Refreshing Lemon Punch
Joann Peterson

2	(3-ounce) packages lemon gelatin	1	(46-ounce) can pineapple juice
3	cups sugar	8	cups cold water
8	cups boiling water	2	quarts ginger ale
10	tablespoons lemon juice		

In a large bowl, dissolve gelatin and sugar in boiling water. Add lemon juice, pineapple juice and cold water. Mix well. Freeze until slushy. To serve, pour mixture into a punch bowl and stir in ginger ale. Yield: 30 servings.

Mama's Punch
Kathy Boyd

1	(46-ounce) can pineapple juice, chilled	1 1/2	pints softened vanilla ice cream
1	pint orange sherbet	3	cups ginger ale, chilled

In a large saucepan, beat pineapple juice, sherbert and ice cream with an electric mixer until creamy. Pour into a punch bowl and add ginger ale just before serving. Yield: 24 servings.

Coffee Punch

Rose Marie Newsom

9   cups boiling water, divided
12 heaping teaspoons instant
    coffee
1   cup sugar
3   heaping tablespoons cocoa

1/2 gallon softened vanilla ice
     cream
1   (16-ounce) container Cool
     Whip

Mix eight cups water and instant coffee in a large saucepan. In a separate saucepan, mix remaining water, sugar, and cocoa. Bring to a boil and pour into coffee. Store in refrigerator in a large jar until ready to serve. This can be made several days ahead. When ready to serve, put refrigerated mixture in a punch bowl. Add ice cream and whipped topping. Blend until creamy. Yield: 20 to 25 servings.

Frozen Punch

Paula Bowen

2   (46-ounce) cans pineapple
    grapefruit juice
1   (6-ounce) can frozen lemon-
    ade

1/2 (6-ounce) can frozen orange
     juice
21/4 cups sugar
3   quarts ginger ale

In a large container, combine juices and sugar. Add ginger ale and stir very little. Freeze. Let thaw 2 to 3 hours before serving. Do not add water or ice. Yield: 50 servings.

Instant Russian Tea
Frances Kelley

2 cups Tang	1 3/4 cups sugar
1 package instant lemonade	1 teaspoon ground cloves
3/4 cup instant tea	2 teaspoons ground cinnamon

In a large bowl, combine all ingredients. Mix well. Store in a jar. Use 1 or 2 teaspoons per cup of hot water. Yield: About 5 cups mix.

Summer Tea
Debbie Segars

2 cups water	1 (6-ounce) can frozen lemon-ade
1 cup sugar	
10 bags Bigelow's Plantation mint tea	1 (6-ounce) can frozen limeade
	Juice of 1 orange

In a saucepan, boil water. Stir in sugar until dissolved. Remove from heat. Steep tea bags in sugar water for 15 minutes. Add lemonade, limeade, and orange juice. Add enough water to make 1 gallon. Yield: 1 gallon.

Sangria
Judy Askins

Peach, small pieces	1 cup lemonade
Orange, small pieces	2 teaspoons sugar
Lemon, small pieces	1 ounce brandy
3 cups red wine	Ice

Add bits of peach, orange, and lemon to pitcher. Add remaining ingredients and lots of ice. Yield: 5 to 6 servings.

Note: Recipe is from Granada, Spain.

★ Soups ★ Stews ★ Sandwiches

Joan Snoddy, Eileen Long,
Sarah Smith, Beth Cox
Mama's junior year
at Coker College

May 2001 was the 50th reunion for Mama's college class. Mama's college roommate, Joan Snoddy Hoffmeyer, and Daddy had a get together at our farm house for the Class of '51 before their festivities started at the college. During the course of preparing for the reunion, Joan was going through old college pictures and ran across some letters that Mama had written to her in 1948. One especially stuck in my mind as I was compiling NeNa's Garden. It read:

"Dearest "Snoddy"
    So you been cooking too? I sure hope you've had better luck than me. I'll never make a cook the way I'm doing now. Howard's getting worried but I won't let him starve. If nothing else, I can give him a sand-wich. I can make them..."

Mama never did love cooking but was a good cook anyway. However, I do remember a lot of toasted pimento cheese sandwiches and chocolate milkshakes when we were growing up.

There's a special kind of freedom
friends enjoy.
Freedom to share innermost thoughts,
to ask a favor,
to show their true feelings.
The freedom to simply be themselves.

Cheeseburger Soup

Ruth Gardner

1/2 pound ground beef	4 cups diced potatoes
3/4 cup chopped onion	1/4 cup all-purpose flour
3/4 cup shredded carrots	8 ounces processed cheese,
3/4 cup diced celery	cubed
1 teaspoon basil	1 1/2 cups milk
1 teaspoon dried parsley flakes	3/4 teaspoon salt
4 tablespoons margarine,	1/2 teaspoon black pepper
divided	1/4 cup sour cream
3 cups chicken broth	

In a 3-quart saucepan, brown beef. Drain and set aside. In the same saucepan, sauté onion and next four ingredients in one tablespoon margarine until vegetables are tender, about 10 minutes. Add broth, potatoes, and beef; bring to a boil. Reduce heat; cover and simmer 10 to 12 minutes or until potatoes are tender. Meanwhile, in a small skillet, melt remaining margarine. Add flour; cook and stir about 5 minutes or until bubbly. Add to soup, bring to a boil. Cook and stir 2 minutes. Reduce heat to low. Add cheese, milk, salt, and pepper. Cook and stir until cheese melts. Remove from heat; blend in sour cream. Yield: 8 servings.

Note: May substitute broth for bouillon cube. Dissolve cube in four tablespoons of water.

Cream of Avocado Soup

Kitty Jackson

2 large avocados, mashed	1/2 teaspoon salt
2 cups light cream	Dash black pepper
1 3/4 cups chicken broth	Dillweed
1 tablespoon lemon juice	

In a medium bowl, combine avocados and next five ingredients. Stir until smooth or use blender to mix. Chill 5 to 6 hours. Garnish with dillweed. Yield: 8 to 10 servings.

Crab and Mushroom Soup

Cynthia Roberson

3	tablespoons butter		1	cup sliced mushrooms
2	cups celery, finely chopped		1	cup crabmeat
1/2	cup parsley, finely chopped		1/4	cup Sauterne cooking wine
1	small onion, minced by hand		2	cups milk
3	tablespoons flour			
1	cup chicken broth			

Melt butter in the top of a double boiler over direct heat. Stir in celery, parsley, and onion. Cook and stir over medium heat until the vegetables are soft and translucent, but not brown. Stir in the flour and cook a few minutes more until the flour begins to be golden. Whisk in the chicken broth, beating until all lumps are gone from the flour. Set the mixture over hot water in the double boiler and steam about 1 hour, until the celery is tender. Stir in the mushrooms, crabmeat, and wine. The recipe may be prepared ahead to this point. At serving time, add the milk and reheat the soup until it is piping hot.
Do not let it cook further, once the milk has been added. Yield: 6 to 8 servings.

Note: A food processor is helpful for chopping the celery and parsley and slicing the mushrooms. Do not put the onion in the processor. It makes the flavor strong and bitter.

Fast Fiesta Soup

Kathy Boyd

2	(10-ounce) cans diced tomatoes and green chilies		1	(15-ounce) can black beans, rinsed and drained
1	(15 1/4-ounce) can whole kernel corn, drained			Shredded Cheddar cheese
				Sour cream

In a saucepan, combine tomatoes, corn, and beans; heat. Garnish servings with cheese and sour cream, if desired. Yield: 4 servings.

Creamy Potato Soup
Edith Cook

6   large baking potatoes peeled
    and diced
1   medium onion, chopped
1   rib celery, chopped
1   carrot, chopped
2   (16-ounce) cans chicken
    broth
1   stick margarine

1/4 cup sour cream
1   (10-ounce) package frozen
     cream style corn, thawed
     Salt and pepper to taste
     Parsley
     Shredded Cheddar cheese
     Bacon, cooked and crumbled
     Green onions, sliced

In a large saucepan or soup pot, boil potatoes, onion, celery, and carrot in chicken broth until tender. Purée in food processor to desired consistency. Return to saucepan. Add margarine, sour cream, and corn. Cook over very low heat until hot. Season to taste. Sprinkle with parsley. Garnish with cheese, bacon or green onions. Yield: 6 to 8 servings.

Cream of Broccoli Soup
Paula Terry

1   (10-ounce) package frozen
    chopped broccoli
2   chicken bouillon cubes
1   cup water

2   cups milk
2   cups cubed Velvetta cheese
1/2 cup all-purpose flour
1   cup half-and-half

In a large heavy saucepan, cook broccoli and bouillon in water. Do not drain. In a blender, blend milk, cheese, and flour. Add this mixture to broccoli. Add half-and-half. Cook, stirring frequently, over medium heat about 15 minutes, until hot and mixture thickens. Yield: 6 servings.

Blender Gazpacho

Susan Crowder

1	clove garlic	1	teaspoon salt
4	ripe tomatoes, cut in eighths	1/4	teaspoon black pepper
1/2	bell pepper, seeded and sliced	2	tablespoons olive oil
1	slim cucumber, peeled and coarsely cut	3	tablespoons red wine vinegar
		1/2	cup ice water

Put all ingredients in a blender in the order listed. Cover and blend on high speed until all ingredients are finely chopped. Serve cold. Garnish with thin cucumber slices, if desired. Yield: 4 servings.

Gazpacho

Beth B. Brown

2	large tomatoes, peeled and chopped	1/4	cup olive oil
1	large cucumber, peeled and chopped	1/3	cup red wine vinegar
		1/4	teaspoon hot pepper sauce
1	medium onion, minced	1/2	teaspoon salt
1/2	bell pepper, chopped		Croutons
1	(4-ounce) jar pimentos, drained		Lemon wedges
			Sour cream
2	(12-ounce) cans tomato juice, divided		

In a large bowl, combine tomatoes and next four ingredients. In a blender, purée one-half of the vegetable mixture and one-half cup tomato juice. Pour purée in with vegetable mixture, remaining tomato juice, olive oil, vinegar, hot sauce, salt and pepper. Chill several hours. Pour into chilled soup bowls. Garnish each serving with croutons, lemon wedges, and sour cream. Yield: 10 (6-ounce) servings.

Healthy Cabbage Soup

Danielle Hall

2-3 pounds tomatoes
1 (1 1/4-ounce) package onion
   soup mix
2-3 chicken or beef bouillon
   cubes
3 quarts water
1-2 heads cabbage, chopped
2 onions, chopped

1 carrot, chopped
1 bell pepper, chopped
2 (11-ounce) cans Mexican
   corn
1 (10 3/4-ounce) can tomato
   soup
Salt and pepper to taste

Blanche tomatoes in a large saucepan or soup pot of boiling water 1 minute. Plunge in cold water, remove skin, and set aside. Dissolve soup mix and bouillon in 3 quarts water. Chop tomatoes, add to soup mixture along with cabbage and next five ingredients. Season to taste. Bring to a boil, and cook about 40 minutes. Yield: 10 servings.

Onion Soup

Becky Brown

6 cups sliced yellow onions
1/4 cup flour
1 stick butter
Salt and pepper to taste

Ac'cent to taste
8 cups beef bouillon
8 slices French bread
Swiss cheese

Sauté onion, flour, and butter in a large saucepan until onion are soft. Add seasonings. Stir in bouillon and simmer 15 minutes. Pour into oven-safe bowls and top with a slice of French bread. Broil until lightly toasted. Top with cheese and return to broiler until melted. Yield: 8 servings.

Peanut Soup

Paula Bowen

3	cups chicken broth	1/8	teaspoon sugar
1	cup peanut butter	1 1/3	cups cream or 1 (13-ounce)
1/8	teaspoon celery salt		can evaporated milk
1/8	teaspoon onion salt		Chopped peanuts

In a large saucepan or soup pot, bring chicken broth to a boil. Reduce heat and add peanut butter. Stir until smooth. Add seasonings and sugar. Stir in cream. Heat but do not boil. Top with chopped nuts. Yield: 6 servings.

Tomato Basil Soup

Wanda Langley-Hassler

4	cups seeded, peeled tomatoes	1/4	teaspoon salt
4	cups tomato juice	1/4	teaspoon cracked black
1/2	cup fresh basil leaves		pepper
1	cup milk	1/2	cup reduced fat cream cheese

In a large saucepan, bring tomatoes and juice to a boil. Reduce heat. Simmer, uncovered, 30 minutes. Transfer tomato mixture to a blender. Add basil. Blend until smooth. Return mixture to saucepan. Stir in milk, salt, and pepper. Add cream cheese. Stir well with a whisk. Cook until thickened. Yield: 8 (one-cup) servings.

Quick but Good Vegetable Soup

Doris Lister

1 (16-ounce) package frozen mixed vegetables
1 (15-ounce) can tomato sauce with onions and garlic

1 (2-pound, 13-ounce) jar Ragù spaghetti sauce
1 pound ground beef
Frozen Irish potato slices

In large soup pot, combine vegetables, sauces, and ground beef. Boil in pot 30 minutes. Add a handful of potato slices and cook 20 more minutes. Yield: 8 servings.

Sparerib Soup

Vernon Boyd

2 pounds lean pork spareribs
1 medium onion, chopped
1 quart water, or more to generously cover spareribs
Salt and pepper to taste
1 (28-ounce) can whole tomatoes, mashed

4 medium white potatoes, peeled and cut in chunks
1 tablespoon sugar (optional)
3-4 shakes Tabasco sauce, (optional)

In a large Dutch oven, combine spareribs, onion, water, salt, and pepper. Cover and bring to a boil. Reduce heat to low, and simmer 2 hours, or until meat is tender and separates from bone. Meat can be chopped at this time, if desired, and bones removed. Add tomatoes and potatoes, sugar, and hot sauce. Cook about 30 minutes. Yield: 8 to 10 servings.

Note: I remember my Mother preparing this when I was a very young child. We have never found such a recipe. Perhaps it was her original.

Spinach and Cheese Tortellini Soup

Lori Tornes

1 bag spinach leaves, chopped	1 can chick-peas or garbanzo
1 Spanish onion, chopped	beans, rinsed and drained
4 (16-ounce) cans chicken	Fresh Parmesan cheese
broth	
1 (9-ounce) package cheese	
tortellini	

In a skillet, sauté spinach and onion in oil until spinach is wilted. Set aside. In a large saucepan, simmer broth to a boil and add cheese tortellini. Cook about 6 minutes only. Add peas to broth. Stir in spinach and onion. Serve hot with Parmesan cheese. Yield: 6 to 8 servings.

Chicken and Cabbage Panade

Pam Newsome

1 cup sliced onion	2 chicken bouillon cubes
1/4 cup margarine or butter	1 tablespoon soy sauce
Touch of olive oil	1 teaspoon minced garlic
4 cups grated cabbage	6 slices French bread, 1/2-inch
1 cup thinly sliced carrots	thick
1 cup sliced fresh mushrooms	1 cup shredded mozzarella
1 quart chicken broth	cheese or Swiss cheese
2 cups cooked chicken,	3 tablespoons Parmesan
chopped	cheese

In a large saucepan, sauté onion in margarine and olive oil until tender. Add cabbage, carrots and mushrooms and cook about 2 more minutes. Add broth, chicken, and next 3 ingredients. Simmer about 30 minutes. Lightly butter bread slices and put on baking sheet and toast in oven. In a small bowl, mix the cheeses together and top the bread slices. Put under broiler until lightly browned. In each soup bowl, place one bread slice and top with panade. Yield: 6 to 8 servings.

Clyde's Chili
Bonnie and Clyde King

1/2	pound pinto beans	1	pound lean ground pork
5	cups canned tomatoes	1/2	cup butter
3	chopped bell peppers	1/2	cup chili powder
2	large chopped onions	2	tablespoons salt
1 1/2	tablespoons oil	1 1/2	teaspoons black pepper
2	cloves garlic, crushed	1 1/2	teaspoons cumin powder
1/2	cup chopped parsley	1 1/2	teaspoons monosodium
2 1/2	pounds ground chuck		glutamate

Wash beans, soak overnight in water. In a large soup pot, simmer in water until tender. Add tomatoes, simmer 5 minutes. In a skillet, sauté bell pepper and onion in oil. Cook until tender. Add garlic and parsley. In a separate saucepan, sauté beef and pork in butter 15 minutes. Add meat to onion mixture. Stir in chili powder. Add meat mixture and remaining spices to beans. Simmer, covered, 1 hour. Cook, uncovered, 30 minutes. Skim fat from top. Yield: 8 servings.

Prestwood Country Club Hot Dog Chili
Catherine Pate

2	pounds very lean ground beef	1	tablespoon prepared mustard
1	medium onion, finely chopped	3	(15-ounce) cans tomato sauce, preferably with onions and peppers
1	(1-ounce) envelope chili seasoning mix		

In a large saucepan, cook beef until browned; drain. Add onion and cook until they begin to look clear. Pour in chili mix and stir thoroughly. Add mustard and tomato sauce. Simmer at least 1 hour to 1 hour and 30 minutes.

Note: I really wanted to give you this recipe for my home made chili which I served on hot dogs when I operated the snack bar at Prestwood. Alex was in high school and a good friend of my son Charlie. This was one of their favorite Saturday noon lunches!

Best Clam Chowder in the World
Fran Perry

8	ounce bacon slab, diced 1/2-inch squares	6	potatoes, peeled and diced
		1 1/2	teaspoon dried thyme
2	tablespoons unsalted butter		Black pepper to taste
2	large onions, diced	2	cups milk
1/4	cup flour	2	cups cream
2	(10-ounce) cans clams	3	tablespoons fresh parsley

In a large saucepan, cook bacon until fat is out and bacon is wilted. Add butter and onion, and cook until wilted. Add flour and cook 5 minutes until mixture is pasty. Pour in clam juice from cans. Add potatoes, thyme, and pepper. Cook 5 minutes. Add clams, milk, and cream. Stir in parsley. Cook over low heat until potatoes are tender. Yield: 10 servings.

Corn Chowder
Robert Braddock
Submitted by Andy Broach

1	pound bacon	2	(10-ounce) packages frozen corn
1	large onion, finely chopped		
4	tablespoons flour	1	carrot, grated
1 1/2	quarts milk	3	cups small diced potatoes
1	pint heavy cream		Salt and pepper to taste

In a large saucepan, cook bacon until brown. Don't overcook! Add onion and flour and mix until you have a roux. Gradually add milk and cream. Stir in corn, mixing well. Add carrot, potatoes, salt, and pepper. Cook over medium heat until a slow boil. Lower heat to keep warm but do not boil. Yield: 15 servings.

Oyster Chowder

Pam Newsome

2	onions, chopped	3	cups water
1	rib celery, chopped	3	chicken bouillon cubes
8	potatoes, diced	3	teaspoons Old Bay seasoning
1	quart mushrooms, sliced	2	teaspoons paprika
4	carrots, sliced	4	shots liquid smoke
1/2	stick margarine		Salt and pepper to taste
1	tablespoon olive oil		Oysters

In a large saucepan, sauté vegetables in margarine and olive oil. Add water and bouillon cubes. Season with Old Bay, paprika, liquid smoke, salt, and pepper. Simmer until potatoes are done. Add oysters and cook until edges curl. Yield: 6 to 8 servings.

Western Chowder

Becky Brown

1	pound round steak, ground	1	(14 1/2-ounce) can stewed tomatoes
2	tablespoons oil	1	(14 3/4-ounce) can cream style corn
	Salt and pepper to taste		
	Ac'cent to taste	1	can water
1	(10 3/4-ounce) can cream of mushroom soup		
1	(10 3/4-ounce) can cream of celery soup		

In a large saucepan, brown meat in oil. Add seasonings to taste. Combine remaining ingredients and mix well. Simmer slowly 20 minutes. Yield: 6 to 8 servings.

Mushroom-Potato Chowder
Wanda Langley-Hassler

2   tablespoons butter
1   small onion, chopped
1   rib celery, chopped
1/2 small bell pepper, chopped
1   (8-ounce) package sliced
     mushrooms
2   cups peeled and diced red
     potatoes

2   cups chicken broth
1/2 teaspoon dried thyme
2   cups milk, divided
1/2 teaspoon black pepper
1/2 teaspoon salt
3   tablespoons all-purpose flour

Melt butter in a large Dutch oven. Add onion, celery, bell pepper, and
mushrooms. Cook until tender. Stir in potatoes, chicken broth, and thyme.
Bring to a boil. Reduce heat and simmer, uncovered, 30 minutes or until
potatoes are tender. Stir in one and one-half cup milk, pepper, and salt.
Combine remaining milk and flour. Blend until smooth. Pour into chowder and
simmer, uncovered, stirring frequently until slightly thickened.
Yield: 11/2-quarts.

Salmon Stew
Judy Brown

1   large onion, chopped
2   tablespoons oil
3   cups Bloody Mary mix, plain
     or spicy

1   (143/4-ounce) can pink
     salmon bone and skin
     removed
     Ketchup

In a 2-quart saucepan, sauté onion in oil until tender. Add Bloody Mary mix
and salmon. Heat through, about 20 minutes. Add ketchup to thicken to your
liking. Serve plain or over rice. Yield: 4 servings.

Brown Stew

Lee Hicks

2	pounds beef chuck, 1 1/2-inch cubes	1	tablespoon salt
	Oil	1/2	teaspoon black pepper
4	cups boiling water	1/2	teaspoon paprika
1	teaspoon lemon juice		Dash allspice or cloves
1	teaspoon Worcestershire sauce	1	teaspoon sugar
1	clove garlic	6	carrots, sliced
1	medium onion, sliced	3	potatoes, quartered
		16	small white onions or 1-2 yellow onions, sliced

In a Dutch oven, brown meat in hot oil. Keep it sizzling and brown on all sides, about 20 minutes. Pour in boiling water. Lower heat and shift meat around to avoid sticking. Add lemon juice and next nine ingredients. Cover tightly and simmer 2 hours. Shift meat around occasionally and add more water, if necessary. Add carrots, potatoes, and onion. Cover and simmer 25 to 30 minutes or until vegetables are tender. Remove vegetables and meat carefully. Place in a casserole dish and thicken stock. Remove bay leaves and pieces of garlic. Pour thickened stock over vegetables. Yield: 6 to 8 servings.

Note: This is an old family recipe taken from my Mother's recipe file. We think it is stew-pendous!

Easy Beef Stew

Marsha Oates

1	pound lean beef, cubed	1/2	cup sherry
2	medium onions, thinly sliced	1	(8-ounce) can mushrooms (optional)
1	(10 3/4-ounce) can cream of mushroom soup		Cooked rice or noodles

Layer beef and onion in a 8x12-inch casserole dish. In a small bowl, mix soup and sherry. Pour over top of beef. Add mushrooms, if desired. Bake at 300 degrees for 3 hours. Serve over rice or noodles. Yield: 4 servings.

Flemish Stew

Kitty Jackson

2 pounds lean stewing beef
2 ounces margarine
1 pound onion, sliced
1 pint beer
  Salt and pepper to taste
  Pinch thyme

2 bay leaves
2 tablespoons flour
4 tablespoons water
4 lumps sugar
1 tablespoon red wine vinegar

Cut beef into 1x3-inch pieces. Brown in a skillet with margarine. Remove to saucepan. Lightly brown onion in same skillet about 10 minutes. Transfer to saucepan with beef. Mix beer into skillet and stir well to remove all sediment from it. Add liquid to saucepan with beef. Add salt, pepper, thyme, and bay leaves. Bring mixture to a boil. Cover and simmer gently 1 hour and 30 minutes to 2 hours and 30 minutes until tender. Blend flour and water to make a smooth paste. Stir into beef mixture. Add sugar and vinegar. Stir continuously 3 minutes until thickened. Yield: 4 servings.

Easy Brunswick Stew

Betty Taylor

2 large potatoes, diced
1 large onion, chopped
2 tablespoons margarine
3 (5-ounce) cans white chunk
  chicken

2 (15-ounce) cans pork barbecue
2 (17-ounce) cans white cream
  style corn
1 (16-ounce) can whole tomatoes

In a medium saucepan, boil potatoes in water until done. Set aside. In a skillet, sauté onion in margarine. In a Dutch oven, combine chicken, pork, corn, tomatoes, and onions. Simmer 45 minutes. Add potatoes just before serving. Yield: 8 servings.

Campfire Brunswick Stew

Angelyn Bateman

2   (10-ounce) cans Castlebury pork barbecue

2   (10-ounce) cans Castlebury beef barbecue

2   (10-ounce) cans Swanson chunk chicken

2   (14 3/4-ounce) cans cream style corn

1/2   stick margarine

In a saucepan, combine all ingredients and heat over the campfire. Great served with cornbread. Yield: 8 to 10 servings.

Note: When Alex and Debbie worked with the MFY of St. Luke Methodist Church, I gave them this recipe to use on a youth camping trip to Sugar Loaf Mountain. My children always enjoyed this meal and have fond memories of their experiences with Alex and Debbie through the MYF group.

Leon Outlaw's Fish Stew

Bill Reaves

1   large onion or 2 medium, diced

2   (10 3/4-ounce) cans tomato soup

1/2-3/4 (14-ounce) bottle ketchup

1/4-1/2 (10-ounce) bottle Heinz 57 sauce

4   soup cans water

1/4   bell pepper, chopped

1   pound of fish per person, lightly salted

Black pepper

Worcestershire sauce

In a skillet, fry onion in just enough grease to saturate onion. Pour off excess grease before adding onion to stew. Set aside. In a large saucepan or soup pot, over high heat, combine soup, ketchup, Heinz 57, water, and bell pepper. Add onions. Blacken top with pepper. Add fish. Reduce heat and cook 30 minutes at a slow boil, stirring several times. Add several dashes of Worcestershire. Yield: 6 servings.

Darlington County Fish Stew
Becky Webb
Submitted by Susan Moore

4	cups uncooked rice	1	(14-ounce) ketchup
1	pound fatback	2	tablespoons black pepper
2	pounds onions, chopped	2	teaspoons red pepper
2	(6-ounce) cans tomato paste	5	tablespoons salt
2	(10 3/4-ounce) cans tomato soup	8	ounces fish per person, deboned and chunked
2	quarts water, more if needed	1/2	stick butter

Prepare rice according to package directions. In a large heavy soup kettle, cook fatback until light brown. Remove and chop. Add onions and cook. Add tomato paste and next six ingredients. Add fatback. Bring to a boil and simmer over low heat 1 hour. Increase heat, add fish and cook 30 to 40 minutes. Add butter about 5 minutes before dish is done. Serve over rice. Yield: 16 to 20 servings.

Corned Beef and Cabbage Sandwich Spread
Denise Kelly

1	(12-ounce) can corned beef, broken up very fine	1	small onion, grated
2	cups grated cabbage	2	tablespoons yellow mustard
1 1/2	cups mayonnaise	3/4	cup sweet relish
4	hard boiled eggs, grated	1	tablespoon hot pepper sauce
			Salt to taste

Combine all ingredients in a large bowl. Mix well. Cover and refrigerate. Will keep for a week or more. Yield: 10 to 15 sandwiches.

Cheesy Chicken Subs

Kathy Boyd

12 ounces chicken breasts, boneless, skinless, cut in strips

1 (1-ounce) envelope Parmesan Italian or Caesar salad dressing mix

1 cup fresh sliced mushrooms

1/2 cup sliced red onion

1/4 cup olive oil or vegetable oil

4 submarine sandwich rolls, split and toasted

4 slices Swiss cheese

Place chicken in a bowl and sprinkle with the salad dressing mix. In a skillet, sauté the mushrooms and onion in oil 3 minutes. Add chicken, sauté 6 minutes or until chicken juices run clear. Spoon mixture onto roll bottoms. Top with cheese. Broil 4 inches from the heat 4 minutes or until cheese is melted. Replace tops. Yield: 4 servings.

The Ultimate Grilled Cheese

Kathy Boyd

1 (3-ounce) package cream cheese, softened

3/4 cup mayonnaise

1 cup shredded Cheddar cheese

1 cup shredded mozzarella cheese

1/2 teaspoon garlic powder

1/8 teaspoon seasoned salt

10 slices Italian bread, 1/2-inch thick

2 tablespoons butter or margarine, softened

In a mixing bowl, beat cream cheese and mayonnaise until smooth. Stir in cheeses, garlic powder, and salt. Spread five slices of bread with the cheese mixture, about one-third cup on each. Top with remaining bread slices. Butter the outside of sandwiches. Cook in a large pan over medium heat until golden brown on both sides. Yield: 5 servings.

Hot Brown
Kathy Boyd

1/3 cup butter, plus 1 tablespoon, divided
1 medium onion, chopped
1/3 cup flour
3 cups milk, heated
1 teaspoon salt
1/2 teaspoon cayenne pepper
4-6 ounces American cheese

2 eggs, well beaten
8 strips bacon
8 slices wheat bread, toasted
2 chicken breasts, cooked and sliced
Parmesan cheese
Paprika

Melt one-third cup butter in a saucepan and add onion. Cook until transparent. Add flour and blend until smooth. Add milk, salt, and pepper. Stir and cook until mixture is thick and smooth. Stir in cheese, eggs, and remaining butter. Continue to cook, stirring until mixture almost reaches boiling. Remove sauce from heat. In a skillet, cook bacon slices until crisp. To assemble: Toast 8 slices of bread. Cut 4 in half diagonally. On 4 ovenproof plates, place cut toast with points turned outward, with one whole slice in the middle. Then layer chicken, sauce, and bacon. Sprinkle generously with cheese and paprika. Broil 2 to 3 minutes. Yield: 4 servings.

Note: Turkey may be substituted for chicken.

Raisin and Nut Sandwich Spread
Hylda Bass

3 eggs
1 cup sugar
2 lemons, juice and zest
1 tablespoon butter

1 cup mayonnaise
1 cup nuts, chopped or ground
1 cup raisins, chopped or ground

In a double boiler, beat eggs and add sugar. Stir in lemon juice and zest. Cook until thickened over moderate heat. Add butter and let cool. Add mayonnaise, nuts, and raisins; mix well. Store in refrigerator. Yield: About 3 cups.

Pimento Sandwich Spread

Jane Sox

1	(5-ounce) can evaporated milk	1	heaping tablespoon mayonnaise
1/2	pound shredded Cheddar cheese		Dash cayenne pepper
2	tablespoons sugar	2	(2-ounce) jars sliced pimentos, mashed
1/2	teaspoon salt		

Place milk in top of a double boiler. Just as it begins to boil, add cheese. Stir mixture, and when it begins to cream, remove from heat. Continue to stir. Add sugar, salt, mayonnaise, pepper, and pimentos. Store in tightly covered container. Store in refrigerator. Yield: 6 to 8 servings.

Stromboli

Kathy Boyd

2	loaves frozen white bread dough	1	pound sliced mozzarella cheese
1/2	cup spaghetti sauce	1/3	pound sliced pepperoni
1	pound sliced turkey or ham	1	(4-ounce) can sliced mushrooms
1	pound sliced provolone cheese		Melted butter
1	pound sliced salami		Oregano

Thaw bread dough at room temperature about 2 hours. Pulling dough lengthwise, stretch each loaf to form a rectangle about 6x12-inches. Spread sauce on dough. Layer meats and cheeses in order given. Top with mushrooms. Roll up like a jelly roll and seal edges. Brush melted butter on top and sprinkle with oregano. Cover with foil. Bake at 350 degrees for 1 hour, uncover, and allow to brown 10 more minutes. Yield: 6 to 8 servings.

Tomato Sandwich Spread

Iris Kennedy

2-3 *large tomatoes, chopped*	1 *(1/4-ounce) package*
1 *pint Hellmann's mayonnaise*	*unflavored gelatin*
1/2 *(2-ounce) jar Hormel real*	3 *tablespoons cold water,*
bacon pieces or more if	*adjust to juiciness of*
desired	*tomatoes*

In a medium bowl, combine tomatoes, mayonnaise, and bacon. In a cup, mix gelatin with water. Pour into tomato mixture and mix well. Let stand in the refrigerator for 6 hours to gel. Spread on loaf bread for sandwiches. Yield: About 20 sandwiches.

Note: Can also be used as a dip with crackers or Bugles.

Vegetable Sandwich Spread

Annie Lea Brown
Submitted by Kathy Boyd

1 *green pepper, finely chopped*	1 *(8-ounce) package cream*
1 *large cucumber, finely*	*cheese, softened*
chopped	*Mayonnaise*
2 *ribs celery, finely chopped*	
1 *medium onion, finely chopped*	

In a medium bowl, combine all vegetables and cream cheese. Add enough mayonnaise for spreading consistency. Yield: About 2 cups.

Venison Tenderloin Sandwiches
Kathy Boyd

2	large onions, sliced	8	venison tenderloin steaks,
2	(4-ounce) cans sliced mush-		3/4-inch thick
	rooms, drained	1/2	teaspoon garlic powder
4	tablespoons butter or	1/4	teaspoon black pepper
	margarine	1/2	teaspoon salt
1/4	cup Worcestershire sauce	4	hard rolls, split

In a skillet, sauté the onion and mushrooms in butter and Worcestershire sauce until onion is tender. Flatten steaks to one-half inch thick, add to skillet. Cook over medium heat until meat is done as desired, about 3 minutes on each side. Sprinkle with garlic powder, pepper, and salt. Place two steaks on each roll, top with onions and mushrooms. Yield: 4 servings.

Oyster Loaf
Kathy Boyd

1	small loaf French bread	Tomatoes, thinly sliced
	Mayonnaise or tartar sauce	Lettuce, shredded
	Hot sauce	Salt and pepper to taste
12	oysters, fried	

Bake French bread slightly underdone. Cool and slice in half lengthwise. Spread each half with mayonnaise or tartar sauce. Cover bottom half with oysters. Sprinkle with hot sauce. Add tomatoes and lettuce. Season with salt and pepper. Top with other half of bread. Yield: 2 servings.

Open-Face Crabmeat Specials

Kathy Boyd

1	pound crabmeat	4	English muffins, split,
4	green onions, minced		buttered and toasted
1	cup sharp Cheddar cheese,		Thick tomato slices
	shredded	8	strips bacon, cooked almost
6	tablespoons mayonnaise		done, broken in half
	Juice of 1 lemon		

In a medium bowl, combine crabmeat and next four ingredients. Place toasted muffin halves on a baking sheet. Top with a tomato slice, a mound of crabmeat mixture. Spread mixture to edges of muffins. Top with two bacon pieces. Broil until bubbly. Yield: 8 servings.

Surprise Sandwiches

Kathy Boyd

8	slices bread, crusts trimmed,	4	eggs, beaten
	divided	2	cups milk
2	cups shrimp or crabmeat or 1	1	(10 3/4-ounce) can cream of
	cup each		mushroom soup
1	onion, diced	1	cup shredded American
1	bell pepper, diced		cheese
1	cup diced celery		Dash of paprika
1/2	cup mayonnaise		

Must prepare the day before serving. Place four slices of bread in the bottom of a greased 9x9-inch pan. In a medium bowl, combine shrimp or crabmeat, onion, bell pepper, celery, and mayonnaise. Spread mixture over bread slices in pan. Top with remaining bread. In a small bowl, combine milk and eggs and pour over the sandwiches. Let stand in the refrigerator overnight. Bake at 325 degrees for 15 minutes. Remove from oven, cover with soup, cheese and paprika. Return to oven and bake for 1 hour. Yield: 4 servings.

★ Salads ★ Fruits ★
Salad Dressings

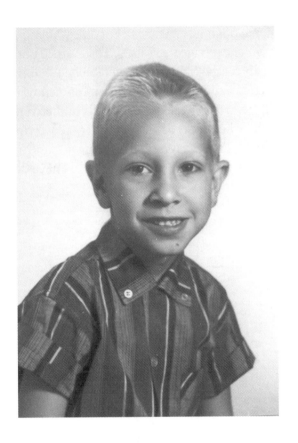

Bo Brown
My older brother
The official jello maker

When it came to cooking, Mama had a real problem when it came to jello. For some unknown reason, every time she made a congealed salad she could never get them to gel! Growing up we drank a lot of jello until my brother, Bo, joined Cub Scouts and learned to make it. He then became the official jello maker at our house. After we got older, Mama didn't have anymore trouble with her congealed salads. They turned out just fine.

My family really teased Mama about her kitchen skills but since I've grown up and had two children of my own, I can somehow understand why she couldn't get the jello to congeal. Three small children running around under foot might have been part of the reason. There were probably days when she didn't know if she was coming or going. Measuring water at that point would almost be impossible. I know because I have days like that!

Let us not love with words or tongue
but with actions and in truth

1 John 3:10

Alex's Friday Night Salad
Dell Gandy

2 heads lettuce, torn	1 (15-ounce) can LeSueur peas,
10 hard boiled eggs, sliced	drained
1 medium onion, sliced	1 cup Miracle Whip salad
2 (16-ounce) packages bacon,	dressing or enough to blend
cooked and crumbled	ingredients together

In a large bowl, layer one head lettuce and one-half of the eggs, onion, bacon, and peas. Add another layer of lettuce and the remaining eggs, onion, bacon, and peas. Spread dressing on top. Right before serving, toss salad together. Yield: 10 to 12 servings.

Note: Alex makes this a lot and takes it to Bob's on Friday nights. We love it!

Spinach Salad and Dressing
Vonciel Holloman

Dressing

2/3 cup light olive oil	1/4 cup apple cider vinegar
1 medium red onion (chop and	2/3 cup sugar
put in dressing - save a few	1/2 teaspoon salt
slices for salad)	1/2 cup ketchup

Salad

2 pounds spinach	4 hard boiled eggs, sliced
16 slices bacon, crisp cooked	Grated Cheddar cheese
and crumbled	

In a medium bowl, mix all of the dressing ingredients together. In serving bowl toss dressing with spinach, bacon, eggs, and cheese. Yield: 6 to 8 servings.

Delicious Salad and Dressing

Marcy Coker

Dressing

3	cloves garlic	1	teaspoon Dijon mustard
1	cup water	2	tablespoons Heinz vinegar
1/4	salt	1/2	cup regular olive oil
1/4	black pepper		

Salad

1	head Romaine lettuce		Pine nuts, toasted
1	tube Parmesan cheese		

For dressing, skin garlic and boil in a cup of water for 5 minutes. Mash garlic in wooden bowl. Add salt, pepper, mustard, and vinegar. Stir with whisk, add oil and mix well. Add lettuce, cheese, and nuts. Toss until greens are evenly coated. Yield: 6 to 8 servings.

Pear-Raspberry Salad

Gail Mobley

4	cups mixed salad greens	1/2	cup Feta Cheese, crumbled
1	(28-ounce) jar sliced Bartlett pears, drained	1	(8-ounce) bottle Ken's Steak House Raspberry-Pecan salad dressing
1	cup fresh raspberries		
1/2	cup toasted pecans		

In a serving bowl, toss first five ingredients together. Just before serving, dress salad with dressing. Toss well. Yield: 6 to 8 servings.

Mixed Greens with Pears, Crumbled Blue Cheese and Pine Nuts

Anne Dawkins

Dressing

1	large shallot, minced
1/2	cup safflower oil
2	tablespoons red wine vinegar
2	tablespoons honey
1	tablespoon Dijon-style mustard

1	tablespoon water
1/8	teaspoon salt
1/4	teaspoon coarsely cracked black pepper

Salad

2	large ripe firm pears, peeled, cut into 1/2-inch dice
12	cups torn mixed greens, red leaf, Boston, curly endive and arugula, washed, crisped and chilled

	Salt
	Freshly ground black pepper
1/3	cup crumbled blue cheese
1/4	cup pine nuts, toasted

For dressing, put ingredients in a jar with tight-fitting lid. Shake vigorously to mix. Can be made a day ahead and refrigerated. Use chilled. Shake well before using. For salad, toss pears with a scant one-fourth cup dressing. Can be done 2 hours ahead and refrigerated. To serve, put greens into large shallow bowl. Toss with remaining dressing. Divide among six chilled serving plates. Sprinkle lightly with salt and pepper. Scatter pears over greens, dividing evenly. Garnish with crumbled cheese and nuts. Serve immediately. Yield: 6 servings.

Note: To toast pine nuts, spread in a single layer on a baking sheet. Bake at 350 degrees until lightly browned and fragrant, about 8 to 10 minutes. Watch carefully so they do not burn.

Becky's Salad
Becky Brown

<u>Topping</u>

1/2 cup walnuts, broken

3 tablespoons sugar

<u>Dressing</u>

1/4 cup oil

2 tablespoons honey

2 tablespoons white wine
vinegar

2 tablespoons dry white wine

1/2 teaspoon ground ginger

<u>Salad</u>

6 cups Romaine lettuce, torn
into small pieces

2 cups fresh oranges, cut into
small pieces

1 1/2 cups pears, chopped, do not
peel

2 ribs celery, diced

3 green onions, thinly sliced

For topping, in a saucepan, combine walnuts and sugar. Cook on low heat,
stirring constantly, until sugar melts and walnuts are coated. Pour out onto
wax paper to cool. When cool break nuts apart. Combine all the dressing
ingredients in a jar that has a tight-fitting lid. Shake well. In a serving bowl,
mix all salad ingredients together. Pour dressing over salad and toss well. Top
with walnuts. Yield: 6 servings.

Taco Salad
Kathy Boyd

2 (16-ounce) cans chili beans,
do not drain

1 (10 1/2-ounce) package corn
chips

2 cups shredded Cheddar
cheese

4 cups chopped lettuce

2 small tomatoes, chopped

1 small onion, chopped

1 (2 1/4-ounce) can sliced ripe
olives, drained

1 1/4 cups salsa

1/2 cup sour cream

In a saucepan, heat beans. Place corn chips on a large platter. Top with
beans, cheese, lettuce, tomatoes, onion, olives, salsa, and sour cream. Serve
immediately. Yield: 8 servings.

Broccoli Salad
Melinda Sansbury

1	cup mayonnaise	1	bunch fresh broccoli florets,
1/4	cup sugar		bite-sized pieces
2	tablespoons white vinegar	1	red onion, chopped finely
1	(16-ounce) package bacon,	1/2-1	cup raisins
	cooked and crumbled	1/2-1	cup walnuts

In a small bowl, combine mayonnaise, sugar, and vinegar. Mix well. Stir in bacon. In a medium bowl, combine broccoli, onion, raisins, and walnuts. Pour dressing over salad and toss until evenly coated. Refrigerate. Yield: 8 to 10 servings.

Cabbage Crunch Salad
Beverly Whisnant

Salad

2-4	chicken breasts, cooked and diced	4	tablespoons toasted sesame seeds or sunflower seeds
2	(3-ounce) packages Ramen chicken flavored noodles, uncooked	4	green onions, sliced
		1	head shredded cabbage
2	(2 1/4-ounce) packages sliced almonds		

Dressing

1	package seasoning mix from Ramen noodles	1	cup oil
		2	teaspoons salt
2	tablespoons sugar or 5 packages Sweet 'n Low	1	teaspoon pepper
		6	teaspoon rice vinegar

In a bowl, combine all salad ingredients and toss. Break up noodles a little. Refrigerate overnight. Mix all dressing ingredients in a small bowl. Refrigerate overnight. To serve, pour dressing over salad and toss well. Yield: 8 to 10 servings.

Napa, Bok Choy Salad
Sylvia Coker

2 (3-ounce) packages oriental Ramen noodle soup mix	1/4 cup cider vinegar
1/2 cup sunflower seeds	2 tablespoons soy sauce
3 tablespoons slivered almonds, chopped	1/2 bok choy, shredded
1/2 cup sugar	1/2 head Napa cabbage, shredded
1/4 cup olive oil	6 green onions, chopped

Remove seasoning packets from soup mix. Set aside. Crumble noodles and combine with sunflower seeds and almonds. Spread on a 15x10-inch jelly roll pan. Bake at 350 degrees for 8 to 10 minutes or until golden brown, set aside. In a saucepan, bring sugar, next three ingredients and one packet of Ramen noodle soup seasoning to a boil over medium heat. Remove from heat and cool. Place bok choy, cabbage, and onions in a large bowl. Drizzle with sugar mixture. Add noodle mixture, tossing well. Serve immediately. Yield: 6 to 8 servings.

Note: This sauce also makes a delicious marinade for chicken to be grilled.

Broccoli Slaw
Vivian Harris

Slaw

1 (16-ounce) package broccoli slaw	3 1/2 ounces sunflower seeds
1 bell pepper, red or green, chopped	2/3 cup slivered almonds
	2 (3-ounce) packages Ramen noodles, broken

Dressing

1 cup oil	1 packet of seasoning from oriental noodles
1/2 cup sugar	
1/3 cup vinegar	

In a large bowl, combine all of the slaw ingredients and toss. Mix all of the dressing ingredients in a jar with a tight-fitting lid. Shake well. Pour over slaw and toss well. Refrigerate. Yield: 8 to 10 servings.

Marinated Coleslaw

Jean Hungerpiller

1 large head cabbage, chopped or shredded	3/4 cup oil
1 bell pepper, sliced	1 teaspoon dry mustard
1 onion, chopped	1 teaspoon celery seed
3/4 cup sugar	3/4 teaspoon granulated garlic
1 cup vinegar	1 teaspoon salt

In a large bowl, combine cabbage, bell pepper, and onion. Sprinkle sugar over top. In a separate bowl, combine remaining ingredients and mix well. Pour over cabbage. Marinate overnight. Yield: 10 to 12 servings.

Marinated Coleslaw

Teresa Hendrix

Dressing

1 pint vinegar	1 teaspoon tumeric
2 1/2 cups sugar	1 1/2 teaspoons celery seed
1 teaspoon mustard seed	1 teaspoon salt

Slaw

1 large head cabbage, shredded	1 (4-ounce) jar pimentos, chopped
1 medium onion, grated	1 1/2 cups cauliflower buds
1 green pepper, finely chopped	

In a saucepan, combine all dressing ingredients. Bring to a boil. Let cool. Place slaw ingredients in a 2-quart dish and pour dressing over mixture. Refrigerate for 12 hours or overnight. Drain before serving. Yield: 15 servings.

Note: Adds a little zest to any meal.

Shrimp Cole Slaw
Robert Braddock
Submitted by Andy Broach

1 pound small shrimp	1/2 teaspoon vinegar
1/2 cup shredded carrots	1 tablespoon diced sweet pickle
1 cup mayonnaise	relish
1 tablespoon sugar	1/2 head cabbage, finely
1/2 teaspoon salt	chopped
1/4 teaspoon black pepper	
1 teaspoon onion salt or 1 small	
onion, finely grated	

Peel and devein shrimp. Cut each shrimp into two pieces. In a saucepan, boil shrimp 3 minutes and set aside to cool. In a medium bowl, add carrots and remaining ingredients. Mix well. Add shrimp and stir together. Let chill... the longer the better, but at least 1 hour. Yield: 6 servings.

Black-Eyed Pea Salad
Mary Ward Baucom

1 large tomato, seeded and chopped	1 cup diced celery
1 bell pepper, chopped	1 (4-ounce) jar diced pimentos, drained
1/3 cup sliced green onions plus 2 sliced green onions, divided	1 (8-ounce) bottle Italian dressing
1 clove garlic, minced	Red cabbage leaves (optional)
6 fresh mushrooms, sliced	
2 (16-ounce) cans black-eyed peas, drained and rinsed	2 tablespoons bacon, cooked and crumbled

In a large bowl, combine tomato, bell pepper, 2 green onions, garlic, and mushrooms. Stir in peas, celery, pimento, and dressing. Cover and chill, stirring occasionally, for 8 hours. Drain salad and spoon onto red cabbage leaves. Sprinkle with bacon and remaining onions. Yield: 8 to 10 servings.

Marinated Bean Salad

Hylda Bass

Salad

1 (15-ounce) can LeSueur peas, drained
1 (14 1/2-ounce) can French style green beans, drained
1 cup celery, chopped
1 red onion, diced

1 (8-ounce) can water chestnuts, drained
1 bell pepper, cubed
1 (11-ounce) can shoe peg corn, drained

Dressing

1 cup apple cider or wine vinegar
1/3 cup salad oil
Salt

1/2 cup sugar
1/2 cup water
Black pepper

Combine salad ingredients in a large bowl and mix. Combine all dressing ingredients in a small bowl and pour over salad. Marinate in refrigerator overnight. Drain before serving. Yield: 10 to 12 servings.

String Bean Salad

Vicki Dorn

Salad

1 (15-ounce) can LeSueur peas, drained
1 (14 1/2-ounce) can French style green beans, drained
4 ribs celery, diced
1 medium onion, chopped

1 (2-ounce) jar pimentos, chopped
1 bell pepper, chopped
1 (15 1/4-ounce) can whole kernel corn, white or yellow

Dressing

1 cup white sugar
1 cup white vinegar

1/2 cup vegetable oil
1 teaspoon salt

Place salad ingredients in a large bowl. In a separate bowl, combine all dressing ingredients and mix well. Stir into salad. Marinate overnight. The longer it marinates the better it is. Yield: 8 to 12 servings.

Vegetable Salad

Miriam Griggs

Salad

6 cups cauliflower, bite-sized pieces

6 cups broccoli florets, bite-sized pieces

1 large red onion, sliced

2 cups cherry tomatoes, halved

1 cucumber, sliced

Dressing

2/3 cup canola oil

1/4 cup vinegar

1 (1-ounce) package Ranch salad dressing mix

In a large bowl, combine salad ingredients. In a small bowl, combine all dressing ingredients; mix well. Pour over salad. Toss well. Marinate in refrigerator about 3 hours before serving. Yield: 8 servings

German Potato Salad

Gus Hoffmeyer

8-10 small red potatoes

1/4 pound bacon or country ham, diced

1 medium onion, diced

1/2 stick butter or margarine

1/2 cup vinegar

Salt and pepper to taste

In a medium saucepan, boil potatoes in skin. Do not overcook. Peel and slice into about three-eighth inch wafers and put in a large bowl. In a skillet, cook the meat and onion on medium heat. If you use bacon, cook crisp and onion light golden brown. Discard grease. To meat and onion, add butter. When butter is melted, add vinegar and mix well. Pour over potatoes in bowl. Pour back and forth (bowl to skillet) several times then let simmer about 30 minutes. Serve hot. Yield: 8 servings

Note: My grandparents had this all the time. I cooked this every Sunday while our children were growing up and they called it "Sunday Potato Salad." Now, I cook it for them and the grandchildren.

Warm Potato Salad

Carol Scarborough

3	tablespoons canola or olive oil	4	hard boiled eggs, chopped
1	packet Goya ham seasoning		Lawry's seasoning salt
1	onion, chopped		Black pepper to taste
6	potatoes peeled and cubed		Duke's mayonnaise
			Bacon bits

In a skillet, sauté onion in oil and ham seasoning. Set aside. In a medium saucepan, cover potatoes with water and bring to a boil. Reduce heat and simmer until tender. Drain. In a large bowl, combine onion, potatoes, eggs, salt, and pepper. Add mayonnaise to evenly coat all ingredients. Top with bacon bits and serve warm. Yield: 6 to 8 servings.

Sweet Potato Salad

Divver Allen

4	medium sweet potatoes	1	teaspoon curry powder
1	cup pineapple chunks, drained	1	teaspoon grated orange zest
1	cup pecans, broken	1/4	teaspoon dried tarragon, can add a little more
1/4	cup orange juice	2	tablespoons half-and-half
1	cup mayonnaise		
1	teaspoon vinegar		

Cook sweet potatoes until tender but firm. Peel. Cut into chunks the size of pineapple chunks. In a large bowl, gently toss potatoes, pineapple, nuts, and orange juice. In a small bowl, combine mayonnaise and next five ingredients. Pour over potato mixture and gently toss. Chill several hours. Arrange on a bed of greens to serve. Yield: 6 servings.

Curried Rice Salad

Judy Brown

1	(10½-ounce) can chicken broth	1/2	teaspoon curry powder
1/2	cup uncooked rice	2	ribs celery, chopped
2	green onions, chopped	3/4	cup mayonnaise
1	tablespoon vinegar	1	(8½-ounce) can LeSueur peas
2	tablespoons oil		

In a saucepan, cook rice in broth. Place hot cooked rice in a medium bowl. Add onions, vinegar, oil, and curry powder. Mix and chill. When cooled, add remaining ingredients. Mix well. Yield: 4 to 6 servings.

Note: Can use chopped chicken or ham to use as main dish.

Fresh Pasta Salad

Hazel Sox

1	(16-ounce) box rotini pasta	1	tomato, chopped
1	(8-ounce) bottle low fat Italian dressing		Salt and pepper to taste
1	cucumber, chopped		Dash lemon pepper
1	bell pepper, chopped		Dash Italian seasoning
			Dash salad seasoning

Cook pasta according to package directions. Drain, rinse and cool. In a large bowl, mix pasta with dressing and remaining ingredients. Yield: 8 servings.

Italian Marinated Salad

Shelia Haney

Salad

1	(8-ounce) can button mushrooms, drained	1	(16-ounce) can artichoke hearts
1	green pepper, cut in 1/2-inch squares	12	small white onions or 6 spring onions with 1-inch green tops
1	carrot, cut lengthwise into squares	1/2	cup stuffed olives
2	cups uncooked cauliflower florets		Cherry tomatoes
			Minced parsley

Dressing

1	teaspoon sugar	1/2	teaspoon black pepper
11/2	cups wine vinegar	2	teaspoons crushed oregano
11/2	teaspoons salt	1/2	cup salad oil or olive oil

In a large bowl combine all salad ingredients, except tomato and parsley. For dressing, in a saucepan, heat sugar and vinegar. Remove from heat and stir in seasonings. Cool. Add oil and mix. Pour dressing over salad. Marinate 24 hours in refrigerator, stirring regularly. Before serving, add tomato and parsley. Yield: 10 to 12 servings

Pasta Chicken Salad

Meridith Hall

1	(16-ounce) package corkscrew pasta	3	tablespoons lemon juice
3	pounds boneless chicken breasts, cooked and cubed	1	tablespoon prepared mustard
		1	medium onion, chopped
1/2	cup Zesty Italian dressing	1	cup chopped celery
1/2	cup mayonnaise		Salt and pepper to taste

Cook pasta according to package directions. Drain. In a large bowl, combine chicken, pasta and dressing. In a small bowl, mix remaining ingredients and fold into pasta mixture. May need to add more dressing before serving. Best made a day ahead. Yield: 12 to 15 servings.

Mediterranean Pasta Salad

Lea Saunders

Salad

2	cups whole grain spiral noodles, uncooked
1	medium red onion, chopped
1	bell pepper, chopped large pieces

1	cup sun-dried tomatoes, packed in oil, sliced
1	cup black olives, sliced
3/4	cup Parmesan cheese

Dressing

1/2	cup olive oil
1/3	cup vinegar
1/3	cup water
1 1/2	teaspoons minced garlic
1	tablespoon balsamic vinegar
1/2	teaspoon oregano

1	teaspoon sugar
1	teaspoon salt
1/2	teaspoon black pepper
2	teaspoons dried basil
1	teaspoon dillweed
1	tablespoon Dijon mustard

Cook noodles according to package directions. Drain. In a large bowl combine noodles and remaining salad ingredients. For dressing, put ingredients in a jar with a tight-fitting lid. Shake to mix and let chill. Pour over noodle mixture. Serve. Yield: 8 to 10 servings.

Note: A favorite in Belgium!

Shrimp Pasta

Teresa Gibson

1	(8-ounce) package angel hair pasta
1/2	pound shrimp, cooked, peeled and deveined
1	cup imitation crabmeat

2	tablespoons capers
2	tablespoons chopped scallions
	Salt and pepper to taste
1	cup mayonnaise

Cook pasta according to package directions. Drain. In medium a bowl, mix shrimp, crabmeat, capers, scallions, salt, and pepper. Add pasta. Stir in mayonnaise. Cover and chill. Yield: 12 servings.

Vegetable Pasta Salad

Judy Knight

1/2 (8-ounce) box pasta
2 bell peppers, chopped
2 ribs celery, chopped
2 (4-ounce) cans pitted black olives, chopped
2 tomatoes, chopped

2 small green onions, chopped
2 cucumbers, chopped
2 carrots, chopped
Kraft Italian Pesto dressing
Salt and pepper to taste

Cook pasta according to package directions. Drain, rinse and cool. In a medium bowl mix pasta and vegetables. Pour dressing over salad to taste. Toss well. Yield: 4 to 6 servings.

Chicken Cranberry Salad

Jane Truett

Layer 1

1 (1/4-ounce) envelope unflavored gelatin
1/4 cup cold water
1 (16-ounce) can whole cranberry sauce

1 (9-ounce) can crushed pineapple
1/2 cup broken walnuts
1 tablespoon lemon juice

Layer 2

1 (1/4-ounce) envelope unflavored gelatin
3/4 cup cold water, divided
1 cup mayonnaise
3 tablespoons lemon juice
3/4 teaspoon salt

2 cups diced cooked or canned chicken
1/2 cup diced celery
2 tablespoons chopped parsley
Walnut halves

For layer one, soften gelatin in one-fourth cup cold water. Dissolve over hot water. Add cranberry sauce, and next three ingredients. Pour into a 10x6-inch dish. Chill until firm. For layer two, soften gelatin in one-fourth cup cold water. Dissolve over hot water. Blend in mayonnaise, remaining water, lemon juice and salt. Add chicken, celery and parsley. Pour over first layer; chill until firm. Cut into squares; invert on salad greens. Top with mayonnaise and walnut halves. Yield: 6 to 8 servings

Chicken Salad

Cathy Gainey

1	five pound hen	2	cups chopped celery
1 1/2	cups mayonnaise	1/4	teaspoon celery salt
2	tablespoons lemon juice	1/4	teaspoon garlic powder
1 1/2	teaspoons salt	1	small onion, chopped
1	teaspoon black pepper		

Wash chicken in cold water, throw fat and giblets away. Place chicken in a large pot of water. Cook on high until boiling begins then turn heat on low and cook 2 hours and 30 minutes to 3 hours or until chicken is tender. Remove chicken from pot to cool. Debone and cut into small pieces. Place in a large bowl and mix with mayonnaise and next seven ingredients. Yield: 8 servings.

Chicken Dill Rice

Flossie Hopkins

1	cup rice	3/4	cup chopped celery
1	(10 1/2-ounce) can chicken broth	1/2	cup mayonnaise
	Enough water to make 2 cups with broth	1	tablespoon Dijon mustard
2	cups cooked chicken, chopped		Fresh dill (about 2 tablespoons)
1	(12-ounce) can artichoke hearts, chopped		Salt to taste

In a medium saucepan, cook rice in broth and water. Let rice cool; add chicken, artichoke, and celery. In a small bowl, mix mayonnaise and mustard and add to rice mixture. Add fresh dill and salt to taste. Yield: 6 to 8 servings.

Grilled Chicken Salad

Susan Crowder

2	cups chopped apples	8	split chicken breasts, deboned
2	cups chopped celery		Barbeque sauce
2	cups chopped grapes		Texas Pete Honey Mustard
1	cup chopped walnuts		Sauce
	Mayonnaise		

In a medium bowl, coat apples and next three ingredients in mayonnaise and refrigerate. Grill the chicken and brush with barbeque sauce while cooking. When done, chop chicken and mix with mustard sauce until moist. Chill this mixture 4 to 6 hours. Stir apple mixture and the chicken together. Add mayonnaise to taste. Yield: 6 to 8 servings.

Pressed Chicken

Sarah Timmons

1	5 pound hen or 2 fryers	2	(1/4-ounce) envelopes
2	cups celery, chopped fine		unflavored gelatin
6	hard boiled eggs, chopped fine	1/2	cup cold water
	Juice of 1 lemon	3	cups skimmed chicken broth
1/2	cup mayonnaise	4	tablespoons sweet
1/2	cup salad dressing		pickle cubes or relish
	Dash salt		

Cook chicken in a large pot of water. Remove chicken from broth and cool. Debone and cut into small pieces. In a large bowl, mix chicken, celery, and eggs. Add lemon juice, mayonnaise, and salad dressing. In a small bowl, dissolve gelatin in cold water. Heat chicken broth and mix with gelatin. Combine with chicken mixture. Stir in pickle. Pour into a 9x13-inch casserole dish and let congeal. Cut into squares and serve on lettuce. Yield: 10 to 12 servings.

Apple-Pineapple-Celery Salad
Kathy Boyd

1 cup or more pineapple juice	3 cups diced apples
1/4 cup water	2 cups diced celery
1/3 cup sugar	1 (15 1/2-ounce) can crushed
1 tablespoon cornstarch	pineapple, drained
1/4 teaspoon ginger	1/4 cup diced cherries

In a saucepan, combine pineapple juice, water, sugar, cornstarch, and ginger. Cook over medium heat, stirring constantly until mixture turns clear. Remove from heat. Cool. In a medium bowl, mix apples, celery, pineapple, and cherries. Pour pineapple mixture over fruit and mix well. Refrigerate overnight. Yield: 10 to 12 servings.

Apple Brosia
Vernon Boyd

1 (12-ounce) can Five Alive Concentrate	5 large apples, peeled and grated
2 cans water	1 (6-ounce) package frozen coconut
1 (6-ounce) can orange juice concentrate	Sugar to taste
1 (20-ounce) can crushed pineapple	Bananas
	Maraschino cherries

Mix first four ingredients in a large bowl. Peel and grate apples and add to mixture. Add coconut and sugar. Can be made 2 or 3 days ahead, but always at least one day before serving. Bananas may be added just before serving. Cherries can be added for color. This will keep for a week. Yield: 15 to 20 servings.

Golden Ambrosia

Martha Moye Peel

1 large or 2 small bananas, cut in 1/4-inch diagonal slices	2 large oranges, sectioned
1 (20-ounce) can unsweetened pineapple chunks, drained, reserve juice	1/3 cup flaked coconut
	1/2 cup cold ginger ale

Dip banana slices in reserved pineapple juice. Layer one half of each fruit in glass serving bowl. Top with one half of the coconut then with layers of the remaining fruits. Chill. Just before serving add ginger ale and top with remaining coconut. Yield: 6 servings.

Mama's Pear Salad

Kathy Boyd

Salad greens	Shredded Cheddar cheese
Canned pear halves, drained	Salad greens
Mayonnaise	

Line a serving plate with salad greens; arrange pear halves on top of greens. Place about 1 teaspoon of mayonnaise in the middle of each pear half. Sprinkle cheese over mayonnaise. Yield: 2 pear halves per serving.

Charlotte Fluff

Jackie Georgius

1   (8-ounce) container light
    Cool Whip
1   (8-ounce) container sour
    cream
1   (8-ounce) can crushed
    pineapple, drained

1   (3-ounce) package orange
    gelatin
1   (11-ounce) can mandarin
    oranges, drained
    Chopped Black walnuts
    (optional)

In a medium bowl, mix first four ingredients. Stir in oranges. Refrigerate. Add nuts before serving if desired. Yield: 6 servings.

Classic Waldorf Salad

Patty Hause

2   cups diced apples
1   cup 1-inch julienne celery
    sticks
1/2 cup broken walnuts
1/4 cup mayonnaise

1   tablespoon sugar
1/2 teaspoon lemon juice
    Dash of salt
1/2 cup heavy cream, whipped

In a large bowl, combine apple, celery, and walnuts. In a mixing bowl, blend mayonnaise, sugar, lemon juice, and salt. Fold in whipped cream. Fold dressing into apple mixture; chill. Yield: 6 servings.

Fruit Salad

Shirley McCutchen

1   (21-ounce) can peach pie filling
2   (20-ounce) cans chunky or
    tidbits pineapple, drained
2   (11-ounce) cans mandarin
    oranges, drained

3   sliced bananas
1   (13-ounce) package frozen or
    fresh strawberries with sugar

In a large bowl, mix all ingredients together and serve. Yield: 18 servings.

Kiwi Salad

Janice Gainey

1 (15 1/4-ounce) can sliced peaches, drained	3-4 bananas, sliced
1 (15 1/4-ounce) can chunky pineapple, drained	1 bunch grapes, halved
1 (15-ounce) can mandarin oranges, drained	1 pint fresh strawberries, halved
1 (3.4-ounce) package instant vanilla pudding mix	3-4 kiwi, sliced

In a large bowl, combine all canned fruit with pudding mix. Marinate overnight. Before serving add fresh fruit. Yield: 14 to 16 servings.

Fruit Fantastic

Gay Pleune

1 (15-ounce) can sliced peaches, drained, reserve syrup	1 (3.4-ounce) box instant vanilla pudding
1 (20-ounce) can chunk pineapple, drained, reserve syrup	1 pint fresh strawberries, halved
	1 cup seedless grapes, halved

In a large bowl, stir one cup of syrup, either pineapple, peach or combination, into dry pudding mix. Beat as directed on box. Fold in prepared fruit. Chill in the refrigerator 2 hours. May be prepared up to 24 hours ahead. Yield: 12 to 14 servings.

Note: Strawberries or grapes may be substituted with 1 pint blueberries or 2 sliced bananas. Bananas must be added just prior to serving.

Heavenly Hash
Kathy Boyd

1   pint heavy cream, whipped
2   cups miniature marshmallows
1   cup pecan pieces, toasted
1   (6-ounce) jar cherries,
    drained and halved

1   cup flaked coconut
1   (15 1/4-ounce) can pineapple
    chunks, drained

In a mixing bowl, combine whipped cream and marshmallows. Refrigerate until chilled. Fold in nuts and next three ingredients. Refrigerate. Serve on salad greens. Yield: 6 to 8 servings.

Watergate Salad
Sandi DeBruhl

1   (3.4-ounce) package
    pistachio pudding mix
1   (20-ounce) can crushed
    pineapple with juice

1   cup miniature marshmallows
1   (8-ounce) container Cool
    Whip
1/2 cup chopped nuts

In a serving bowl, mix dry pudding mix with next four ingredients. Refrigerate until chilled. Yield: 8 servings.

Frozen Fruit Salad

Deborah Crawford

1 (8-ounce) container peach
   yogurt
1 (8-ounce) container sour
   cream
3/4 cup powdered sugar
   Juice of 1 lemon

2 bananas, sliced
1 (8-ounce) can crushed
   pineapple, drained
1/4 cup sliced maraschino
   cherries

In a medium bowl, gently mix all ingredients thoroughly and pour into a greased 8x8-inch pan. Cover with plastic wrap and freeze. Remove from freezer 10 minutes before serving. Slice and serve. Yield: 8 servings.

Note: Very refreshing!

MaMa's Frozen Fruit Salad

Annie Lea Brown
Contributed by Kathy Boyd

2 tablespoons sugar
2 tablespoons vinegar
2 eggs, beaten
15 marshmallows

1 cup heavy cream, whipped
1 (15 1/4-ounce) can fruit
   cocktail
   Chopped nuts

In a saucepan, cook sugar, vinegar, and egg until thickened. Fold in marshmallows. Let cool. Add whipped cream, fruit cocktail, and nuts. Pour into a 9x13-inch glass dish and freeze. Cut into slices. Yield: 12 to 15 servings.

Note: This was my grandmother's recipe that she had from the 1940's.

Cherry Salad
Barbara Frampton

1   (14 1/2-ounce) can tart pie red
    cherries, drain, reserve juice
1/2 cup sugar
1   (3-ounce) package cherry
    jello

1/2 teaspoon unflavored Knox
    gelatin
1/2 cup chopped nuts

In a saucepan, combine cherry juice and enough water to equal amount of liquid jello package calls for. Add sugar and bring to boil. In a mixing bowl, combine jello and gelatin. Pour hot sugar mixture over jello, stirring to dissolve. Add cherries and nuts. Pour into a mold or small oblong casserole. Refrigerate. This can be made several days ahead. Yield: 4 servings

Note: After a midday Thanksgiving feast, we always have this salad for supper along with turkey sandwiches.

Cranberry-Raspberry Salad
Kathy McCall

1   (3-ounce) package raspberry
    jello
1   (3-ounce) package lemon
    jello
1 1/2 cups boiling water

1   (10-ounce) package frozen
    raspberries
1   cup cranberry-orange relish
1   cup Sprite

Topping

1   cup sour cream
1   teaspoon sugar

1/4 teaspoon ginger
    Dash salt

In a medium bowl, dissolve jello in boiling water. Stir in raspberries, breaking apart with fork. Add cranberry-orange relish. Chill until cold but not set; this happens quickly. Pour in Sprite gently to avoid foaming. Stir in an up and down motion. Chill until partially set. Turn into a 5 1/2 cup mold. In a small bowl, combine all topping ingredients. Can put in center of a ring mold. Garnish with raspberries on top. Yield: 10 servings

Cranberry Salad

Mary Lutie Fletcher

1 1/2 cups boiling water
1 (6-ounce) package or
   2 (3-ounce) packages
   raspberry jello
1 (20-ounce) can crushed
   pineapple

1 cup chopped nuts
1 apple, peeled and grated
1 (12-ounce) container Ocean
   Spray Cran-Fruit for chicken
   cranberry orange flavor

In a medium bowl, mix boiling water with jello. Let jello cool and thicken. Add remaining ingredients. Put into a mold or 8x8-inch glass dish. Place in refrigerator to congeal several hours or overnight. Yield: 8 servings.

Note: Especially good with Thanksgiving or Christmas dinners. Buy several of the Cran-Fruit for chicken around the winter holidays or you will not be able to find it.

Grandmama's Congealed Salad

Marla Prozzi

1 (6-ounce) lime jello
2 cups boiling water
6 1/4 ounces miniature
   marshmallows
1 (8-ounce) package cream
   cheese, softened

1 (8-ounce) can crushed
   pineapple
1 cup chopped nuts
1 (12-ounce) container Cool
   Whip

In a medium bowl, dissolve jello in water; add marshmallows. Cool for a few minutes. Beat cream cheese into mixture. Add pineapple, nuts, and whipped topping. Blend well and put into a mold or 9x13-inch glass dish. Refrigerate. Yield: 12 servings.

Grape-Blueberry Congealed Salad

Jean Beasley

2 (3-ounce) packages grape jello	1 cup sour cream
1 cup hot water	1 (8-ounce) package cream cheese, softened
1 (21-ounce) can blueberry pie filling	1/2 cup sugar
1 (20-ounce) can crushed pineapple with juice	1/2 cup finely chopped pecans

In a medium bowl, dissolve gelatin in hot water. Add pie filling and pineapple; mix well. Pour into a 9x13-inch glass dish. Chill until set. Combine cream cheese, sour cream, and sugar in a small bowl. Beat with electric mixer until smooth. Spread over congealed gelatin. Sprinkle with pecans. Yield: 12 servings.

Orange Buttermilk Salad

Sylvia Chapman

1 (6-ounce) package orange jello	2 cups buttermilk
1 (20 ounce) can crushed pineapple, do not drain	1 (12-ounce) container Cool Whip
	1 cup chopped nuts

In a saucepan, mix dry jello and pineapple. Bring to a boil, stirring constantly. Remove from heat and cool. Stir in buttermilk. Fold in whipped topping. Stir in nuts. Pour into a 9x13-inch glass dish. Refrigerate until congealed. Yield: 8 to 10 servings

Note: Can use sugar free jello and fat free whipped topping.

Orange-Pineapple and Almond Salad

Betsy Stanton

1 (6-ounce) package orange jello	1 (15 1/2-ounce) can crushed pineapple
14 large marshmallows	1 (2 1/4-ounce) package slivered almonds
1 (3-ounce) package cream cheese	2 cups Cool Whip
2 cups boiling water	

In a large bowl, combine first three ingredients and pour boiling water over and beat until marshmallows are dissolved. Put in refrigerator and congeal slightly. Add pineapple, almonds, and whipped topping. Pour into a 9x13-inch dish and refrigerate until congealed. Yield: 8 to 10 servings.

Strawberry Congealed Salad

Tammy Douglas

2 (6-ounce) packages straw-berry jello	1 (20-ounce) can crushed pineapple
4 cups hot water	2 (10-ounce) cartons frozen strawberries, thawed
2-3 bananas, sliced	
1 cup chopped pecans	

Topping

2 (8-ounce) package cream cheese	1 cup sugar
1 (8-ounce) carton sour cream	1 1/2 teaspoons vanilla
	Chopped nuts

In a medium bowl, dissolve jello in hot water. Add bananas and next three ingredients. Refrigerate until congealed. For topping, beat all ingredients together until smooth. Spread over congealed jello. Sprinkle with nuts. Yield: 10 to 12 servings.

Strawberry Pretzel Salad

Jenny Forbes

First Layer

1 cup pretzels, crushed	2 tablespoons sugar
1 stick butter, softened	

Second Layer

1 (8-ounce) container Cool Whip	1 cup sugar
1 (8-ounce) package cream cheese	

Third Layer

2 (3-ounce) packages strawberry jello	1 (10-ounce) package frozen strawberries, not completely thawed, do not drain
2 cups hot water	

Preheat oven to 350 degrees. For first layer, combine all ingredients in a small bowl and press in 9x13-inch pan. Bake at 350 degrees for 10 minutes. Cool completely. In a small bowl, combine all ingredients for second layer and beat until smooth. Spread over pretzel mixture. For third layer, in a medium bowl, dissolve jello thoroughly in hot water. Mix with strawberries and refrigerate until mixture begins to gel. Pour over other layers and let congeal completely. Yield: 10 to 12 servings.

Blue Cheese French Dressing

Sloan Brittain

1 teaspoon sugar	3 tablespoons vinegar
1/2 teaspoon salt	1/2 cup salad oil
1/2 teaspoon dry mustard	1/3 cup (2-ounce) blue cheese,
1/2 teaspoon paprika	crumbled

Put all ingredients in a jar with a tight-fitting lid. Shake well before using. Keeps well for weeks in the refrigerator. Yield: About 1 cup.

Auntie's Bleu Cheese Dressing

Judy Brown

1/2 pound bleu cheese, softened	1 1/4 teaspoons white pepper
2 cups mayonnaise	1/2 teaspoon dry mustard
1 cup buttermilk	1/2 teaspoon salt
1/2 cup coffee cream	1/2 tablespoon Ac'cent
6 drops Tabasco	
1 1/2 tablespoons lemon juice	

Place softened cheese in a medium bowl. Add all other ingredients and blend well. Will keep in the refrigerator for several weeks. Yield: 2 pints.

French Dressing

Glenn Cannon

10 tablespoons olive oil	2 tablespoons lemon juice
3 tablespoons tarragon vinegar	3 teaspoons seasoned salt

Put all ingredients in a jar with a tight-fitting lid. Shake well. Yield: 1 cup.

Avocado and Roquefort Dressing

Kathy Boyd

1 ripe avocado, quartered	1/2 teaspoon salt
1 cup sour cream	1 clove garlic, crushed
3 tablespoons milk	1 teaspoon Worcestershire
1 tablespoon Roquefort cheese	sauce
2 tablespoons lemon juice	

Mix all ingredients in a blender. Keeps well in refrigerator. Yield: 1 cup.

Poppy Seed Fruit Dressing

Geri Jernigan

3/4 cup sugar
1 1/2 teaspoons onion salt
1 teaspoon ground mustard

1/2 cup red wine vinegar
2/3 cup vegetable oil
1 tablespoon poppy seeds

In a small bowl, mix all ingredients except poppy seeds. With electric mixer, beat on medium speed 2 to 3 minutes. Add poppy seeds. Store in refrigerator. Yield: About 1 1/2 cups.

Thousand Island Dressing

Kathy Boyd

1 cup mayonnaise
1/2 cup chili sauce
2 tablespoons finely minced onion

3 tablespoons sweet pickle relish
3 hard boiled eggs, chopped

In a small bowl, combine all ingredients. Mix well. Refrigerate at least 3 hours. Yield: About 1 1/2 cups.

★Bread ★ Breakfast ★

Howard Brown and Alex Brown
Daddy and Alex enjoying breakfast.

Daddy and Alex often meet in the mornings to start their days off with a good breakfast and sharing time with one another. There doesn't have to be a lot of talk, just being together and knowing how much each other cares.

Sharing time and loving one another are priceless gifts. They are gifts that can not be bought and we need to possess. Often we become too busy in our lives and don't take the time to give the greatest gifts that are buried within ourselves. They are meant to be given away. We must give of ourselves to help others grow. Put your love to practice.

Above all, love each other deeply, because love covers
a multitude of sins. Offer hospitality to one another
without grumbling. Each one should use whatever gift
he has received to serve others, faithfully administering
God's grace in its various forms.

1 Peter 4: 8-10

Banana-Raisin Bread

Jacqueline Segars

2 eggs	1 cup chopped nuts
4 very ripe bananas, mashed	Light raisins soaked in white
1 (181/4-ounce) package yellow	wine
cake mix	1 teaspoon vanilla

Preheat oven to 325 degrees. Grease and flour two 9x5-inch loaf pans. In a mixing bowl, beat eggs; add bananas. Pour in cake mix and mix well. Stir in nuts, raisins and vanilla. Pour batter into prepared pans. Bake at 325 degrees for 30 minutes. Yield: 2 loaves.

Note: Slice thin and make small sandwiches with butter. Can use small loaf pans to make three small loaves.

Cinnamon Rolls

Kathy Boyd

1/3 cup sugar	Cherries (optional)
1/4 teaspoon cinnamon	Jelly (optional)
1/4 cup melted butter	1/2 cup chopped pecans
1 (10-ounce) can refrigerated	
biscuits	

Preheat oven to 350 degrees. Grease and flour a 9-inch round pan. In a resealable plastic bag, mix sugar and cinnamon. Pour butter in a small bowl. Dip biscuits in butter and then shake in sugar mixture. Place in prepared pan. Indent the center of each biscuit with thumb. Place a cherry or jelly in center. Sprinkle pecans over top. Bake at 350 degrees for 20 to 25 minutes. Yield: 10 rolls.

Quick Caramel Rolls

Laura Crouch

1 (25-ounce) package frozen Parkerhouse style roll dough	1 cup brown sugar
	1 stick melted margarine
1 (3.4-ounce) box butterscotch pudding, not instant	1 cup chopped nuts

Grease a Bundt pan. Place frozen doughs balls in bottom of pan. Sprinkle remaining ingredients over dough balls, one ingredient at the time in order given. Leave overnight. Bake next morning at 350 degrees for 20 to 25 minutes. Cool 3 minutes then turn out of pan. Yield: 10 servings.

Note: We serve these every Christmas morning!

Peach Bread

Jane Truett

Peach Purée

6-8 peaches, about 1 pound sliced	1/2 cup sugar
1 teaspoon asorbic acid (fruit fresh)	Pinch salt

Bread

1 1/2 cups sugar	1 teaspoon cinnamon
1/2 cup shortening	1 teaspoon soda
2 eggs	1 teaspoon baking powder
2 1/4 cups fresh peach purée	1/4 teaspoon salt
2 cups all-purpose flour, unsifted	1 teaspoon vanilla
	1 cup finely chopped pecans

Preheat oven to 325 degrees. Grease and flour two 9x5-inch loaf pans. For peach puree, mash peaches with or without peel. Whiz in a blender. Add ascorbic acid, sugar and salt. Whiz all together in a blender. In a mixing bowl, cream sugar and shortening together. Add eggs and mix thoroughly. Add peach puree and dry ingredients; mix well. Stir in vanilla and pecans. Pour into prepared pans. Bake at 325 degrees for 55 minutes to 1 hour. Cool a few minutes before removing from pan. Yield: 2 loaves

German Streusel Coffee Cake

Anne Goodson

Cake

3 eggs, beaten	2 cups all-purpose flour
2/3 cup hot milk	2 tablespoons sugar
1/4 cup soft butter	1 teaspoon salt
1 package dry yeast	

Crumbly Topping

1/2 cup sugar	1/4 cup butter
2/3 cup flour	1/2 teaspoon cinnamon '

Glaze

1 cup powdered sugar	1/4 teaspoon vanilla
1 tablespoon melted butter	1-2 tablespoons milk

Preheat oven to 350 degrees. Grease a 9x13-inch pan. In a saucepan, warm eggs, milk, and butter over low heat. Transfer egg mixture to a medium bowl and mix with all dry ingredients. Beat 3 minutes. Pour into prepared pan. For topping, in a small bowl, mix all ingredients together and sprinkle over batter. Let rise 30 minutes. Bake at 350 degrees until golden brown. Combine all glaze ingredients in a small bowl; mix well. Pour over warm cake. Yield: 6-10 servings.

Pistachio Nut Coffee Cake

Kae Dawkins

1 (181/4-ounce) box yellow cake mix	2 eggs
1 (3-ounce) package pistachio nut pudding mix	1 (8-ounce) container sour cream
1/2 cup cooking oil	1/2 cup sugar
	1 tablespoon cinnamon

Preheat oven to 350 degrees. Lightly grease a Bundt pan. In a mixing bowl, cream cake mix, pudding mix, oil and eggs. Stir in sour cream. In a small bowl, mix sugar and cinnamon and set aside. Pour one half of the cake mixture in prepared pan. Sprinkle one half of the sugar mixture in the center and swirl around. Pour in remaining cake batter and sprinkle with remaining sugar mixture. Bake at 350 degrees for 1 hour. Yield: 18 to 20 servings.

Sour Cream Coffee Cake

Cecelia Alford

Filling

1 cup chopped pecans	21/4 teaspoons cinnamon
3/4 cup brown sugar	

Cake

3 cups all-purpose flour	11/2 cups sugar
41/2 teaspoons baking soda	3 eggs
41/2 teaspoons baking powder	2 teaspoons vanilla
1/2 teaspoon salt	1 (16-ounce) container sour
2 sticks butter	cream

Preheat oven to 375 degrees. Grease a 12-inch Bundt pan. In a small bowl, combine all filling ingredients. Set aside. In a separate bowl combine flour, baking soda, baking powder, and salt. In a mixing bowl, cream butter and sugar. Add eggs one at the time. Beat well after each addition. Stir in vanilla. Alternate adding flour mixture and sour cream to creamed mixture and mix well. Pour two cups of batter into prepared pan. Sprinkle three-fourths of filling on top of batter. Pour two and one-half cups of batter on top of filling. Add remaining filling and cover with remaining batter. Bake at 375 degrees for 1 hour. Cool about 10 minutes. Sprinkle with powdered sugar. Yield: 16 to 20 servings.

Strawberry Bread

Debbie Brown

1 cup butter or margarine	1 teaspoon salt
11/2 cups sugar	1 teaspoon cream of tartar
1 teaspoon vanilla	1/2 teaspoon baking soda
1/2 teaspoon lemon extract	1 cup strawberry preserves
4 eggs	1/2 cup sour cream
3 cups all-purpose flour	1 cup pecans (optional)

Preheat oven to 350 degrees. Grease and flour two 9x5-inch loaf pans. In a bowl, cream butter and sugar. Add vanilla and lemon. Stir in eggs. Sift flour with salt, cream of tartar, and soda in a large bowl. In a small bowl, mix preserves and sour cream. Alternately add cream mixture and preserves to dry ingredients. Stir in nuts. Bake at 350 degrees for 50 minutes. Yield: 2 loaves.

Zucchini Bread

Judy Morehead

3	eggs, well beaten	1	teaspoon soda
2	cups sugar	2	teaspoons cinnamon
1	cup salad oil	2	cups grated zucchini (peeling
2	cups all-purpose flour		and all)
1	teaspoon salt	1	cup chopped nuts
1/4	teaspoon baking powder	1	teaspoon vanilla

Preheat oven to 350 degrees. Grease and flour two 9x5-inch loaf pans. In a large bowl, combine first three ingredients. In a separate bowl, sift together flour and next four ingredients. Add to egg mixture. Add zucchini, nuts, and vanilla. Pour into prepared pans. Bake at 350 degrees for 45 minutes. Yield: 2 loaves.

Note: Great with a good cup of coffee!

Poppy Seed Bread

Annabelle Snipes

1	(18-ounce) package moist Betty Crocker Butter Pecan cake mix, pudding in mix	1/3	cup poppy seeds
		1	cup warm water
		1	cup corn oil
1	(3-ounce) package coconut cream or toasted coconut instant pudding mix	4	eggs

Preheat oven to 325 degrees. Grease and flour two 5x3-inch loaf pans. In a large bowl, combine dry ingredients with warm water. Add oil, then eggs. Mix well with an electric mixture on medium speed. Pour into prepared pans. Bake at 325 degrees for 45 to 60 minutes. Check at 30 minutes using tester to see if it comes out dry and clean. Yield: 2 loaves.

Sweet Potato Bread

Jane Sox

8-10 medium size sweet potatoes,
    boiled and peeled
21/2 sticks butter or margarine
1   teaspoon nutmeg

21/2 teaspoons cinnamon
21/2 cups sugar
3/4 cup self-rising flour
1   tablespoon vanilla

Preheat oven to 350 degrees. Grease and flour a 9x5 loaf pan. In a large bowl, mash potatoes; add butter and next five ingredients. Mix well. Pour into prepared pan. Bake at 350 degrees until browned. Yield: 1 loaf.

Note: May add 1 cup chopped nuts or 1 cup chopped nuts and 1 cup raisins. Mix nuts and raisins with 1/4 cup flour and fold into potato mixture.

Six Week Bran Muffins

Angelyn Bateman

2 cups All Bran cereal
2 cups boiling water
4 eggs
3 cups sugar
1 cup oil
1 quart buttermilk

3 cups all-purpose flour
5 teaspoons soda
2 teaspoons salt
1 teaspoon cinnamon
1 (9-ounce) box raisins
  (optional)

In a medium bowl, pour water over the bran cereal and let stand while mixing other ingredients. In a separate bowl, mix remaining ingredients. Add bran cereal mixture; mix well. Spoon into greased muffin pan or paper liners filling two-thirds full. Bake at 400 degrees for 20 minutes. This mixture will keep in a covered container in the refrigerator for six weeks. Yield: 48 large muffins.

Note: I have a fond memory of Anne Dawkins popping in the back-door with a container of this delicious mix and saying " I brought you something and having a great big smile."

Corn Muffins

Frances Kelley

2	cups cornmeal	1	egg
1	teaspoon baking soda	1	cup buttermilk
	Pinch salt	1	tablespoon Crisco, melted

Preheat oven to 425 degrees. Grease a muffin pan or a 8x8-inch baking dish. In a medium bowl, sift all dry ingredients together. In a separate bowl, mix egg, buttermilk and shortening together. Add egg mixture to dry ingredients and mix well. Pour into prepared pan. Bake at 425 degrees for 20 minutes or until brown. Yield: 12 servings.

Morning Glory Muffins

Glenn Cannon

2	cups all-purpose flour	1/2	cup coconut
1 1/3	cups sugar	1/2	cup chopped nuts
2	teaspoons baking soda	1	(8-ounce) can crushed
1	teaspoon ground cinnamon		pineapple, drained
1/2	teaspoon salt	1	cup vegetable oil
2	cups grated carrots	3	eggs, lightly beaten
1/2	cup raisins	2	teaspoons vanilla extract

Preheat oven to 350 degrees. In a large bowl, combine first five ingredients; stir in carrot and next four ingredients. Make a well in center of mixture. In a separate bowl, combine vegetable oil, eggs; and vanilla. Add to flour mixture, stirring until just moistened. Place paper baking cups in muffin pans. Spoon into cups, filling two-thirds full. Bake at 350 degrees for 25 minutes or until golden brown. Remove from pans immediately. Yield: 22 muffins.

Onion Popovers
Carol Coggeshall

1	cup all-purpose flour	1	teaspoon parsley flakes
1/2	teaspoon salt	1	cup milk, whole or 2%
1	teaspoon minced onion flakes	2	eggs, slightly beaten

Preheat oven to 450 degrees. Grease muffin pan or custard cups. In a medium bowl, combine all ingredients. Stir with a fork just until smooth. Spoon into muffin pan filling three-fourths full or one-half full in custard cups. Bake at 450 degrees for 20 minutes; reduce heat to 350 degrees and bake an additional 10 to 15 minutes or until a dark golden brown. If any are leftover, freeze and reheat at 375 degrees for 5 to 8 minutes. Yield: 10 to 12 servings.

Sausage Muffins
Stephanie McCullum

2	cups self-rising flour	1	pound bulk sausage, browned
1	stick butter, melted	1	(8-ounce) package grated
1	(8-ounce) container sour cream		Cheddar cheese

Preheat oven to 350 degrees. Grease a muffin pan or use paper baking cups. Mix flour, butter, and sour cream in medium bowl. Stir in sausage and cheese. Spoon into prepared muffin pan filling one-half full. Bake at 350 degrees for 25 minutes. Yield: 12 muffins.

Daddy's Cheese Biscuits
Kathy Boyd

6	tablespoons shortening	1/4	teaspoon black pepper
2	cups self-rising flour		Pinch cayenne pepper
1/2	cup milk	1	cup grated Cheddar cheese

Preheat oven to 450 degrees. In a mixing bowl, cut shortening into flour. Add milk and mix; stir in peppers and cheese. Turn out on floured board and knead gently. Roll out to a 1/2-thickness. Cut with biscuit cutter. Bake at 450 degrees until golden brown. Yield: 18 biscuits.

Charleston Biscuits
Vermelle King

2 cups self-rising flour	1/2 pint sour cream
1 1/2 sticks butter, melted	

Preheat oven to 350 degrees. Combine all ingredients in a medium bowl. Drop by heaping teaspoonfuls into small muffin pans. Bake at 350 degrees for about 20 minutes. Yield: 35 to 40 muffins.

Note: Freezes well after they have been cooked. Good with luncheon dishes or brunches.

Quick Corn Biscuits
Kathy Boyd

3/4 stick butter	1 (8 1/2-ounce) can cream style
1 1/2 cups Bisquick	corn

Melt butter on a sided baking sheet. Mix baking mix and corn. Drop by teaspoonfuls on baking sheet. Turn each biscuit to coat with butter. Bake at 400 degrees for 20 minutes or until golden brown. Yield: 18 biscuits.

Miss Henrietta's Biscuits
Karen Jeffords

10 level tablespoons Crisco	2/3 cup buttermilk
2 cups self-rising flour, sifted	

Preheat oven to 450 degrees. In a mixing bowl, cut shortening into flour. Add milk and mix. Turn out onto a floured board and knead gently. Roll out dough to a 1/4 to 1/2-inch thickness. Cut with biscuit cutter and place on a ungreased baking sheet. Bake at 450 degrees for 12 to 15 minutes. Yield: 18 biscuits.

Red Lobster Biscuits

Wilma Casstevens

2   cups biscuit baking mix
3/4 cup grated sharp Cheddar
     cheese
1/2 cup cold water

1/4 cup butter
1/2 teaspoon garlic powder
1   teaspoon parsley flakes
1/2 teaspoon Italian seasoning

Preheat oven to 400 degrees. Mix biscuit mix, cheese, and water in a medium bowl. Drop by large spoonfuls onto a greased baking sheet. Bake at 400 degrees for about 10 minutes. While biscuits are baking, in a saucepan, melt butter and add garlic, parsley, and Italian seasoning. When biscuits are done, remove baking sheet from the oven and brush immediately with butter mixture. Serve hot. Yield: 16 biscuits.

Sweet Potato Biscuits

Kathy Boyd

3/4 cup mashed, cooked sweet
     potatoes
2/3 cup milk
4   tablespoons melted butter

4   teaspoons baking powder
1   tablespoon sugar
1/2 teaspoon salt
1 1/4 cups all-purpose flour

Preheat oven to 450 degrees. Grease a baking sheet or spray with nonstick cooking spray. In a large bowl, mix potatoes, milk, and butter. In a separate bowl, sift together remaining ingredients. Add to potato mixture and mix until it makes a soft dough. Turn out on floured board and toss lightly until outside looks smooth. Roll out dough to a 1/2-inch thickness and cut with biscuit cutter. Place on prepared pan and bake at 450 degrees until brown. Yield: 18 biscuits.

Whipping Cream Biscuits

Fannie Rodgers

1   (20-ounce) box Bisquick   1/2   pint heavy cream, can use
                                          light

Preheat oven to 450 degrees. In a large bowl, make a well in the center of
the biscuit mix. Pour cream into center and stir until dough becomes stiff.
Turn dough out on floured board and knead until it becomes dry. Pinch off
dough to biscuit size and mash flat. Place on ungreased baking sheet. Bake at
450 degrees until golden brown. Yield: 15 to 20 biscuits.

Sausage Biscuits

Beverly Whisnant

2   (9 1/2-ounce) cans refrigerated   3   beaten eggs
    butter biscuits   Dash dry mustard
1   pound bulk sausage   Dash Worcestershire
1   cup grated Cheddar cheese   Dash black pepper

Preheat oven to 400 degrees. Spray 2 muffin pans with nonstick cooking
spray. Press biscuits in muffin pans forming cups. In a skillet, brown sausage;
remove from heat and drain grease. Stir in cheese and eggs. Add mustard,
Worcestershire, and pepper to taste. Fill dough cups with egg mixture. Bake
at 400 degrees for 12 minutes. Yield: 20 biscuits.

Aunt Flora's Ice Box Rolls

Jenny Rogers

2	yeast cakes	1	cup hot milk
1/2	cup water (lukewarm to rise quickly)	2/3	cup shortening
6-7	cups flour	1/2	cup sugar
1	teaspoon baking powder	2	eggs, beaten
1	tablespoon plus 1/2 teaspoon salt, divided		

Dissolve yeast cakes in water. In a medium bowl, sift the flour, baking powder, and one-half teaspoon salt together. In a separate bowl, pour hot milk over shortening, sugar, and remaining salt; let cool. After cooled, add eggs and part of the flour, yeast, and the remaining flour. Mix this with a spoon; no kneading. It shouldn't be too stiff. Cover with a damp cloth and let rise until double in bulk. Put in refrigerator until ready to make rolls (At this point, dough can stay in the refrigerator two to three days). On floured board, roll dough out a little at the time and cut with biscuit cutter. Place on a baking sheet and brush with butter, then fold over. Let them rise until doubled. Bake at 400 degrees for 10 minutes. Yield: 100 small rolls.

Note: You may cook the rolls half way and then freeze.

Broccoli Cornbread

Donna Tucker

1	(10-ounce) package chopped broccoli	6	ounces cottage cheese, small curd
4	eggs beaten	1	teaspoon salt
1	stick melted butter or margarine	1	(8-ounce) box corn muffin mix
1	chopped onion, optional		

Preheat oven to 400 degrees. Cook broccoli according to package directions; drain thoroughly. In a medium bowl, mix all ingredients together. Spray a 9x13-inch pan with nonstick cooking spray. Pour batter into pan. Bake at 400 degrees for 25 to 30 minutes. Yield: 15 to 20 servings.

Cornbread

Beth Brown

Submitted by Kathy Boyd

1	cup flour	1	cup yellow corn meal
1/4	cup sugar	1	egg, beaten
4	teaspoons baking powder	1	cup milk
3/4	teaspoons salt	1/4	cup shortening, melted

Preheat oven to 425 degrees. Grease an 8x8-inch baking pan. In a medium bowl, sift all dry ingredients together. Add egg, milk, and shortening, stirring well. Pour into prepared pan. Bake at 425 degrees for 20 to 25 minutes. Yield: 6 to 8 servings.

Hobo Dream Cornbread

Ressie Cassidy

1	cup self-rising cornmeal	1	onion finely chopped
1	cup self-rising flour	1	cup milk
1	egg		Pinch of salt
1	(8 1/2-ounce) can cream style corn	3/4	cup cooking oil
		1/4	teaspoon cayenne pepper
1	cup grated sharp Cheddar cheese	1/4	teaspoon baking powder

Preheat oven to 355 degrees. In a large bowl, combine all ingredients; mix thoroughly. Pour into a well-greased iron frying pan. Bake at 350 degrees until top is lightly browned. Yield: 6 to 8 servings.

Thad Saleeby's Mexican Cornbread
J E Winburn

1/2 pound ground beef or sausage	2 small onions, chopped
1 1/2 cups self-rising meal	1 small bell pepper, chopped
2 tablespoons self-rising flour	1/2 cup oil
2 teaspoons salt	1 cup buttermilk
1/2 teaspoon soda	3 (2 tablespoons) jalapeño
1 1/2 cups shredded sharp cheese	peppers, chopped
2 eggs	

Preheat oven to 375 degrees. Grease a 8x8-inch pan. In a skillet, brown meat; drain. In a medium bowl, mix all ingredients together thoroughly. Pour into prepared pan. Bake at 375 degrees for 35 minutes. Yield: 8 to 10 serv-

Sour Cream Cornbread
Ann Atkins

3/4 cup yellow corn meal	3/4 teaspoon salt
1 cup unsifted all-purpose flour	1 cup sour cream
1/4 cup sugar	1/4 cup milk
2 teaspoons double-acting baking powder	1 egg, beaten
1/2 teaspoon soda	2 tablespoons shortening, melted

Preheat oven to 425 degrees. Grease 8x8-inch pan or corn stick pan. In a medium bowl, mix all ingredients just enough to blend. Pour into prepared pan. Bake at 425 degrees for about 20 minutes. Yield: 8 to 10 servings.

Amish Baked Oatmeal

Susan Crowder

1	cup oil	4	teaspoons baking powder
1	cup honey	2	cups milk, can use skim, 2%
4	eggs		or whole
2	teaspoons salt	6	cups uncooked oatmeal

Preheat oven to 350 degrees. Grease an 9x13-inch baking pan. In a mixing bowl, combine oil, honey, and eggs. Add salt, baking powder, milk, and oatmeal. Blend well. Pour into prepared pan. Bake at 350 degrees for 35 to 40 minutes. May top with milk, yogurt, or fruit; or serve plain. Yield: 10 to 12 servings.

Note: This recipe can be halved and baked in an 8x8-inch pan for 30 minutes.

Blueberry Oven Pancakes

Debbie Bell

2	cups Bisquick original baking mix	2	eggs
1	cup milk	1	cup fresh or frozen blue- berries,
2	tablespoons sugar		if frozen, thaw and drain
2	tablespoons vegetable oil		

Preheat oven to 425 degrees. Grease an 10x15-inch jelly roll pan. In a mixing bowl, beat all ingredients except blueberries with a wire whisk or hand beater until well blended. Fold in blueberries. Spread mixture in prepared pan. Bake at 425 degrees for 14 to 16 minutes or until top is light golden brown. Cut into 12 pieces. Serve immediately. Yield: 12 servings.

Wade's Wonderful Pancakes

Annabelle Snipes

Pancakes

2 1/4 cups buttermilk

2 eggs

3 tablespoons vegetable oil

1/3 cup sour cream, regular or fat free

2 cups self rising flour

3 tablespoons sugar

1 tablespoon baking powder

Fruit and Nut Spread

1/3 cup butter or margarine

1/2 cup sifted powdered sugar

1/2 cup diced fresh or canned fruit, peaches (yummy fresh) apricots or nectarines

1/4 cup chopped or slivered pecans or almonds

1 teaspoon lemon juice

In a large bowl, combine buttermilk, eggs, oil, and sour cream. Beat with a whisk to blend well. Add flour and sugar to liquids and beat to remove lumps. Add baking powder and blend well. Batter should be consistency of rich egg nog. In a frying pan, pour in one-fourth of batter. When top surface bubbles evenly and edges look cooked; flip over. For spread: in a mixing bowl, with electric mixer, cream the butter until light; gradually add sugar and beat until fluffy. Fold in remaining ingredients. Serve at room temperature with warm syrup. Yield: 4 servings.

Note: Our grandchildren love these pancakes made by Daddy Wade! Recipe doubles well. For waffles add flour to batter to make thicker. If preparing for dessert, make ahead, cool completely, and seal in plastic bag.

Brunch Egg Casserole
Kathy Boyd

2   pounds bulk sausage
1   pound sharp Cheddar
    cheese, shredded
4   cups sour cream

Salt and pepper to taste
Paprika to taste
10 eggs, beaten

Preheat oven to 350 degrees. In a skillet, brown sausage; drain. In a 9x13-inch glass dish layer one-half the cheese, one-half of the sour cream, and sausage . Then add the remaining cheese and sour cream. Add salt, pepper, and paprika to the eggs. Pour on top of the layers. Bake at 350 degrees for 30 minutes. Yield: 12 to 15 servings.

Note: This is a Christmas morning tradition at our house with garlic cheese grits and cinnamon rolls! Can prepare a day ahead, refrigerate overnight and bake the next morning.

Breakfast Pizza
Kelly Harper

1   pound bulk sausage
1   (8-ounce) can refrigerated
    crescent rolls
1   cup frozen hash browns,
    thawed
1   cup shredded sharp Cheddar
    cheese

5   eggs
1/4 cup milk
    Salt and pepper or seasoned
    salt
2   tablespoons Parmesan cheese

Preheat oven to 375 degrees. In a skillet, brown sausage; drain. Arrange crescent rolls on bottom of 9x13-inch baking dish, pressing edges together. Layer sausage, hash browns, and cheese over dough. In a small bowl, beat eggs and milk together. Pour over top. Sprinkle with salt, pepper, and Parmesan cheese. Bake at 375 degrees for 20 to 25 minutes. Yield: 6 to 8 servings.

Note: May use a prepared pie crust instead of rolls. May use ham or bacon instead of sausage. Add chopped chilies or onions.

Bacon and Cheese Breakfast Pizza

Lauren Brown

1/2 pound bacon	1 1/2 cups sour cream
Pastry for (9-inch) pie crust	2 tablespoons chopped fresh
2 cups shredded Swiss cheese	parsley
4 eggs	

Preheat oven to 425 degrees. In a skillet, cook bacon until browned and crumble. Set aside. Roll pastry to fit a 12-inch pizza pan. Bake at 425 degrees for 5 minutes. Sprinkle bacon and cheese evenly over crust. In a small bowl, beat eggs, sour cream, and parsley until smooth. Pour mixture over pizza. Bake at 325 degrees for 25 minutes or until pizza is puffy and lightly browned. Yield: 4 to 6 servings.

Garlic Cheese Grits

Kathy Boyd

1 (6-ounce) roll garlic cheese, divided	2 eggs
	1/2 cup milk
4 cups cooked grits	1 stick butter, melted

Preheat oven to 350 degrees. Cut three-fourths of cheese into small pieces. Add to hot grits to melt cheese. In a medium bowl, beat eggs and milk. Add to grits mixture. Stir in butter, mixing well. Pour into a 2-quart greased casserole dish. Dot with remaining cheese. Bake at 350 degrees for 45 minutes. Yield: 6 to 8 servings.

Nassau Grits

Bill Stokes

1   pound sliced bacon
2   green peppers, finely
    chopped
2   medium onions, finely
    chopped
1 1/2 cups ham, finely ground
    (optional)

1   (28-ounce) can whole
    tomatoes, chopped*
1 1/2 cups white grits
    Garlic to taste
    Seasoned salt to taste

In a skillet, cook bacon until crisp. Remove bacon and set aside. Pour off all but 2 tablespoons of drippings from skillet. Sauté onion and bell pepper until soft. Add ham and stir well. Sauté over low heat 15 minutes. Add tomatoes, garlic, and salt. Simmer 30 minutes. In a medium saucepan, cook grits according to package directions. When grits are cooked, add tomato mixture and mix well. Crumble bacon and stir into grits saving a little to sprinkle on top. Yield: 12 servings.

Note: *May use a smaller can of chopped tomatoes and a can of tomatoes and green chilies to equal 28 ounces.

Party Grits

Linda Drayton

1   pound sliced bacon
2   green peppers, finely
    chopped
2   medium onions, finely
    chopped

1   (28-ounce) can whole
    tomatoes, chopped
1 1/2 cups finely ground ham
1 1/2 cups white hominy grits
    Chicken broth

In a skillet, cook bacon until crisp; drain on paper towel. Pour off all but 2 to 3 tablespoons of drippings from skillet. In same skillet, cook onion and bell pepper 7 to 8 minutes or until soft. Add the tomatoes and simmer, uncovered, 30 minutes. Stir in ham. In a medium saucepan, cook grits according to package directions using chicken broth in place of the water. When grits are cooked, add ham mixture and stir well. Serve hot with crumbled bacon on top. Yield: 12 servings.

Grits-Sausage Casserole
Harriet Foster

1 1/2 cups quick cooking grits
1 pound bulk pork sausage or turkey sausage
1 1/2 cups shredded Cheddar cheese

1 egg beaten
2 tablespoons picante sauce
1 tablespoon minced onion

Preheat oven to 350 degrees. Grease 2-quart shallow casserole dish. Cook grits according to package directions. In a skillet, cook sausage until brown; crumble; drain. Combine grits, sausage, and other ingredients. Pour into prepared dish. Bake at 350 degrees for 30 minutes. Yield: 4 servings.

Note: May be made ahead and refrigerate overnight before baking.

Company Breakfast
Deb Walters

1 pound bulk sausage
4-6 slices bread
8 eggs or Eggbeaters
1 1/2 cups milk

1 cup grated Cheddar cheese
1 teaspoon dry mustard
Salt and pepper to taste

Grease a 8x11-inch or 9x13-inch pan. In a skillet, brown meat; crumble and drain. Cut bread in cubes. Put into prepared pan. Spread sausage over bread. In a medium bowl, beat eggs with milk; add cheese, mustard, salt, and pepper. Pour egg mixture over bread and sausage. Cover with plastic wrap. Refrigerate overnight. Put in a cold oven and bake at 350 degrees for 35 minutes. Yield: 6 to 8 servings.

Derby Eggs

Marsha Oates

1	pound bulk sausage	1	cup mayonnaise
12-14	hard boiled eggs, sliced in half	1	(8-ounce) can sliced mushrooms
2	(103/4-ounce) can cream mushroom soup		Chives to taste
			Salt and pepper to taste

Preheat oven to 350 degrees. In a skillet, cook sausage until brown; crumble and drain. Place eggs in a 3-quart casserole. Sprinkle sausage over top of eggs. In a mixing bowl, combine soup, mayonnaise, mushrooms and seasonings. Pour mixture over eggs. Bake at 350 degrees until bubbly and hot. Yield: 10 to 12 servings.

Ham Soufflé

Lea Saunders

16	slices sandwich white bread, cut off crust, divided	1/2	teaspoon dry mustard
8	slices Cheddar cheese or 12-ounces grated	1/2	teaspoon salt
		2	cups corn flakes
1	(16-ounce) package sand-wich ham, finely chopped	1/2	cup melted butter
6	eggs	3	(103/4-ounce) cans cream of mushroom soup
3	cups milk	3/4	soup can cooking sherry

Place eight slices of bread in the bottom of a greased 9x13-inch glass casserole dish. Top with cheese slices or grated cheese. Sprinkle ham over cheese and cover with remaining bread. In a medium bowl, beat eggs and milk together; add spices. Pour egg mixture over bread and place in refrigerator overnight. Next morning, in a bowl, mix corn flakes with melted butter and spread over casserole. Bake at 350 degrees for 1 hour or until eggs or set. In a saucepan, combine soup and sherry. Heat until hot. Serve as a sauce over the casserole. Yield: 10 servings.

Note: All time favorite. Delicious!

Sausage and Egg Quiche

Peggy Harrison

1 pound hot bulk sausage	1 cup grated Cheddar cheese
1 small onion, chopped	2 tablespoons flour
2 eggs, beaten	1 (9-inch) deep dish pie crust
1/2 cup mayonnaise	

Preheat oven to 400 degrees. In a skillet, brown sausage with onion; drain. Add eggs and next three ingredients and mix well. Pour into pie crust. Bake at 400 degrees for 30 minutes. Yield: 6 to 8 servings.

Sausage Casserole

Debbie Galloway

2 pounds bulk sausage	1 (10 3/4-ounce) can cream of
1 cup grits	mushroom soup
4 cups water	2 cups grated sharp Cheddar
Salt and pepper to taste	cheese, divided
6 eggs	

Preheat oven to 350 degrees. In a skillet, brown sausage; drain. Cook grits with water, salt, and pepper according to package directions. Add sausage, eggs, soup, and one-half of cheese to grits. Pour into a 9x11-inch glass dish. Top with remaining cheese. Bake at 350 degrees for 40 minutes. Yield: 8 to 10 servings.

Sausage and Gravy Toast

Robert Braddock
Submitted by Andy Broach

1	pound bulk sausage	1	cup milk
1/4	cup flour	1/2	cup water
1	teaspoon salt	8	slices toast
1	teaspoon black pepper		

In a skillet, cook sausage until browned; crumble. Make sure sausage is done but not overcooked. Sprinkle flour over top and stir in salt, and pepper. Add milk and mix well. Add water and stir. Serve over hot toast. Yield: 6 servings.

Weekender Special

Tru Lawton

10	slices bacon	1 1/2	cups milk
1/2	cup bell pepper, chopped	1	teaspoon seasoned salt
8	green onions, chopped	1	teaspoon dry mustard
1	pound fresh mushrooms, chopped	1	teaspoon thyme
3	tablespoons sherry	4	cups Gruyère cheese, grated, divided
12	eggs		

Grease a 9x13-inch baking dish. In a skillet, cook bacon until crisp; drain and chop. In same skillet, sauté bell pepper, onion and mushrooms until limp. Add sherry, heating until sherry evaporates. In a large bowl, beat eggs and next four ingredients together. Add bacon, bell pepper mixture and three cups of cheese. Pour into prepared pan. Cover and refrigerate overnight. Bake at 350 degrees for 40 minutes. Sprinkle with remaining cheese and bake 5 minutes longer. Let stand 20 minutes before serving. Yield: 8 servings.

Scrambled Egg Casserole

Debbie Brown

Cheese Sauce

2   tablespoons butter
21/2 tablespoons flour
2   cups milk
1/2 teaspoon salt

1/8 teaspoon black pepper
4   ounces Cheddar
     cheese, shredded

Casserole

1   cup cubed or ground country
     ham
1/4 cup chopped green onions
7   tablespoons melted butter,
     divided

12   eggs
1   (4-ounce) can sliced
     mushrooms, drained
21/4 cups soft breadcrumbs
1/8 teaspoon paprika

For cheese sauce, in a heavy skillet melt butter on low heat. Blend in flour and cook 1 minute. Gradually add milk and cook over medium heat until thickened, stirring constantly. Add salt, pepper, and cheese. Stir until cheese melts and mixture is smooth. Set aside. In a large skillet, sauté ham and onion in three tablespoons melted butter until onion is tender. Add eggs and cook over medium-high heat, stirring to form soft curds. When eggs are set, stir in mushrooms and cheese sauce. Spoon egg mixture into a greased 9x13-inch baking dish. Combine remaining butter and breadcrumbs, mixing well. Spread evenly over egg mixture. Sprinkle with paprika. Cover and refrigerate over-night. Bake, uncovered, at 350 degrees for 30 minutes or until heated through. Yield: 8 to 10 servings.

★ Seafood ★

Howard and Beth Cox Brown
June 7, 1950
Mama and Daddy cutting cake on their wedding day

Mama and Daddy were married on June 7, 1950 in Conway, South Carolina. They were married for 49 and a half years. All marriages have their ups and downs but I would consider their marriage made in heaven. They remained devoted to each other through the years. I am blessed to have such a good example to follow.

A wife of noble character who can find?
She is worth far more than rubies.
Her husband has full confidence in her
and lacks nothing of value.
She brings him good, not harm,
all the days of her life.

Proverbs 31:10-12

Crab Cakes
Beth Brown
Submitted by Kathy Boyd

1/4	cup bell pepper, finely chopped
12	saltines, crushed
1/4-1/2	cup onion, finely chopped
1	tablespoon Worcestershire sauce

1	egg, slightly beaten
1	tablespoon mayonnaise
2	teaspoons salt
	Dash black pepper
1	pound fresh crabmeat
1/4	cup oil

In a large bowl, combine all ingredients except oil and mix well. Shape into eight 3-inch patties. In a skillet, fry patties in hot oil until browned. Turn once. They take about 4 minutes to cook. Yield: 4 servings.

Crabmeat Quiche
Kathy Boyd

1/2	cup mayonnaise
2	tablespoons flour
2	eggs, beaten
1/2	cup milk
2	(6-ounce) cans Alaska crabmeat
8	ounces Swiss cheese, grated

1/3	cup green onions, chopped
1/4	cup bell pepper, diced
1	(4 1/2-ounce) can sliced mushrooms, drained
4	slices bacon, cooked and crumbled
1	(9-inch) unbaked pie crust

Preheat oven to 350 degrees. In a medium bowl, mix mayonnaise, flour, eggs, and milk. Add crabmeat and remaining ingredients. Spoon into pie crust and bake at 350 degrees for 40 to 45 minutes. Yield: 6 to 8 servings.

Crabmeat Casserole
Mary Parnell

1	cup sweet milk	3	slices bread, cubed
3	eggs beaten	2	tablespoons mayonnaise
1/2	stick butter	1	teaspoon minced onion
1	teaspoon horseradish		Salt and pepper to taste
1	teaspoon Worcestershire		Shredded Cheddar cheese
	sauce		Paprika
1	(71/2-ounce) can crabmeat		

Preheat oven to 350 degrees. In a large bowl, mix all ingredients except cheese and paprika. Pour into a 2-quart casserole dish and bake at 350 degrees for 30 minutes. Five minutes before removing from the oven, sprinkle with cheese and paprika. Return to oven until cheese melts. Yield: 6 servings.

Crab Salad Rolls
Cynthia Roberson

1	pound crabmeat	1/2	cup salad dressing or
1/2	cup celery, finely chopped		mayonnaise
1/2	cup cucumbers or pickles,	2	tablespoons soft butter
	finely diced	4	hot dog buns
1/4	cup green onions, chopped		

In a medium bowl, combine crabmeat with celery and next three ingredients. Chill until ready to serve. Spread butter on outer sides of hot dog buns. Toast under broiler on both sides until golden brown. Spoon the crabmeat into buns. Serve while buns are still warm. Yield: 4 servings.

Crab Soufflé From Aunt Kate Barbie

Becky Brown

1	cup milk	1/2	pound crabmeat
3	eggs, beaten	2	slices white bread
1/2	stick butter or margarine	2	tablespoons mayonnaise
1	heaping tablespoon	1	teaspoon grated onion
	horseradish		Salt and pepper to taste
1	tablespoon Worcestershire		Shredded Cheddar cheese
	sauce		

Preheat oven to 350 degrees. In a large bowl, mix all ingredients except cheese. Pour into a 9-inch baking dish. Bake at 350 for 25 minutes. Take out of oven and sprinkle with cheese. Cook an additional 5 minutes. Yield: 6 servings.

Note: This crab soufflé was served at my Aunt Kate's boarding house 40 years ago. She served meals "family style" for .50 cent to $1.00. The menu always included two meats, several vegetables, a congealed salad, and a variety of desserts - and always tiny, hot, homemade biscuits!

Blackened Fish

Byron Greene

1	tablespoon paprika	1	teaspoon black pepper
1	tablespoon onion powder	1/2	teaspoon oregano (optional)
1/2	teaspoon thyme		Melted unsalted butter
2	teaspoons salt		Thick grouper fillets
1	teaspoon garlic powder		
1	teaspoon white pepper		

In a small bowl, thoroughly mix all dry ingredients together. Heat cast iron frying pan until it is smoking. Dip fillets in butter. Sprinkle the flesh side with seasoning and place flesh side down in smoking pan 2 to 3 minutes. Season and turn fillets. Cook until done, about 2 minutes. Yield: 1 fillet per serving.

Jamie's Grouper
Beth and Jamie Morphis

1 (1-ounce) envelope Ranch
   salad dressing mix
1/2 cup sour cream
1/2 cup mayonnaise

   Grouper filets, 3/4-inch thick
1 (2.8-ounce) can french fried
   onion rings

Preheat oven to 375 to 400 degrees. Spray a 9x13-inch baking dish with nonstick cooking spray. In a medium bowl, combine dry dressing mix, sour cream, and mayonnaise. Mix well. Dredge filets in dressing mixture. Place in prepared dish. Bake at 375 to 400 degrees for 12 to 15 minutes. Remove from oven and top with onion rings. Put under broiler until onions are browned. Transfer from baking dish to serving platter. Yield: 1 fillet per person.

Flounder Roll-Ups with Blue Cheese Stuffing
Kathy Boyd

1 stick melted butter, divided
1/4 cup minced fresh parsley
1 medium tomato, chopped
1/2 cup minced celery
1/4 cup firmly packed blue
   cheese

3 cups soft breadcrumbs
1 egg, beaten
1/2 teaspoon salt
1 3/4 pounds flounder fillets
   Juice of 1 lemon

Preheat oven to 350 degrees. Grease a 1 1/2-quart baking dish. In a skillet, combine one-half of butter, parsley, tomato, and celery. Cook 10 minutes over medium heat, stirring often. Remove from heat. Crumble cheese into mixture. Add breadcrumbs, egg, and salt, mixing well. Spread mixture on fillets; roll up, fasten with toothpicks. Place in prepared dish. In a small bowl, mix remaining butter and lemon juice. Pour over fish rolls. Bake at 350 degrees about 30 minutes or until fish flakes easily. Yield: 6 servings.

Fish Filets Eleganté

Ruby Perry

1   (1-pound) package frozen
    fish filets, thawed
    Black pepper to taste
2   tablespoons butter or
    margarine

1   (10³/4-ounce) can cream of
    shrimp soup
1/4 cup Parmesan cheese
    Paprika to taste

Preheat oven to 400 degrees. Arrange filets in a greased 8x8-inch baking dish. Sprinkle with pepper. Dot with butter. Spread soup over top and sprinkle with cheese and paprika. Bake at 400 degrees for 25 minutes.

Salmon Loaf

Ressie Cassidy

1   (16-ounce) can red salmon
2   eggs, lightly beaten
3   slices soft bread, crumbled

1   teaspoon salt
1/4 cup butter, melted
1 1/2 cup milk

Preheat oven to 350 degrees. In a large bowl, thoroughly mix all ingredients. Place in a greased 9x5-inch loaf pan. Bake at 350 degrees for 1 hour. Yield: 4 to 6 servings.

Tuna Pasta Casserole

Dollie Cummings

1   (8-ounce) box macaroni
2   cups frozen mixed vegetables,
    thawed
2   tablespoons melted butter
1   (10³/4-ounce) can cream of
    mushroom soup

1   cup milk
1 1/2 cups shredded mozzarella
    cheese
1/8 teaspoon black pepper
1   (12-ounce) can chunk light
    tuna, drained

Cook pasta according to package directions; drain. In a large skillet, sauté vegetables in butter until tender. Stir in soup, milk, cheese, and pepper. Cook over medium heat, stirring frequently, until cheese melts. Stir in pasta and tuna. Cook until thoroughly heated. Yield: 4 to 6 servings.

Barbequed Shrimp

Mark and Kim Prozzi

1 stick butter	1 teaspoon cayenne pepper
1/3 cup Worcestershire sauce	1 teaspoon thyme
1 pound raw shrimp, peeled and deveined	1 teaspoon oregano
	2 teaspoons rosemary
1 teaspoon salt	6-8 cloves garlic, chopped
1 teaspoon black pepper	Italian breadcrumbs

Preheat oven to 400 degrees. In a saucepan, melt butter and add Worcestershire sauce. Pour into a 9x13-inch glass baking dish. Add shrimp to sauce. In a small bowl, combine salt and next six ingredients; sprinkle over shrimp. Top with Italian breadcrumbs. Bake at 400 degrees for 10 to 15 minutes. Serve with French bread and use sauce to dip bread. Yield: 4 servings.

Beaufort Shrimp n Grits

George Garbade

	Grits	3 tablespoons flour
10-12	slices bacon	Salt and pepper to taste
1/2	cup chopped onion	3 tablespoons Worcestershire sauce
1/3	cup bell pepper	
2	pounds raw shrimp, peeled and deveined	1/4 cup ketchup
		5 drops Tabasco sauce
2 1/2	cups water	

Cook grits according to package directions. Brown bacon in a Dutch oven. Remove bacon and set aside. In bacon drippings, sauté onion and bell pepper When onion turns a golden brown color, add shrimp; turning mixture until shrimp turn pink. Add water and simmer several minutes. Do not cover at any time. Make a paste out of the flour and a little water and add to mixture. Stir in salt, pepper, Worcestershire, ketchup, and Tabasco. Cook slowly until sauce thickens. Crumble bacon and spread over shrimp before serving. Serve over grits. Yield: 8 servings.

Note: Great for breakfast or brunch. Serve with green beans or asparagus.

Beaufort Shrimp Creole

Lewis Brown

10-12 slices bacon
1/2 cup onions, chopped
1 cup bell pepper, chopped
3 (16-ounce) cans diced
tomatoes
1 (15-ounce) can tomato
sauce
1 cup ketchup

1 teaspoon salt
2 tablespoons Worcestershire
sauce
3 tablespoons sugar
2 pounds small boiled shrimp,
peeled
Cooked rice

In a 6 to 8-quart Dutch oven, brown bacon. Remove bacon and set aside; drain excess drippings if desired. Sauté onion and pepper about 10 minutes. Add tomatoes, tomato sauce, and ketchup. Bring to a light boil and add salt and Worcestershire. Break bacon into small pieces and add to sauce. Reduce heat and simmer 30 minutes. Stir in sugar. Add shrimp a few at the time. Simmer another 30 minutes. Serve over rice. Yield: 10 to 12 servings.

Bourbon Street Shrimp

Minnie Bryant

1/4 cup butter
3 tablespoons chives
1 (8-ounce) carton fresh
mushrooms, sautéed
Pepper to taste
1 teaspoon soy sauce

2 (103/4-ounce) cans cream of
shrimp soup
1 cup sour cream
1/4 cup sherry
1 1/2 pounds small-medium
shrimp

Combine all ingredients in a large saucepan. Cook over moderate heat 10 to 15 minutes. Serve over your favorite pasta or rice. Also good over grits. Yield: 4 to 6 servings.

Chinese-Style Shrimp

Lee Hicks

2 cucumbers	2 teaspoons salt
2 tablespoons vegetable oil	1 teaspoon sugar
1/2 cup sliced celery	2 teaspoons cornstarch
1/2 cup bell pepper strips	1/3 cup white wine
1 pound raw shrimp, peeled and deveined	

Scoop the seeds out of cucumber, peel and cut lengthwise into slices 1-inch thick. In a heavy frying pan or wok; heat the oil. Sauté the cucumber, celery, and bell pepper 3 to 5 minutes, being careful not to burn the vegetables. Add shrimp, salt, and sugar. In a small bowl dissolve the cornstarch in the wine and add to mixture. Bring to a boil and simmer about 3 to 5 more minutes. Yield: 4 servings.

Note: Great served hot over Carolina Plantation rice!

Coconut Shrimp

Danielle Hall

16 large raw shrimp, peeled and deveined	1 cup flour
3 eggs	2 cups shredded coconut
	6-8 cups oil

Split shrimp down the center, cutting almost but not completely through. In a small bowl, beat eggs. Put the flour in a separate bowl and the coconut in a small bowl. Dredge the shrimp in the flour and then the egg. Roll in the coconut, coating well. In a large saucepan, heat oil to 325 degrees and fry shrimp for 5 to 6 minutes or until golden brown. Yield: 4 servings.

Note: Best served with mango chutney!

Dill Shrimp Cream Loaf

Gus Hoffmeyer

1	loaf French bread	1	pint sour cream
2	sticks butter	1	pint heavy cream
1 1/2	pounds small shrimp, peeled		Dill seed

Preheat oven to 325 degrees. Slice French bread into 1-inch slices almost through. Place the bread on a piece of aluminum foil large enough to wrap around the loaf so it will not leak. Put butter in a 12-inch frying pan over medium heat and melt. Add shrimp and cook for two minutes. Take shrimp out and set aside. Pour the butter over the bread so that it goes between the slices and covers the bread. Wrap the bread completely in the foil, making sure it does not leak. Put the bread on a baking pan and bake at 325 degrees for 30 minutes. While the bread is cooking, in a medium bowl, mix the creams together. Pour into the pan shrimp were cooked in. Bring to a boil and add shrimp. Cook 1 1/2 minutes. When bread is done, unwrap and put one slice on a plate and cover with the shrimp sauce. Sprinkle with dill seed to taste. Yield: 6 to 8 servings.

Note: Rich but good!

Daufuskie Shrimp

Bobbie Kelley

7	slices bacon, chopped	1/4	cup cocktail sauce
2	medium onions, diced	1/2	teaspoon salt
1	large bell pepper	1/8	teaspoon black pepper
3	jalapeño peppers, seeded	2	pounds large raw shrimp,
4	cloves garlic, minced		peeled and deveined
2	(28-ounce) cans diced		Cooked grits
	tomatoes		

In a deep skillet, cook the bacon. Remove and set aside. Sauté the onion, peppers, and garlic in drippings. Stir in tomatoes and next three ingredients. Simmer 1 hour. Stir in the shrimp and cook 5 minutes. Serve over grits. Sprinkle bacon on top. Yield: 8 generous servings.

Shrimp and Asparagus Casserole
Britney Jeffords

2   (15-ounce) cans asparagus spears, drained, divided
8   slices sharp Cheddar cheese
1   (103/4-ounce) can cream of shrimp soup

20   boiled shrimp, peeled and deveined

Preheat oven to 350 degrees. Place one can of asparagus in a covered baking dish. Top with four slices of cheese and 7 shrimp. Repeat layers and pour shrimp soup on top. Sprinkle remaining shrimp on top. Bake at 350 degrees for 20 minutes. Yield: 4 to 6 servings.

Shrimp and Crab Casserole
Meredith McIntyre

1 1/2 cups butter
3   tablespoons chopped onions
1 1/2 cups flour
6   cups milk
1 1/2 cups heavy cream
9   egg yolks, beaten
6   tablespoons parsley
1 1/2 teaspoons paprika
1 1/2 cups sliced sautéed mushrooms

3   tablespoons mustard
3   tablespoons Worcestershire sauce
6   pounds (91/110) cooked shrimp, peeled and deveined
12   dashes Tabasco sauce
1   pound crabmeat
Swiss cheese, shredded
Buttered breadcrumbs

Preheat oven to 350 degrees. In a large saucepan, melt butter and sauté onion. Add flour and make roux. Stir in milk and all other ingredients; mixing well. Put into individual casseroles or a 9x13-inch baking dish and top with Swiss cheese and breadcrumbs. Bake at 350 degrees until lightly browned and bubbly. Yield: 15 to 16 servings.

Shrimp and Rice

Judy Brown

1 cup uncooked rice	1/3 cup soy sauce
2 1/2 cups chicken broth	1/2 teaspoon garlic powder
1 pound raw medium shrimp, peeled and deveined	5 green onions, chopped, divided
1/3 cup peanut oil	3/4 cup chopped cashews

In a saucepan, cook rice according to package direction using chicken broth instead of water. In a large skillet, sauté shrimp in oil; add soy sauce, garlic powder, and two onions. Stir until hot and shrimp done. Serve over cooked rice. Garnish with remaining onions and cashews. Yield: 4 servings.

Shrimp Fried Rice

Anne Dawkins

2 teaspoons peanut oil	2 cups cooked rice
2 cups onion, chopped	1/2 teaspoon sugar
1 (3 1/2-ounce) can mushrooms, chopped and drained	2 eggs, slightly beaten
	1/4 cup soy sauce
1 (8-ounce) can water chestnuts, chopped	2 cups cooked shrimp, chopped
	1-2 tablespoons green onions

Heat frying pan or wok; add oil and cook onions until golden brown. Add mushrooms and water chestnuts and cook 1 minute. Stir in cold rice; mix well and cook an additional 2 minutes. Add sugar, eggs, soy sauce, and shrimp. Cook until heated through and golden brown in color. Spoon on serving plate and top with green onions. Yield: 4 to 6 servings.

Note: Ham, chicken or bacon could be used in place of the shrimp. Eggs can be omitted.

Southern Shrimp
Kathy Harris

1/2 cup chopped celery	1 pound sharp Cheddar cheese, grated
1/2 cup chopped bell pepper	
1 large chopped onion	1 (10 3/4-ounce) can tomato soup
1 (8-ounce) can sliced mushrooms	
4 tablespoons bacon grease	3 pounds shrimp, cooked, peeled and deveined, can use frozen
2 tablespoons Worcestershire sauce	1 cup raw rice, cooked

Preheat oven to 350 degrees. In a skillet, sauté vegetables in bacon grease. In a large bowl, combine all of the ingredients. Pour into a 9x13-inch casserole dish. Bake at 350 degrees for 20 minutes or until bubbly. Yield: 12 to 15 servings.

Wild Rice and Shrimp
Beth Brown
Submitted by Kathy Boyd

3 tablespoons bell pepper, chopped	1/2 teaspoon Worcestershire sauce
3 tablespoons onion, chopped	1/2 teaspoon dry mustard
3 tablespoons butter, melted	1/2 teaspoon black pepper
2 1/2 pounds raw shrimp, peeled and deveined	1/2 teaspoon salt
1 (10 3/4-ounce) can cream of mushroom soup	1/2 cup cubed Cheddar cheese
	1 (6-ounce) package Uncle Ben's Wild Rice, original recipe, cooked
1 1/2 tablespoons lemon juice	

Preheat oven to 350 degrees. In a skillet, sauté pepper and onion in butter; remove with slotted spoon and place in a large bowl. Put shrimp in same skillet with butter and sauté until pink. Add to onion mixture. Thoroughly mix in all other ingredients. Spoon into a 9x13-inch baking dish and bake at 350 degrees for 35 minutes. Yield: 8 to 10 servings.

Note: Freezes well.

Pawleys Island Oyster Pie

Anne Dawkins

1	quart oysters	1	cup cracker crumbs, divided
1	teaspoon black pepper	1/4	cup butter or margarine
1	teaspoon minced onion		
1	teaspoon Worcestershire sauce		

Preheat oven to 350 degrees. In a large bowl, combine oysters, pepper and next two ingredients. Mix gently but coat thoroughly. Place one-half of the oysters in a 8x8-inch baking dish. Sprinkle with one-half of the crumbs and dot with butter. Repeat layers and dot generously with butter. Bake at 350 degrees for 35 minutes or until oysters are hot and top is browned. Serve immediately. Yield: 8 servings.

New Orleans Oyster Casserole

Beth Brown

Submitted by Kathy Boyd

3	(10-ounce) packages frozen chopped spinach	4	dozen oysters, drained, chopped, reserve liquid
3	sticks butter	3/4	cup chopped fresh parsley
1	teaspoon thyme	1/2	cup Parmesan cheese
1 1/2	cups chopped green onions	2	tablespoons Pernod (anise liqueur)
1	cup chopped celery		
1	large clove garlic, crushed	1	teaspoon salt
2	tablespoons Worcestershire sauce	1/2	teaspoon black pepper
1 1/2	cups seasoned breadcrumbs	1/4	teaspoon cayenne pepper

Preheat oven to 375 degrees. Prepare spinach according to package directions. Set aside. In a large skillet over moderate heat, melt butter; add thyme and next three ingredients. Sauté 5 minutes; add Worcestershire sauce and breadcrumbs. Stir well 5 minutes or until breadcrumbs are toasted. Gently stir in oysters, one-half of the liquid, parsley, cheese, and Pernod. Cook 2 to 3 minutes or until oysters curl. Add spinach, salt, pepper, and cayenne pepper. Mix well. Place in a 3-quart casserole and bake at 375 degrees for 20 to 25 minutes. Yield: 8 to 10 servings.

The Gullah House Gumbo

Anne Dawkins

3-3 1/2	pound broiler-fryer	1	(16-ounce) can tomato purée
3	large onions, 1 quartered, 2 chopped, divided Celery leaves	1	cup fresh corn or 10-ounce package frozen whole kernel, thawed
1	teaspoon salt		
6	slices bacon, finely chopped	1	cup fresh okra or 10-ounce package frozen sliced okra, thawed
1	pound smoked sausage 1/4-inch slices	1	teaspoon chopped thyme
2	bell peppers, chopped	1	pound raw shrimp, peeled and deveined
2	ribs celery, chopped		
3	cloves garlic, minced		
3	tomatoes, peeled and chopped		

Combine chicken, one quartered onion, celery leaves and salt in a large Dutch oven; add water to cover. Bring to a boil; cover, reduce heat, simmer 40 minutes or until chicken is tender. Remove chicken, reserving broth and discarding onion, and celery leaves. Skin, bone and cut chicken into bite size pieces. Set aside. Cook bacon and sausage in a large Dutch oven over medium heat until bacon is crisp. Remove bacon and sausage, reserving one tablespoon of drippings in Dutch oven. Crumble bacon; set aside bacon and sausage. Add two chopped onion, bell pepper, celery, and minced garlic to drippings; cook over medium heat until vegetables are tender. Add chicken, bacon, sausage, reserved broth, tomatoes, and next four ingredients. Bring mixture to a boil; reduce heat, and simmer, uncovered, 1 hour and 20 minutes. Add shrimp and cook 10 minutes. Yield: 11 cups.

Seafood Gumbo

Curt and Cindy Griggs

1/4 pound Italian sweet or spicy sausage
1 tablespoon olive oil
1 small onion, chopped
1 medium rib celery, chopped
1/2 cup bell pepper, seeded and chopped
2 (141/2-ounce) cans chicken broth
1 (28-ounce) can crushed tomatoes
1 (11-ounce) bag frozen okra
2 tablespoons all-purpose flour
1/2 cup water
1 teaspoon salt

1/4 teaspoon black pepper
1 tablespoon dried thyme
1 bay leaf
1/2 teaspoon dried oregano
1/2 teaspoon dried basil
1 teaspoon creole (or Old Bay) seasoning
1 teaspoon Worcestershire sauce
3 scallions, finely chopped
1/2 pound raw shrimp, peeled and deveined, cut in thirds
1/2 pound crabmeat
1/4 cup chopped fresh parsley

Place sausage in saucepan and fill with water to cover. Bring to a boil and cook 3 to 4 minutes. Drain and set aside. In a large pot over medium-high heat the oil. Add onion, celery and bell pepper. Cook until vegetables are tender but not browned; about 5 minutes, stirring occasionally. Add the chicken broth, tomatoes, okra, and reserved sausage. Cover and bring to a boil. Continue cooking, covered, over high heat 5 minutes. In a small bowl, whisk together the flour and one-half cup water. Stir the flour mixture, salt, spices, and Worcestershire sauce into the sausage mixture; cover and cook over high heat another 10 minutes. Add the scallions, shrimp, and crabmeat. Reduce to medium heat and cook 5 minutes. Remove the bay leaf, stir in the parsley and remove from the heat. Cover and let sit 5 minutes. Serve over rice. Yield: 6 servings.

Seafood Thermidor

Judy Brown and Lilyanne Inabinet

2	tablespoons butter		White wine
2	tablespoons flour	1	teaspoon black pepper
1/2	cup milk		Splash of lemon juice
1/2	cup half-and-half		Salt to taste
1	cup grated Cheddar cheese	2	pounds cooked shrimp
1	cup grated Romano cheese	1/2	pound raw scallops
1	teaspoon thyme		Parmesan cheese
1	teaspoon garlic powder		

Preheat the oven to 350 degrees. Grease a 2-quart baking dish. In a large saucepan, mix butter and flour and make a paste; add milk and half-and-half stirring until smooth. Add cheeses, thyme, and garlic. Use white wine to thin the sauce. Add the next five ingredients; mix well. Pour into prepared dish. Cover with Parmesan cheese. Bake at 350 degrees for 30 minutes. Yield: 6 servings.

Baked Seafood with Artichokes

Kathy Boyd

3	tablespoons butter	1	tablespoon sherry
3	tablespoons flour	1	cup sharp Cheddar cheese,
1	pint half-and-half		grated
1	teaspoon Worcestershire	1	pound crabmeat
	sauce	2	pounds shrimp, cooked
1	teaspoon paprika	1	(14-ounce) can artichoke
1	tablespoon lemon juice		hearts, diced
2	tablespoons ketchup		Breadcrumbs
	Salt and pepper to taste		

Preheat the oven to 400 degrees. Grease a 11x17-inch baking dish. In a saucepan over medium heat, combine butter and flour and make paste. Pour in half-and-half, stirring until smooth. Add Worcestershire, paprika, and next three ingredients. Stir in sherry and cheese. In prepared dish, layer one-half crabmeat, one-half shrimp, one-half artichokes, and one-half cream sauce. Repeat layers. End with cream sauce. Top with breadcrumbs. Bake at 400 degrees for 20 minutes. Yield: 8 servings.

★ Meats ★

Howard and Beth Brown
June 9, 1990
Mama and Daddy dancing at our garden party

On Mama and Daddy's 40th wedding anniversary, June 7, 1990, Edwin and I were married very quietly at home and celebrated with a garden party on June 9th. Just as my parents had begun their marriage 40 years earlier, they were now helping us celebrate our beginning.

This is love:
not that we loved God,
but that he loved us and sent his son
as an atoning sacrifice
for our sins.

1 John 4:10

Boeuf Bourguignon

Jenny Forbes

10 small or 5 medium onions, sliced
2 tablespoons bacon grease
2 pounds lean beef, 1-inch cubes
1 1/2 tablespoons flour
Pinch marjoram

Pinch thyme
Salt
Black pepper
1/2 cup beef bouillon
1 cup dry red wine
1/2 pound mushrooms, sliced

In a heavy deep skillet, cook onions in bacon grease until browned. With a slotted spoon remove onion and place in a bowl. In same drippings, cook beef until browned. Add a little more grease if necessary. When browned on all sides, sprinkle flour over beef and add a generous pinch of marjoram, thyme, salt, and pepper. Stir in beef bouillon and wine, mixing well. Simmer on low 3 hours and 30 minutes. Mixture should bubble occasionally. The liquid may evaporate some, so add a little more bouillon and wine (1 part stock to 2 parts wine) as necessary to keep the beef covered. Put onion and mushrooms in beef mixture and cook 45 minutes to 1 hour. If needed, add more bouillon and wine. The sauce should be thick and dark brown. Yield: 6 to 8 servings.

Crock Pot Steak and Gravy

Kathy Boyd

1/3 cup all-purpose flour
6 beef cube steaks
1 tablespoon vegetable oil
1 large onion, sliced
3 cups water, divided
1 (.75-ounce) envelope mushroom gravy mix

1 (.875-ounce) envelope brown gravy mix
1 (.75-ounce) envelope onion gravy mix
Hot mashed potatoes or cooked noodles

Place flour in a large resealable bag. Add steaks, a few at the time, and shake until coated. In a skillet, cook the steaks in oil until browned on both side. Transfer to a crock pot. Add onion and 2 cups of water. Cover and cook on low for 8 hours or until tender. In a medium bowl, stir together gravy mixes with remaining water. Pour into crock pot and cook for 30 minutes. Serve over potatoes or noodles. Yield: 6 servings.

Chopped Steak Noodle Bake
Adele Camp

2	tablespoons butter or margarine	1	(8-ounce) package noodles
1	pound ground round steak	1	(8-ounce) package cream cheese
1	clove garlic, crushed	1	cup sour cream
	Salt and pepper to taste	6	scallions, chopped
1	tablespoon sugar	1/2	cup shredded sharp Cheddar cheese
2	(8-ounce) cans tomato sauce		

Preheat oven to 350 degrees. Melt butter in a skillet, toss in ground steak, breaking up into small pieces. Cook until browned. Add garlic and next three ingredients. Cook slowly for 15 minutes. Cook noodles according to package directions. In a medium bowl, mix the cream cheese and sour cream together until smooth; add scallions with some green tops. Season with salt and pepper. In a 9x13-inch baking dish, put one-third of the noodles in the bottom of dish. Spread with one-third of the cream cheese mixture. Cover with one-third of the meat sauce. Repeat layers ending with meat sauce. Sprinkle cheese over top. Bake at 350 degrees until bubbly. Yield: 6 servings.

Punk's Favorite Corned-Beef Hash
Kitty Jackson

1/4	cup ketchup	1/2	teaspoon prepared mustard
1	tablespoon lemon juice or vinegar	1	(16-ounce) can corned-beef hash
2	teaspoons brown sugar	8	teaspoons Parmesan cheese
1	teaspoon Worcestershire sauce		

Preheat oven to 350 degrees. In a medium bowl, combine ketchup and next four ingredients. Slice hash into 4 pieces and place in a 8x8-inch glass dish. Top each slice of hash with ketchup mixture and two tablespoons Parmesan cheese. Bake at 350 degrees for 20 minutes. Yield: 4 servings.

Chuck Roast Barbeque
Debbie Bell

2 1/2 pounds boneless chuck roast, trimmed
2 small onions, chopped
1 (12-ounce) Coke
1/3 cup Worcestershire sauce
1 1/2 tablespoons apple cider vinegar or white vinegar
1 1/2 teaspoons beef bouillon granules

3/4 teaspoon dry mustard
3/4 teaspoon chili powder
1/4 teaspoon cayenne pepper, may add more
3 cloves garlic, minced
1 cup ketchup
1 tablespoon margarine
6 hamburger buns

Place roast in a 3 1/2 to 4-quart electric slow cooker; add onions. Combine cola and next seven ingredients; cover and chill one cup of the sauce. Pour remaining sauce over the roast. Cover and cook on high 6 hours or on low for 9 hours or until roast is very tender. Remove roast and onions from cooker with a slotted spoon; put in a large bowl and shred meat with two forks. In a saucepan, combine the reserved sauce, ketchup and butter. Cook over medium heat, stirring constantly until heated. Pour over meat, stirring gently. Spoon meat mixture into buns. Yield: 6 servings.

Russian Roast
Beverly Whisnant

1 (1 1/4-ounce) envelope onion soup mix
2 (8-ounce) bottles Russian salad dressing
4 pounds chuck beef roast

Fresh baby carrots
1 (14 1/2-ounce) can whole potatoes
Onions, cut in wedges

Heat electric slow cooker to high. Pour in soup mix and dressing; mix well. Add carrots and onion. Place meat in cooker. Add potatoes. Cook on high about 1 hour, then turn to medium and cook 7 to 8 hours or until meat is tender. Yield: 8 servings.

Mary's Tenderloin Deluxe

Mary Zimmerman

3	pounds whole beef tenderloin	1	tablespoon soy sauce
2	tablespoons softened butter	1	teaspoon Dijon wine mustard
1/4	cup scallions		Dash ground black pepper
2	tablespoons butter	3/4	cup extra dry vermouth

Let meat sit at room temperature 2 to 3 hours. Preheat oven to 400 degrees. Rub beef with softened butter. Place on a rack in a broiling pan, bake, uncovered, for 20 minutes. In a saucepan, sauté scallions in butter until tender. Add soy sauce, mustard, and pepper; mix well. Stir in vermouth and heat just to boiling. Pour sauce over meat and bake another 20 to 25 minutes to serve medium-rare. Baste frequently. Remove from oven and let stand 10 minutes. Cut into 1-inch slices. Yield: 8 servings.

Sirloin Tips

Patti Shelly

2 1/2	pounds sirloin tip steak, cut in strips	2	cloves garlic, sliced
2	tablespoons cooking oil	1/2	teaspoon onion salt
2	(10 1/2-ounce) cans beef consommé	1	(3 1/2-ounce) jar mushrooms (optional)
1/2	cup burgundy wine	2	large tablespoons cornstarch
2	tablespoons soy sauce	1/2	cup water
			Cooked rice

In a large skillet, brown meat in oil. Stir in consommé and next five ingredients. Heat to boiling. Reduce heat, cover, simmer 1 hour. In a small bowl, blend cornstarch and water together. Pour over meat mixture. Turn heat up and cook to boiling; about 1 minute. Serve over rice. Yield: 6 servings.

Note: Can be used for buffet in a chafing dish.

American Ravioli

Betty Taylor

1	(8-ounce) box macaroni	1	(16-ounce) can tomato sauce
1	pound ground beef	1/2	can water
1	onion, chopped		
1	(10¾-ounce) can cream of mushroom soup		

Preheat oven to 400 degrees. Cook macaroni according to package directions; drain. In a skillet, brown beef and onion; drain off excess grease. Add mushroom soup, tomato sauce, and water. Stir in macaroni, mixing well. Pour into a 2-quart casserole dish. Bake at 400 degrees for 30 minutes. Yield: 8 servings.

Baked Spaghetti

Anna Laura McElveen

1½	pounds ground beef	1	(10¾-ounce) can tomato soup
	Garlic to taste		
	Salt and pepper to taste	1	(8-ounce) can tomato sauce (optional)
2	large onions, chopped		
1	large bell pepper, chopped	1	(3.8-ounce) can black olives, reserve juice
1	pound coarsely grated Cheddar cheese	1	(16-ounce) box spaghetti

Preheat oven to 350 degrees. In a skillet, brown beef, seasonings, onion, and bell pepper. Add cheese, soup, tomato sauce, and olives. Rinse sauce can with olive juice and add to beef mixture. Cook until cheese melts. Cook spaghetti according to package directions; drain. Add meat mixture to spaghetti, mixing well. Pour into two 9x13-inch baking dishes. Bake at 350 degrees for 30 to 35 minutes. Yield: 8 servings.

Cheeseburger Pie
Kathy Boyd -

2 (9-inch) unbaked pie crusts	Salt and pepper to taste
1 1/2 cups celery, chopped	1 pound ground beef
1 1/2 cups onion, chopped	1 (16-ounce) can tomatoes
1/2 cup bell pepper, chopped	2 tablespoons mustard
Butter	1/2 cup shredded Cheddar cheese

Preheat oven to 400 degrees. Prebake one pie crust 5 minutes and set aside. In a large skillet, sauté celery, onion, and bell pepper in butter until tender. Add beef, salt and pepper; cook until beef is browned and drain off any excess grease. Add tomatoes and mustard and simmer 45 minutes. Sprinkle cheese over bottom of prebaked pie crust. Spoon meat mixture over cheese. Top with remaining pie crust. Pierce pie crust with fork to allow steam to escape. Bake at 400 degrees for 45 minutes. Yield: 6 to 8 servings.

Italian Ground Beef Casserole
Judy Brown

1 pound lean ground beef	1/2 cup sour cream
1/2 cup chopped onion	1 (8-ounce) can refrigerated
1 (8-ounce) can tomato sauce	crescent rolls
1 (1.37-ounce) envelope dry spaghetti sauce mix	3/4 cup grated Parmesan cheese
1 1/2 cups shredded mozzarella cheese	2 tablespoons melted butter or margarine

Preheat oven to 375 degrees. In a skillet, cook ground beef and onion until beef is browned; drain. Add tomato sauce and spaghetti mix. Stir until bubbling hot. Pour meat mixture into a 9x13-inch baking dish. In a small bowl, combine mozzarella cheese and sour cream; spread over the meat mixture. Separate crescent rolls into two triangles and place on top of cheese mixture. Sprinkle Parmesan cheese and butter over dough. Bake at 375 degrees for 25 to 30 minutes. Yield: 6 servings.

Lasagna

Dana Carpenter

1	pound lean ground beef	1/4	teaspoon garlic powder
1	(10-ounce) package lasagna	1	bell pepper, chopped
	noodles	1	medium onion, chopped
1 1/2	teaspoons salt	1/2	cup Parmesan cheese
1/2	teaspoon black pepper	1	pound mozzarella cheese,
1	(16-ounce) can tomatoes		shredded
1	(12-ounce) can tomato paste	6	ounces Cheddar cheese,
2	tablespoons parsley flakes		shredded
1	tablespoon whole basil		

Preheat oven to 350 degrees. In a large saucepan, brown beef and drain. Cook noodles according to package directions; drain. Add all ingredients except cheeses to meat and simmer 15 minutes. In a greased 9x13-inch baking dish layer one-half of the noodles, one-half of the cheeses and one-half of the meat sauce. Repeat layers. Bake at 350 degrees for 30 minutes. Yield: 10 servings.

Pizza Bake

Carol Freeman

2	(8-ounce) cans refrigerated	1	(16-ounce) jar tomato sauce
	crescent rolls, divided	1	cup shredded Cheddar cheese
1	pound ground beef	1	cup shredded mozzarella
1	(1.5-ounce) package Sloppy		cheese
	Joe seasoning mix		

Preheat oven to 350 degrees. Spray a 9x13-inch baking dish with nonstick cooking spray. Separate one can of rolls into two triangles and line the bottom of the dish. In a skillet, cook the ground beef until browned; drain. Add seasoning mix and tomato sauce to meat, mix well. Pour meat mixture over the dough. Sprinkle with cheeses. Separate the remaining can of rolls into two triangles and spread over cheeses. Bake at 350 degrees for 30 minutes. Yield: 8 servings.

Not Your Mother's Meatloaf
Wanda Langley-Hassler

2	eggs	2	teaspoons garlic powder
4	tablespoons milk	1/2	teaspoon salt
8	tablespoons ketchup, divided	1/4	teaspoon black pepper
4	tablespoons Worcestershire	1/4	teaspoon celery seeds
	sauce	2	slices bread, crumbled
1	teaspoon Dijon style mustard	1	pound lean ground beef

Heat oven to 450 degrees. In a small bowl, beat egg, milk, two tablespoons ketchup, and next six ingredients with a fork. Add bread crumbs and beef. Mix well. Place in a loaf pan and cover with remaining ketchup. Bake at 450 degrees for 25 to 30 minutes. Yield: 6 servings.

Patrice's Meatloaf
Patrice Heustess

1 1/2	pounds ground beef	3	tablespoons Heinz 57 sauce
1	egg, slightly beaten	3	tablespoons ketchup
1	cup soft Italian style		Dash Worcestershire
	breadcrumbs		Salt and pepper to taste
1/2	cup milk		

Preheat oven to 350 degrees. In a large bowl, combine all ingredients and mix thoroughly. Shape into a loaf and place on a lightly greased baking pan. Bake at 350 degrees for 1 hour. Yield: 6 servings.

Vidalia Onion Meal
Ruby Perry

1	thick ground beef patty	Butter or margarine
1	thick slice potato, 1 1/2-inch	Salt and pepper to taste
1	thick slice onion, 1 1/2-inch	

Preheat oven to 350 degrees. Place patty on aluminum foil. Top with remaining ingredients and close foil around to seal. Bake at 350 degrees for 1 hour and 20 minutes. Yield: 1 serving.

Stuffed Bell Peppers
Gayle McDonald

4	large bell peppers	1	medium onion, chopped
1-2	pounds ground beef		(optional)
1	cup uncooked rice		Salt and pepper to taste
1	egg	1	(46-ounce) can tomato juice

Cut tops off peppers and hull out centers using a teaspoon. In a large bowl, mix beef, rice, egg, and onion. Add salt and pepper. Stuff mixture into peppers. Place in a large saucepan on stove top. Cover with tomato juice. Cook on low heat 3 hours. Can also cook in oven at 350 degrees for 3 hours. Yield: 4 servings.

Creamy Ham and Potatoes
Kathy Boyd

4	medium red potatoes, thinly sliced	1/2	teaspoon salt
		1/2	teaspoon black pepper
2	medium onions, finely chopped	1	(10 3/4-ounce) can cream of mushroom soup
1 1/2	cups cubed fully cooked ham	1 1/3	cups water
2	tablespoons margarine	1	cup shredded Cheddar cheese
2	tablespoons all-purpose flour		

In a slow cooker, layer potatoes, onions, and ham. In a saucepan, melt margarine. Stir in flour, salt, and pepper until smooth. In a small bowl combine soup and water; gradually stir into flour mixture. Bring to a boil and stir constantly about 2 minutes or until thickened. Pour over ham. Cover and cook on low 8 to 9 hours or until potatoes are tender. Sprinkle with cheese before serving. Yield: 4 servings.

Ham and Green Bean Casserole

Olive Timberlake

1	(14 1/2-ounce) can French style beans, drained
2	cups ham, cooked and diced
1	(10 3/4-ounce) can cream celery soup
1	cup grated sharp Cheddar cheese

3/4	cup mayonnaise
2	teaspoons lemon juice
1 1/2	teaspoons prepared mustard
	Herb Stuffing

Preheat oven to 350 degrees. Spread beans in a 2-quart casserole. Cover with ham. In a bowl, combine soup and next four ingredients. Pour over ham. Top with herb stuffing. Bake at 350 degrees for 30 minutes. Yield: 4 servings.

Barbeque Pig

Wayne McCutchen

1	(100-125 pounds) pig
1/2	box of salt or to taste
1	gallon vinegar
1	ounce cayenne pepper

2	ounces black pepper
4	ounces crushed red pepper
	Juice of 4 lemons

Have pig split for barbeque, which is split down the breast bone but not cut all the way through. Leave skin on back. Lay belly side down on an outside grill, using wire under the pig to turn it over after it has cooked. Cook at 250 to 300 degrees for 10 to 12 hours. Turn pig over and take out all the bone and fat. Salt to taste. On an outside stove, mix vinegar and next four ingredients in a large pot and heat to almost boiling point. Pour sauce over pig on grill with a dipper or metal cup. Simmer 1 hour. It is ready to taste and enjoy! Yield: 125-130 servings.

Note: This is always Christmas lunch at our house!

Busy Day Chops
Ginger Holland

1   cup uncooked rice
1   (10³/₄-ounce) can French
    onion soup
1   (10¹/₂-ounce) can beef broth
1   (8-ounce) can mushrooms,
    drained

Bell pepper, chopped
(optional)
Onion, chopped (optional)
Celery, chopped (optional)
4-6 boneless pork chops

Preheat oven to 350 degrees. Spray a 2¹/₂-quart casserole dish with a non-stick cooking spray. In a medium bowl, mix rice, soup, broth and mushrooms. Add bell peppers, onion and celery if desired. Pour into prepared dish. Place pork chops on top and cover. Bake at 350 degrees for one hour and 30 minutes. Yield: 4 to 6 servings.

Cheesy Pork Chops
Harriet Foster

4   pork chops, 1-inch thick
    Salt and pepper to taste
1   large onion, cut in 4 slices

1   tablespoon plus 1 teaspoon
     mayonnaise
1/2 cup Parmesan cheese

Preheat oven to 325 degrees. Sprinkle chops with salt and pepper; place in a greased 12x8-inch baking dish. Top each chop with onion slice. Spread each onion slice with 1 teaspoon mayonnaise. Sprinkle with cheese. Bake, uncovered, at 325 degrees for 1 hour or until chops are tender and cheese is browned. Yield: 4 servings.

Grilled Cajun Pork Tenderloin

Geri Jernigan

2	tablespoons paprika	1/2	teaspoon black pepper
1	teaspoon salt	1	teaspoon thyme
2	teaspoons onion powder	1	teaspoon oregano
2	teaspoons garlic powder		Pork tenderloin
2	teaspoons cayenne pepper		
1 1/2	teaspoons ground white pepper		

Put all dry ingredients in a shaker jar; shake vigorously. Rub mixture all over tenderloin. Cook over medium grill (350 degrees) until 170 degrees internal temperature is reached. Cooking time is about 45 minutes to 1 hour depending on size of tenderloin.

Note: Store remaining cajun rub in a tight fitting jar to use later. Also, a regular pork loin may be used. Cooking time will increase. A large loin will require about 2 hours of cooking time.

Crock Pot Pork Loin

Beverly Whisnant

Pork loin roast	Jane's Original Crazy
1/2-1 cup Dale's steak seasoning	Pepper

Turn slow cooker on high to preheat. Place meat inside and pour seasoning over meat to lightly coat. Sprinkle with pepper. Turn cooker to low and cook for 8 hours. Yield: 8 servings.

Creole Sausage and Rice Bake

Dr. Carl Hughes

1	pound bulk sausage	1/2	cup milk
3	cups cooked rice	1	(4-ounce) can sliced mush-
2	cups grated sharp Cheddar		rooms, drained
	cheese, divided	2	teaspoons creole (cajun)
3	eggs, beaten		mustard
1	(10 3/4-ounce) can cream of	1/4	teaspoon onion powder
	mushroom soup		

In a skillet, cook sausage until brown and crumbly; drain fat and set aside. Combine rice and one-half cup cheese. Spread in a 8x12-inch baking dish. Sprinkle with sausage. In a large bowl, combine eggs and next five ingredients, mix well. Pour mixture over sausage. Bake, covered, at 350 degrees for 35 minutes. Sprinkle with remaining cheese and bake, uncovered, an additional 5 minutes. Yield: 8 servings.

One Meal Bean Dish

Angelyn Bateman

1 1/2	pounds bulk sausage	1	(15-ounce) can wax beans,
1	cup chopped celery		drained
1	cup chopped onion	1	(15-ounce) can lima beans,
1	tablespoon mustard		drained
1	cup brown sugar	1	(16-ounce) can kidney beans,
1	(6-ounce) can tomato paste		drained
1	(10 3/4-ounce) can tomato	1	(15-ounce) can hot chili
	soup		beans
1	(14 1/2-ounce) can green	1	(15-ounce) can pork and
	beans, drained		beans

Preheat oven to 350 degrees. In a large saucepan, cook the sausage, celery, and onion until meat is browned; drain. Add mustard and next three ingredients. Simmer 30 minutes. Add green beans and next five ingredients. Put into a casserole dish larger than a 11x14-inch. Bake at 350 for 1 hour. Serve with cornbread. Yield: 18 -20 servings.

Sausage Casserole

Mary Nance

1 cup celery, chopped	1 (10³/4-ounce) can chicken
1 cup onion, chopped	noodle soup
Olive oil	1 soup can water
1 pound bulk sausage	1 cup water
1 (10³/4-ounce) can cream	1 cup rice uncooked
mushroom soup	

Preheat oven to 325 degrees. In a skillet, sauté celery and onion in oil. In a skillet, cook sausage until browned; drain. In a large bowl, mix soups and water together. Stir in rice, vegetables and sausage. Pour into a 9x13-inch casserole dish. Bake, uncovered, at 325 degrees for 1 hour. May need to add water if rice is not cooked. Yield: 4 to 6 large servings.

Note: This recipe was shared in the teacher's lounge at Thornwell school, I believe. Our family never tired of it, and often shared it and good times around our kitchen table. It is great with a large salad, stewed apples and garlic bread to make a hearty group of eaters very happy.

Sausage and Bean Casserole

Susan Moore

1 pound bulk sausage	1 bell pepper, chopped
1 1/2-2 pounds ground beef	1/2-3/4 cups ketchup
1 medium onion, chopped	2 (15-ounce) cans pinto beans

Preheat oven to 350 degrees. In a skillet, cook sausage and beef until brown and crumbly; remove from skillet with slotted spoon. In same skillet, sauté onion and bell pepper until tender. Place meat back in skillet and add ketchup and beans, mix well. Pour mixture into a 9x13-inch baking dish. Bake at 350 degrees for 30 minutes. Yield: 8 servings.

Note: Great with tacos!

Sausage Rice Casserole

Nancy Creech

1	pound bulk sausage	1	(10³/₄-ounce) can cream
1/2	cup celery, chopped		chicken soup
1/2	cup onion, chopped	1	soup can water
1	(10³/₄-ounce) can cream of	1	cup rice
	mushroom soup	1	(2-ounce) jar pimentos

Preheat oven to 325 degrees. In a skillet, brown sausage, celery, and onion; drain. Mix remaining ingredients with sausage and place in a 9x13-inch casserole dish. Bake at 325 degrees for 1 hour and 30 minutes. Yield: 6 to 8 servings.

American Style Pizza

Catherine Pate

1	(16-ounce) box Pillsbury hot	1	teaspoon prepared mustard
	roll mix		Salt and pepper to taste
2	(8-ounce) cans tomato sauce	2	tablespoons oregano
1	medium onion, chopped	1	pound bulk sausage
1	pound smoked sausage, thinly	1/2	pound grated sharp Cheddar
	sliced like pepperonis		cheese

Preheat oven to 400 degrees. Prepare crust according to directions on box of roll mix. Spread into two medium pizza pans. In a large saucepan, pour in tomato sauce and rinse each can with one-half can of water and add to sauce. Add onion, smoked sausage and next three ingredients. Cook sauce on low heat about 1 hour. Thinly spread sauce over tops of pizza dough. In a skillet, cook sausage until brown and crumbly; drain well. Spread sausage over sauce mixture and top with grated cheese. Bake at 400 degrees until crust in browned and sauce is bubbly. Yield: 8 servings.

Sausage Stuffed Shells
Debby Gaddy

1-2	*pounds sausage*	*1*	*teaspoon paprika*
1	*(12-ounce) box jumbo shells*	*2*	*teaspoons seasoned salt*
1	*(36-ounce) carton cottage*	*1*	*teaspoon black pepper*
	cheese	*1/2*	*teaspoon salt*
1	*cup grated mozzarella cheese*	*2*	*eggs*
1	*cup Parmesan cheese*		*Spaghetti sauce*

Preheat oven to 350 degrees. Spray a 9x13-inch baking dish with nonstick cooking spray. In a skillet, cook sausage until brown and crumbly; drain well. Set aside. Cook shells according to directions on box. Be careful that they do not stick and do not overcook. When done, pour water off and fill with cold water; let shells cool in water. When stuffing shells, pick up one at the time to work with so they don't dry out. In a large bowl, mix cottage cheese and next seven ingredients. Stir in sausage, mix well. Stuff shells generously with sausage mixture. Place in prepared dish. Generously spoon spaghetti sauce over shells. Cover with foil and bake at 350 degrees for 20 to 25 minutes. Yield: 36 shells.

★ Poultry ★ Game ★

Alex Brown and Beth Brown
Alex and Mama
March 1999

During the last months of Mama's life she learned of Alex's diagnosis of colorectal cancer. She battled myelodysplasia for years and put up with chemotherapy and blood transfusions, but not once did I hear her complain. She would always tell us she was feeling okay even though we knew she didn't. She kept living to the fullest and really never let us know how bad she felt. Alex was going through chemotherapy and radiation and would sit and talk to Mama in the mornings. She would tell him to pray each day for God to give him strength to make it through the day. As we were going through some old trunks after her death, we saw how in those last months she had organized and left notes for us so we would know what everything was and to whom it had belonged. Her love for her family was unconditional. Mama had faith, hope and unselfish love. Hopefully, that part of her will live on in us and we will pass it on to our children.

Love is patient, love is kind.
It does not boast, it is not proud.
It is not rude, it is not self-seeking,
it is not easily angered,
it keeps no records of wrong.
Love does not delight in evil
but rejoices with truth.
It always protects, always trusts,
always hopes, always perseveres.

1 Corinthians 13: 4-7

Barbeque Chicken

Judy Pigg

	Chicken pieces	4	tablespoons sugar
2	sticks butter	4	tablespoons A-1 sauce
6	tablespoons vinegar	2	dashes Tabasco
8	tablespoons Worcestershire sauce	1/2	teaspoon dry mustard
			Pinch of cayenne pepper

Preheat oven to 350 degrees. Place chicken skin side down in a baking dish. Size of dish depends on amount of chicken pieces used. In a medium saucepan, combine butter and next seven ingredients and bring to a boil. Remove from heat. Brush sauce on chicken and baste every 15 minutes. Bake at 350 degrees for 1 hour. Yield: 1 to 2 pieces chicken per serving.

Barbequed Chicken Sauce

Stephanie Stanley

1	teaspoon salt	1/3	cup oil
1/2	teaspoon black pepper	1/2	cup hot water
1	tablespoon paprika	1/3	cup vinegar
1	tablespoon sugar	1	tablespoon Worcestershire sauce
1	medium onion, finely chopped		
1	cup ketchup		

In a medium saucepan, blend salt, pepper, paprika, and sugar. Add onion, ketchup, oil, and water. Heat to boiling and remove from heat; add vinegar and Worcestershire. This is enough sauce for 2 to 3 chickens. To cook a chicken, place chicken pieces in a glass baking dish and cover with foil. Bake at 350 degrees for 1 hour. Drain off liquid and add sauce. Continue cooking 30 more minutes. Remove foil and cook 10 to 15 minutes. Yield: 1 to 2 pieces chicken per person.

Chicken Almandine
Marsha Oates

1	(10¾-ounce) can cream of celery soup	1/2	cup chopped onion
1	(10¾-ounce) can cream of mushroom soup	1	(2-ounce) jar diced pimentos
		2	cups cooked rice
1	(10¾-ounce) can cream of chicken soup	2	cups grated Cheddar cheese, divided
2½-3	cups cooked chicken, cubed	1	(2¼-ounce) package slivered almonds

Preheat oven to 350 degrees. In a large bowl, mix soups, chicken and next three ingredients together. Add one-half of the cheese; mix well. Put into a 3-quart casserole dish or two 1½-quart dishes. Top with remaining cheese and almonds. Bake at 350 degrees for 30 minutes. Yield: 6 to 8 servings.

Easy Chicken-In-Wine
Elizabeth Cook

6	chicken breast halves	2	tablespoons chopped fresh parsley
	Salt and pepper		
1/2	cup butter	4	tablespoons lemon juice
1	cup chopped green onions	1	cup white wine
3	tablespoons Worcestershire sauce		Pinch rosemary
1	(4-ounce) can sliced mushrooms, drained		

Preheat oven to 275 degrees. Salt and pepper chicken. In a Dutch oven or large casserole dish, brown chicken in butter. Add remaining ingredients and cover. Bake at 275 degrees for 2 hours. Yield: 4 to 6 servings.

Chicken Bog (For Four)
Kay Holley

2	large chicken breasts	1	large chopped onion
	Salt	1	slice hot sausage, patty
	Black pepper		1-inch thick
	Cayenne pepper	6	tablespoons butter
8	shakes of Tabasco sauce	1	cup rice, not instant

In 3 or 5-quart saucepan, cover chicken with water. Bring to a boil; cover, reduce heat and simmer until chicken is tender. Remove chicken from broth and cool. Reserve broth. Pull chicken from bones and break into pieces. In same saucepan with broth, add a few cups of water to broth if needed. Add salt and next five ingredients. Bring to boil and boil 5 to 10 minutes. Stir in butter, rice, and chicken pieces. Cover and simmer about 20 minutes. Yield: 4 servings.

Chicken Broccoli Casserole
Donna Stokes

1	stick margarine	1	(10-ounce) package frozen
1	(8-ounce) package		broccoli, thawed
	Pepperidge Farm Stuffing mix	1	(10 3/4-ounce) can cream of
4	cups cooked and diced		broccoli soup
	chicken breasts	1	(10 3/4-ounce) can cream of
	Salt		chicken soup
	Black pepper	2	cups chicken broth
3	hard boiled eggs, chopped		

Preheat oven to 325 degrees. In a saucepan, melt margarine and remove from heat. Stir in stuffing mix. Put one-half of stuffing mixture in bottom of a 9x13-inch baking dish. Top with chicken and next four ingredients. In a medium bowl, mix soups with broth and pour over chicken mixture. Top with remaining stuffing mix. Bake at 325 degrees for 1 hour. Yield: 6 to 8 servings.

Chicken Casserole

Donna Tucker

1	(3-3 1/2-pound) broiler-fryer	1	stick butter, melted
1	medium onion, chopped	1	(10 3/4-ounce) can cream
1	rib celery, chopped		mushroom soup
1	(8-ounce) package	1	(10 3/4-ounce) can cream of
	Pepperidge Farm		celery
	herb-stuffing mix	2	soup cans chicken broth

Preheat oven to 350 degrees. Combine chicken, onion and celery in a Dutch oven. Bring to a boil; cover, reduce heat and simmer 40 minutes or until chicken is tender. Remove chicken, reserving broth. Discard onion and celery. Skin, bone and cut into bite-sized pieces. Mix stuffing mix and butter in a medium bowl. Place one-half mixture in a 9x13-inch baking dish and spread chicken over top. In a medium bowl, mix soups and broth; pour over chicken. Sprinkle with remaining stuffing mixture. Bake at 350 degrees for 1 hour. Yield: 6 to 8 servings.

Herb Chicken

Tacky Vosburgh

2	cups corn flakes, crushed	1	tablespoon garlic powder
1/2	cup Parmesan cheese		Salt and pepper to taste
1	tablespoon thyme	10-12	large chicken breasts,
1	tablespoon oregano		boneless and halved
1	tablespoon parsley flakes		Melted butter

Preheat oven to 350 degrees. In a large bowl, mix corn flakes and next six ingredients. Dip chicken in melted butter and then in corn flake mixture. Place in a 10x14-inch baking dish. Bake at 350 degrees for 1 hour. Yield: 10 to 12 servings.

Chicken Crunch Casserole

Minnie Bryant

1 sleeve Ritz crackers, crushed	1 cup diced celery
1 stick margarine, melted	1 small onion, chopped
1 (10 3/4-ounce) can cream of mushroom or chicken soup	1 (4-ounce) package slivered almonds
3/4 cup mayonnaise	2 cups cooked spaghetti noodles
2 cups cooked white chicken, chopped	

Preheat oven to 350 degrees. In a small bowl, mix crackers and margarine; set aside. In a large bowl, combine remaining ingredients. Spoon into a 3-quart baking dish. Spread cracker mixture over top of casserole. Bake at 350 degrees for 35 minutes. Yield: 8 servings.

Creamy Baked Chicken Breasts

Marie Shirley

4 whole chicken breasts, split, skinned and boned	1/4 cup dry white wine
8 (4x4) slices Swiss cheese	1 cup herb-seasoned stuffing mix
1 (10 3/4-ounce) can cream of chicken soup	1/4 cup butter, melted

Preheat oven to 350 degrees. Arrange chicken in a lightly greased 9x13-inch baking dish. Place cheese slices on top. In a small bowl, combine soup and wine. Spoon mixture over chicken. Mix stuffing mix and butter together in a small bowl. Sprinkle on top of soup mixture. Bake at 350 degrees for 45 to 55 minutes. Yield: 8 servings.

Chicken and Olives
Vivian Holliday

1   whole chicken, skinned
1/4   cup olive oil
1/2   (12-ounce) bottle red wine vinegar
    Salt and pepper to taste

    Garlic salt to taste
1   Diced onion
1-2   tablespoons ketchup
1   (4-ounce) bottle capers
1   (7-ounce) bottle green olives

In a Dutch oven or large saucepan, brown chicken in olive oil. Add vinegar, dry seasonings, and onion. Stir in ketchup. Add olives and capers. Cook on low heat on stovetop 1 hour, stirring occasionally. Transfer to a 9x13-inch baking dish and bake at 350 degrees for 30 to 45 minutes. Yield: 4 to 5 servings.

Chicken Rice Casserole
Rochelle Miller

1   cup uncooked long-grain rice
1/2   cup chopped onion
1/4   cup butter or margarine
2 1/4 cups chicken broth
1/2   cup bell pepper
1/2   cup diced celery
1 1/2 cups chopped, cooked chicken

1   (3-ounce) can sliced mushrooms, drained
1   cup shredded mild Cheddar cheese
    Sliced green olives

Preheat oven to 350 degrees. In a medium skillet, brown rice and onion in butter over medium heat, stirring occasionally. Add chicken broth, cover and cook 10 minutes. Add bell pepper and celery. Cook, covered, about 15 minutes longer or until rice is tender, stirring occasionally. Add chicken and mushrooms; mix well. Transfer to a 1 1/2-quart casserole dish. Bake, covered, at 350 degrees for 15 to 20 minutes. Remove from oven and cover with cheese. Return to oven until cheese melts. Garnish with olives. Yield: 5 to 6 servings.

Chicken and Rice Special

Retha Chapman

11/4 cup uncooked rice
1   (103/4-ounce) can cream of
     celery soup
1   (103/4-ounce) can cream of
     chicken soup
1   (103/4-ounce) can cream of
     mushroom soup

1   can hot water
1   (4-ounce) can mushroom
     pieces (optional)
     Salt and pepper to taste
6-8 chicken pieces
2   tablespoons melted margarine
     Paprika

Preheat oven to 275 degrees. In a medium bowl, combine rice and next six ingredients. Spread rice mixture in a 9x13-inch baking dish. Arrange a single layer of chicken pieces on top of rice mixture. Pour melted margarine over chicken and sprinkle with paprika. Bake at 275 degrees for 2 hours and 30 minutes. Yield: 6 to 8 servings.

Note: Sunday lunch time. Cook while at church.

Chicken and Bean Casserole

Greta Hawkins

2   (141/2-ounce) cans green
     beans
6   chicken breasts, cooked and
     cut in bite-sized pieces
1   (10-ounce) Cream of Cheddar
     cheese soup
1/3 cup milk

1/3 cup breadcrumbs
6   slices bacon, cooked and
     crumbled
1/2 cup grated sharp Cheddar
     cheese

Preheat oven to 350 degrees. Drain beans and place on bottom of a 3-quart casserole dish. Cover with chicken. In a small bowl, mix soup with milk and pour over chicken. Combine breadcrumbs and bacon in a small bowl and sprinkle over soup. Bake at 350 degrees for 25 minutes. Remove from oven and top with cheese. Return to oven and bake an additional 5 minutes. Yield: 5 servings.

Chicken and Sausage Casserole

Benton Boyd

1	large fryer	2	(10¾-ounce) cans cream of
1	(6-ounce) package Uncle		mushroom soup
	Ben's Wild Rice mix	1	(8-ounce) jar sliced
1	pound bulk sausage		mushrooms (optional)
2	medium onions, chopped		Buttered breadcrumbs

Preheat oven to 350 degrees. Cook chicken in a large pot of water, with one teaspoon of salt added, for 1 hour. Remove chicken from broth and cool. Pull chicken from bones, discarding bones and skin. Cut chicken into bite-sized pieces. Cook rice according to package directions, using chicken broth in place of water. In a large skillet, cook sausage until browned and crumbly; remove sausage with a slotted spoon. Drain off any excess grease. In same skillet, sauté onions in sausage drippings. Add sausage, soup, chicken, rice, and mushrooms; mix well. Pour into a 9x13-inch baking dish. Top with breadcrumbs. Bake at 350 degrees for 30 minutes. Yield: 8 servings.

Chicken Supreme

Amanda Crocker

2	cups cooked noodles	1	(10¾-ounce) can cream of
1	cup cooked and diced		chicken soup, may use two
	chicken		cans
1	cup sour cream	1	teaspoon salt
1/2	teaspoon sage	1/4	teaspoon black pepper

Preheat oven to 350 degrees. In a medium bowl, mix all ingredients. Pour into a 2-quart baking dish. Bake at 350 degrees for 20 to 25 minutes. Yield: 4 to 5 servings.

NeNa's Chicken Pie

Beth Brown
Submitted by Kathy Boyd

1   large fryer, 3 pounds
2-3 hard boiled eggs, sliced
1   (10 3/4-ounce) can cream of
    chicken soup
1   (10 3/4-ounce) can cream of
    celery soup

1 1/2 soup cans chicken broth
1   stick margarine
1   cup self-rising flour
1   cup buttermilk

Preheat oven to 350 degrees. Cook chicken in a large pot of water, adding 1 teaspoon salt, for 1 hour. Remove chicken from broth and cool. Skin, bone and tear into small bite-sized pieces. Place in bottom of a 9x13-inch baking dish. Place eggs on top of chicken. In a small bowl, mix soups and broth. Pour over chicken and eggs. In a saucepan, melt butter, add flour stirring until smooth. Pour in buttermilk, mixing well. Pour over top of casserole. Bake at 350 degrees for 1 hour. Yield: 6 to 8 servings.

Deb's Pot Pie

Vicki Roberson

1   (10-ounce) can white chunk
    chicken, drained
1   (5-ounce) can white chunk
    chicken, drained
1   (15-ounce) can Veg-All,
    drained

2   (15-ounce) cans cream of
    potato soup
    Salt and pepper to taste
2   (9-inch) deep dish pie crust,
    unbaked

Preheat oven to 350 degrees. In a large bowl, combine chicken, vegetables and soup; mix well. Pour mixture into one unbaked pie crust and cover mixture with other unbaked pie crust. Pierce crust with a fork to allow steam to escape. Bake at 350 degrees for 1 hour. Yield: 8 servings.

Easy Chicken Pie
Anna Laura McElveen

1   large fryer, 3 pounds
    Salt and pepper
1   (16-ounce) package frozen
    mixed vegetables
1   (10¾-ounce) can cream
    chicken soup

1   cup chicken broth
1   cup all-purpose flour
1/2   teaspoon baking powder
1   cup milk

Preheat oven to 350 degrees. Grease a 9x12-inch baking dish. Cook chicken in a large pot of water, with salt and pepper added, for 1 hour. Remove chicken from broth and cool. Pull bones from chicken, discarding all bones and skin. Cut in bite-sized pieces. In a medium saucepan, combine vegetables, soup, and broth and cook 5 minutes. Place chicken in prepared dish. Pour vegetable mixture over chicken. In a medium bowl, combine flour, baking powder, and milk and stir until smooth. Pour over vegetable mixture. Bake at 350 degrees for 1 hour and 15 minutes. Yield: 6 to 8 servings.

Grandmother's Chicken Stew
Ginger Manning

1   large fryer or hen
    (4-5 pounds)
4   slices bacon
6   large onions, sliced
1   (14-ounce) bottle ketchup
4   tablespoons Worcestershire
    sauce
1/4   teaspoon cayenne pepper

1   teaspoon black pepper
1   teaspoon salt
1   stick margarine
1/2   cup flour
1/2   cup water
4   hard boiled eggs, sliced
    Cooked rice

In a large pot, cook chicken in three cups of water for 1 hour. Remove chicken; reserve broth. Skin, bone and cut chicken into chunks. In same large pot, cook bacon until browned. Add onions to bacon; steam until tender, not browned. Add ketchup and next five ingredients. Add the reserved 3 cups broth. In a small bowl, combine flour and water to make a paste and add to mixture. Cook until smooth and creamy. Add chicken and eggs. Serve over rice. Yield: 8-10 servings

Hawaiian Chicken
Shannon Haas

6 boneless chicken breast
1 (8-ounce) bottle Russian salad
  dressing
1 (11/4-ounce) envelope onion
  soup mix
1 (15-ounce) can mandarin
  oranges

1 (20-ounce) can pineapple
  chunks
1 (12-ounce) jar apricot
  preserves

Preheat oven to 350 degrees. Place chicken in a 9x13-inch baking dish. In a
medium bowl, combine all remaining ingredients and mix well. Pour over
chicken. Bake, covered, for 1 hour. Thicken sauce with flour.
Yield: 6 servings.

Herbed Chicken Fettuccine
Kathy Boyd

1-2 teaspoons salt-free seasoning
1 teaspoon poultry seasoning
1 pound boneless skinless
  chicken breast, cut in 1-inch
  strips
2 tablespoons olive oil
4 tablespoons butter, divided
2/3 cup water
2 tablespoons teriyaki sauce

2 tablespoons onion soup mix
1 (11/4-ounce) envelope savory
  herb and garlic soup mix,
  divided
1 (8-ounce) package fettucine
2 tablespoons Parmesan
  cheese
1 tablespoon Worcestershire
  sauce

Combine seasonings in a small bowl; sprinkle over chicken. In a skillet, sauté
chicken in oil and two tablespoons butter 5 minutes. Add water, teriyaki
sauce, onion soup mix, and two tablespoons savory herb and garlic soup mix.
Bring to a boil. Reduce heat; cover and simmer 15 minutes. Cook fettucine
according to package directions. Drain; add to chicken mixture. Add cheese,
Worcestershire sauce, remaining butter, and remaining herb and garlic soup
mix; Toss to coat. Yield: 4 servings.

Sarah's Favorite Lemon and Basil Chicken

Mary Ward Baucom

4-5 boneless chicken breasts or
   favorite pieces
   Salt and pepper
4-5 fresh basil leaves

1 lemon, thinly sliced
4-5 cloves garlic, bruised and
   peeled
1/4 cup olive oil

Preheat oven to 400 degrees. Spray or grease a 9x13-inch baking dish. Place chicken in dish and sprinkle both sides with salt and pepper. Place a basil leaf or two on each piece of chicken and top with a few lemon slices. Add garlic to the dish. Drizzle all with olive oil. Bake at 400 degrees for 30 minutes. Baste occasionally with pan juices. If using chicken with bone, bake a little longer. Yield: 4 to 5 servings.

Hot Chicken Soufflé Supreme

Barbara Grant

13 slices white bread,
   divided
5 chicken breasts, boned,
   cooked and cubed
1 cup bell pepper,
   chopped
1/2 cup pimentos, chopped
1 cup celery, chopped
1 teaspoon salt

   Black pepper to taste
1 cup mayonnaise
5 unbeaten eggs
3 cups milk
2 (10 3/4-ounce) cans cream of
   mushroom soup
2 cups grated Cheddar cheese

Trim and cube 4 slices of bread. Place on bottom of a 3-quart casserole dish. In a large bowl, combine chicken, vegetables, salt, pepper, and mayonnaise; mix well. Spoon over bread. Trim remaining bread and cube or crumble and place on top of chicken mixture. In a medium bowl, combine eggs and milk and pour over bread. Refrigerate one hour or overnight. When ready to bake, spoon soup over top. Bake at 325 degrees for 1 hour or until set. Sprinkle with cheese the last few minutes of baking. Yield: 14 servings.

Turkey Seasoning

Andy Eaddy

2 ounces salt
2 ounces black pepper
2 ounces crushed red pepper
2 ounces garlic powder

2 ounces chili powder
2 ounces Ac'cent
   Peanut oil

In a large bowl, combine all dry ingredients and mix well. This seasoning will season two to three turkeys. Rub turkey with peanut oil and then coat with seasoning 24 to 36 hours prior to cooking. Refrigerate. Put turkey in a roasting pan. Bake at 300 to 350 degrees for four minutes per pound or grill slowly on outdoor grill at 225 to 250 degrees.

Oven Smoked Turkey

Anne Brown Dawkins

1   (10-12 pound) turkey
1/4 cup vegetable oil
1/4 teaspoon garlic salt or
    powder

1/2 cup seasoned salt
4   tablespoons liquid smoke
1/4 cup black pepper

Preheat oven to 350 degrees. Grease a large brown paper bag. Wash meat and pat dry; set aside. In a small bowl combine oil, garlic, salt, liquid smoke, and pepper; mix well. Rub turkey thoroughly inside and out. Put turkey in the bag and tie with a string. Place on baking sheet and roast 3 hours and 30 minutes. Remove from oven and let stand at room temperature at least 30 minutes before untying bag. Yield: 20 to 24 servings.

Cajun Ducks At The High Dollar Camp
Jimmy Atkins

6	whole ducks	3	(10 1/2-ounce) cans beef broth
	Tony Chachere's seasoning	3	(10 1/2-ounce) cans chicken
1	cup bacon drippings		broth
4	onions chopped	1/2	cup red wine
3	bell peppers, chopped	1	(16-ounce) package baby
4	ribs celery, chopped		carrots
1	tablespoon minced garlic	1	(8-ounce) package sliced
2	tablespoons Kitchen Bouquet		mushrooms
2	tablespoons Worcestershire		
	sauce		

Preheat oven to 350 degrees. Season ducks inside and out with Tony Chachere's seasoning. In a Dutch oven roaster, brown ducks in bacon drippings and remove. In same roaster, combine onion and next 5 ingredients and cook until tender. Add ducks, beef broth and next four ingredients. Bake covered at 350 degrees for 3 hours, occasionally checking for tenderness and liquid level. Yield: 8 servings.

Note: May substitute salt, pepper, and, cayenne pepper for Tony Chachere's seasoning. Serve over rice with Duck Camp White Bean recipe on page 240.

Quail With Sour Cream And Bacon
Kathy Boyd

16	thin slices Canadian bacon	1	cup sour cream
	Salt and pepper to taste	1	(10 3/4-ounce) can cream of
16	quail		mushroom soup
16	slices bacon		

Preheat oven to 275 degrees. Line a greased 9x13-inch baking dish with Canadian bacon. Season quail with salt and pepper. Wrap each in 1 slice of bacon. Arrange quail on top of Canadian bacon. In a medium bowl, combine sour cream and soup. Spoon over quail. Bake at 275 degrees for 3 hours. Yield: 12 servings.

Grilled Venison Tenderloin

Edwin Boyd

Venison tenderloin
Bacon

Italian dressing
Allegro marinade

Wrap tenderloin in bacon strips and secure with toothpicks. Place in 9x13-inch glass dish and pour equal amount of dressing and marinade over top. No certain amount. It depends on size of tenderloin or if preparing more than one. Marinate overnight in refrigerator. Place on preheated grill and cook about 20 minutes, turning frequently. Meat should be pale pink inside. Serve immediately. Yield: 4 to 6 servings.

Scandanavian Venison

Andy Eaddy

1   (8-ounce) package egg
    noodles
1   pound ground venison,
    seasoned
2   onions, chopped

Dill weed to taste
1   (10¾-ounce) can cream of
    mushroom soup, undiluted
1   (8-ounce) carton sour cream

Cook noodles according to package directions. In a skillet, combine venison and onion. Cook until venison is browned and onion tender. Add dill to taste. Stir in soup and sour cream and mix well. Serve over noodles. Yield: 4 to 6 servings.

Note: Add other condiments or substitute venison for ground beef.

Mustard Fried Venison

Edwin Boyd

5 *Venison steaks, cubed*	*Flour*
Mustard	*Salt and pepper to taste*
Heinz 57 sauce	

In a large bowl, marinate venison in mixture of two-thirds mustard and one-third Heinz 57 sauce 2 to 3 hours. Combine flour, salt, and pepper. Dredge venison in flour and deep fry in hot oil until golden brown. Yield: 5 servings.

★ Vegetables ★
Side Dishes

Howard and Beth Brown
Joan and Gus Hoffmeyer
1994 Coker College alumni trip
Charleston, South Carolina

Mama and Joan met at Coker College and ended up being roommates and life long friends. They shared the same wedding dress and had families close in age to each other. We spent many a summer vacation at Surfside Beach at the Hoffmeyer's beach house. Seven kids and four adults in the house. We had a great time. There was a lot of family fun. I think the adults were having fun too! We would go crabbing and shrimping at the bridge in Murrells Inlet and play on the beach. One night during the week we would all go out to eat and to the big rides in Myrtle Beach. We would also jump on the trampolines in Garden City across the street from Sam's Corner. That was one of our favorite things.

Take time with your children and build memories with them. They will look back to their childhood and feel happiness. Teach them the importance of family and friends.

Now about brotherly love
we do not need to write to you,
for you yourselves have been taught
by God to love each other.

1 Thessalonians 4:9

Asparagus Casserole

Doris Chaplin

1 (10¾-ounce) can cream of asparagus soup
1 cup Ritz cracker crumbs, divided
1 cup grated Cheddar cheese, divided

3 hard boiled eggs, grated or chopped
   Black pepper
1 (15-ounce) can of asparagus spears, reserve juice

Preheat oven to 350 degrees. In a medium bowl, combine soup, one-half of the crumbs, one-half of cheese, eggs, and pepper. Cut asparagus into one and one-half inch pieces and add to the soup mixture. Pour in one-fourth cup of asparagus juice and mix well. Spread into a lightly greased 8x8-inch baking dish. Sprinkle remaining cheese over mixture and top with remaining crumbs. Bake at 350 degrees for 30 minutes. Yield: 6 servings.

Asparagus and Pea Casserole

Susan Moore

1 (15-ounce) can LeSueur peas, drained
1 (15-ounce) can asparagus spears, drained
3 hard boiled eggs, sliced

1 (10¾-ounce) can cream of mushroom soup
3 tablespoons water
1/2 stick butter
   Grated Cheddar cheese

Preheat oven to 350 degrees. Pour peas in a 8x8-inch casserole dish. Arrange asparagus spears over peas and top with eggs. In a small bowl, combine soup with water and mix well. Pour soup over casserole. Dot with butter and top with cheese. Bake at 350 degrees for 30 minutes. Yield: 6 servings.

Marinated Asparagus

Dorothy Brown

1/2 cup sugar	1/2 teaspoon celery seeds
1/4 cup white vinegar	1/2 teaspoon salt
1/4 cup water	1 (15-ounce) can asparagus
3 whole cloves	spears, drained
1 cinnamon stick	

In a saucepan, bring first seven ingredients to a boil. Place asparagus in a bowl and pour mixture over top. Marinate, covered, 6 to 24 hours in the refrigerator. Serve cold or hot after draining off liquid. Yield: 4 servings.

Note: May also serve as individual salads. Place spears on salad greens, top with egg slices and pimento strips.

Curry's Baked Beans

Debbie Dawkins

1/2 pound bacon	1 tablespoon whole mustard
1/2 large onion, chopped	seeds
1/2 bell pepper, chopped	1-2 (31-ounce) cans pork and
1 1/2 cups ketchup	beans
1 1/2 cups brown sugar	

Preheat oven to 350 degrees. In a skillet, cook bacon. Remove and set aside. In drippings, sauté onion and bell pepper. Add ketchup, brown sugar, and mustard seed, mix well. Cook until bubbling. Drain beans and pour into a 1 1/2-quart casserole dish. Pour onion mixture into beans and mix well. Bake at 350 degrees for 30 minutes or until hot and bubbly. Yield: 5 to 12 servings

Note: Can substitute mustard for mustard seeds.

Best In The West Beans

Gail Funderburk

1/2	pound ground beef	2	tablespoons molasses
10	slices bacon, chopped	1/2	teaspoon chili powder
1/2	cup onion, chopped	1/2	teaspoon black pepper
1/3	cup packed brown sugar	1	(16-ounce) can kidney beans,
1/3	cup granulated sugar		drained
1/4	cup ketchup	1	(16-ounce) can pork and
1/4	cup Kraft barbeque sauce		beans
2	tablespoons prepared mustard	1	(16-ounce) can lima beans
1/2	teaspoon salt		

Preheat oven to 350 degrees. In a large skillet, cook ground beef and bacon; drain. Add onion and cook until tender. Add sugars and next seven ingredients; mix well. Stir in beans. Pour mixture into a 3-quart casserole dish. Bake at 350 degrees for 1 hour. Yield: 10 to 12 servings.

Bean Casserole

Marcia Camp

3	(14 1/2-ounce) cans Blue Lake green beans, drained, reserve juice	1/2	cup vinegar
		1	onion, sliced in rings
1/2	cup sugar		Bacon strips

Preheat oven to 325 degrees. In a small bowl, combine a little juice from beans with sugar and vinegar. Pour beans in a 2-quart baking dish. Pour sugar mixture over beans. Spread onion over beans. Top with bacon. Bake, covered, at 325 degrees for 2 hours. Yield: 6 to 8 servings.

Dinnertime Green Beans

Beth Brown
Submitted by Kathy Boyd

2 1/2 pounds green beans, tipped
6 tablespoon butter
1 pound mushrooms, sliced

5 chopped scallions
Salt and pepper to taste

Drop the beans in a large pot of boiling water, and after it returns to a boil, cook 7 minutes. Drain under running cold water. Set aside. Just before serving, melt butter in a large skillet and sauté mushrooms and scallions 2 minutes. Add the beans, salt, and pepper. Toss 2 minutes and serve. Yield: 8 servings.

Duck Camp White Beans

Jimmy Atkins

3 tablespoons cooking oil
1 large onion, chopped
1 large bell pepper, chopped
2 ounces tasso, cut in
   small pieces
1 (4 1/2-ounce) can chopped
   green chilies

2 (15 1/2-ounce) cans Trappy's
   navy beans
2 (15 1/2-ounce) cans Black
   Runner cream white beans
1/2 can water

Preheat cooking oil in a 6 to 8-quart pot. Sauté onion, bell pepper, and tasso until soft. Add chilies. Pour in beans and water. Cover and cook on low heat 1 hour. Serve over rice or with gravy. Great with duck or fried fish. Yield: 6 to 8 servings.

Note: Can substitute country ham pieces for tasso and navy beans for white beans.

Three Bean Casserole

Lee Langston

4	slices bacon	3/4	cup brown sugar
1	medium onion, chopped	1/4	pound American cheese,
1	(16-ounce) can pork and		cubed
	beans	1/3	cup ketchup
1	(16-ounce) can lima beans,	2	tablespoons Worcestershire
	drained		sauce
1	(16-ounce) can kidney beans,		Parmesan cheese
	drained		

Preheat oven to 350 degrees. In a large pot, cook bacon; drain. Add all remaining ingredients and mix well. Pour into a greased 2-quart casserole. Sprinkle with cheese. Bake at 350 degrees for 30 minutes. Yield: 8 to 10 servings.

Broccoli and Rice Casserole

Vonceil Holloman

1	stick butter	1	(8-ounce) jar Cheese Whiz
1	cup chopped onion	1	(10¾-ounce) can cream of
1	cup chopped celery		mushroom soup
1	(10-ounce) package chopped	3	cups cooked rice
	broccoli, thawed and drained		

Preheat oven to 350 degrees. Melt butter in a skillet and sauté onion and celery 2 to 3 minutes or until tender. Add broccoli and cheese, stirring to melt cheese. Add soup and rice. Mix well. Pour into a 9x13-inch casserole dish or smaller. Bake at 350 degrees about 35 minutes or until hot and bubbly. Yield: 8 to 10 servings.

Note: May be prepared a day ahead and then baked.

Hot Cabbage
Gus Hoffmeyer

6	slices bacon or 1 cup cured ham, diced	3	tablespoons Worcestershire sauce
1	head cabbage, 6-inch diameter	1	teaspoon cornstarch
1	onion, 3-inch diameter	1/3	cup water
2	tablespoons vegetable oil		Salt and pepper to taste

Sauté bacon or ham in a skillet over medium heat. Drain on paper towel. Empty sauté pan of any grease. Core cabbage and cut into quarters, slice into three-eights inch slices and place in same skillet. Slice onion into one-eighth inch slices and add to cabbage. Pour in oil and mix. Cover and cook. In a cup, put cornstarch in water and mix. When cabbage mixture begins to steam add cornstarch mixture. As cabbage begins to get tender, add Worcestershire sauce and meat. Steam about 10 more minutes or until very tender. Yield: 6 to 8 servings.

Cheese Pudding
Harriette Crouch

12	slices bread	2 1/2	cups milk
	Butter	1	teaspoon salt
1/2	pound sharp Cheddar cheese, grated	4	eggs, beaten

Preheat oven to 275 degrees. Generously butter bread and cut into cubes. Layer in a 2-quart baking dish, alternating with cheese. In a medium bowl, combine milk, salt, and eggs; mixing well. Pour mixture over bread and cheese. Let stand several hours before baking. Bake at 275 degrees for about 45 minutes. Yield: 6 servings.

Note: Make sure dish is large enough as this will rise a great deal.

Cheese Cloud

Jacqueline Segars

12 slices white bread, crust trimmed and cut in half	1/2 teaspoon yellow mustard
	1 tablespoon grated onion
1/2 pound shredded Cheddar cheese, divided	1/4 teaspoon salt
	1/4 teaspoon cayenne pepper
4 eggs	Paprika
2 1/2 cups whole milk	

Preheat oven to 325 degrees. Arrange six slices bread on the bottom of 8x12-inch baking dish. Cover with one-half of the cheese. Arrange remaining bread on top of cheese. In a medium bowl, beat egg and next five ingredients. Pour over bread. Cover bread with remaining cheese. Sprinkle paprika over top. Bake at 325 degrees for 30 to 45 minutes. Yield: 12 servings.

Note: May be made a day ahead, refrigerated overnight and then baked.

Carrots Au Gratin

Cindy DeFoor

1 tablespoon margarine	1 cup shredded American cheese
1/3 cup chopped onion	
3 tablespoons flour	8 cups sliced carrots, cooked, drained
1/2 teaspoon salt	
1/4 teaspoon black pepper	1 tablespoon parsley flakes
1 1/2 cups milk	1/2 cup corn flake crumbs

Preheat oven to 350 degrees. Melt margarine in a saucepan and sauté onion over low heat. Add flour, salt and pepper. Stir in milk. Increase heat to medium and cook until bubbly and thickened, stirring constantly. Add cheese and stir until smooth. Stir in carrots and parsley flakes. Spread mixture into a shallow 1 1/2-quart baking dish. Sprinkle with crumbs. Bake at 350 degrees for 20 minutes or until bubbly and crumbs are golden brown. Yield: 9 servings.

Carrots in Horseradish Sauce

Patty Holley

1 (16-ounce) package fresh baby carrots	2 teaspoons horseradish sauce, or more to taste
3/4 cup mayonnaise	1 cup buttered breadcrumbs
1 tablespoon minced onion	

Preheat oven to 350 degrees. Place carrots in a small bowl with a small amount of water and cook for 4 minutes in microwave. Reserve two tablespoons of liquid from carrots. Place carrots in a 8x8-inch baking dish In a small bowl, combine reserved liquid, mayonnaise, onion, and horseradish. Top with breadcrumbs. Bake a 350 degrees for 30 minutes. Yield: 4 servings .

Carrot Nuggets

Adele Camp

2 pounds carrots, sliced round	1/2 cup salad oil
1 bell pepper, sliced	1/2 cup vinegar
1 onion, sliced	2 tablespoons sugar
1 (10 3/4-ounce) can tomato soup	

In a saucepan, cook carrots until tender; drain. In a medium bowl, combine carrots, bell pepper, and onion. In a separate bowl, combine remaining ingredients and mix well. Pour mixture over vegetables. Refrigerate. Marinate for 24 hours. Yield: 6 to 8 servings.

Corn Casserole

Susan Coker

1 (15-ounce) can cream-style corn	1 (8-ounce) container sour cream
1 (15-ounce) can whole kernel corn, do not drain	1 (8 1/2-ounce) box Jiffy cornbread mix
1 stick melted butter	

Preheat oven to 350 degrees. In a large bowl, use a wire whisk to blend all ingredients together. Pour into a greased 2-quart casserole dish. Bake, uncovered, at 350 degrees for 45 minutes or until set. Yield: 8 to 10 servings.

Corn Casserole

Tena Coker

1	stick butter	1	(8-ounce) container sour
1	(15-ounce) can cream-style		cream
	corn	1	(8½-ounce) box Jiffy
1	(15-ounce) can whole kernel		cornbread
	corn, do not drain		

Preheat oven to 375 degrees. In a 10-inch casserole dish, melt butter in microwave. In a large bowl, combine remaining ingredients. Mix well. Pour over butter and stir slightly. Bake at 375 degrees for 45 minutes. Yield: 8 to 10 servings.

Angel Corn

Betty Sullivan

2	cups frozen Green Giant	Salt and pepper to taste
	white shoe peg corn, cooked	4 tablespoons grated Swiss
1	cup heavy cream	cheese
3	tablespoons melted butter	Whipped cream
3	eggs, separated	
	Dash of nutmeg	

Preheat oven to 350 degrees. Grease a 1½-quart baking dish. In a large bowl, combine corn, cream, butter, egg yolks, nutmeg, salt and pepper. In a separate bowl, beat egg white until stiff and fold into corn mixture. Pour into prepared dish. Sprinkle with cheese and top with whipped cream. Bake at 350 degrees for 20 minutes. Increase heat to 375 degrees and bake 10 more minutes. Yield: 4 servings.

Note: Not good to prepare this ahead. Tends to get too soupy. Can double recipe and bake in a 3-quart baking dish to serve 6 to 8.

Corn and Macaroni Casserole

Diane Ollis

1	(15-ounce) can cream-style corn	1/2	cup melted butter
1	(15-ounce) can whole kernel corn, do not drain	1/4	cup chopped onion
		1/4	cup chopped bell pepper
			Salt and pepper to taste
1	cup uncooked macaroni	1 1/2	cups cubed Velvetta cheese

Preheat oven to 350 degrees. In a medium bowl, combine all ingredients; mix well. Spread into a 9x13-inch casserole dish. Bake at 350 degrees for 25 minutes. Remove from oven and stir. Return to oven and bake another 25 minutes or until macaroni is done. Yield: 6 to 8 servings.

Corn Pudding

Mary Brown

3	tablespoons butter	1	(15-ounce) can cream-style corn
1/4	cup all-purpose flour		
1/2	cup sugar	1	cup evaporated milk
3	eggs, beaten	1/2	teaspoon black pepper
1	(15-ounce) can whole kernel corn, drained		

Preheat oven to 325 degrees. Spray a 1-quart casserole dish with nonstick cooking spray. Melt butter in a saucepan over low heat. Stir in flour and sugar, mixing well. Remove from heat and stir in eggs. In a medium bowl, combine corn, milk, and pepper. Add butter mixture and stir well. Pour into prepared casserole dish and bake at 350 degrees for 30 to 40 minutes or until firm. Yield: 4 to 6 servings.

My Aunt's Corn Pudding

Jeannie Gainey

1	stick butter	5	tablespoons sugar
2	(16-ounce) packages frozen corn	2	cups milk
		4	eggs
3	tablespoons flour		Salt and pepper to taste

Preheat oven to 350 degrees. Melt butter in a 9x13-inch casserole dish. In a large bowl, combine remaining ingredients and mix well. Pour corn mixture over butter. Bake at 350 degrees for 30 to 35 minutes or until brown on top and firm in the middle. Yield: 6 servings

Cauliflower

Harriet Foster

1	medium head cauliflower	1	tablespoon chopped onion
2	tablespoons water	1	teaspoon mustard
1/2	cup mayonnaise	1/2	cup shredded Cheddar cheese

In a covered casserole dish, microwave the cauliflower in water 8 to 9 minutes on high. In a small bowl, combine mayonnaise, onion, and mustard; spoon on top of cauliflower. Sprinkle with cheese. Microwave at 50% power to melt cheese. Let stand 2 minutes, then serve immediately. Yield: 4 servings.

Scalloped Eggplant

Kathy Boyd

1	medium eggplant, peeled and cubed	1 1/2	cups crumbled soda crackers
			Black pepper
1/2	cup minced onion	1 1/4	cups milk
3	teaspoons salt, divided	6	tablespoons melted butter

Preheat oven to 375 degrees. Cook eggplant, in a pot of boiling water, with onion and two teaspoons of salt. Boil about 5 minutes or until tender but not mushy; drain. Spread one-half of cracker crumbs in a greased 8x8-inch baking dish. Spoon eggplant mixture over crackers. Sprinkle with remaining salt and pepper. Top with remaining crackers. Pour milk into corners of baking dish to cover bottom. Pour butter over top. Bake at 375 degrees for 45 minutes. Yield: 4 servings.

Creole Eggplant
Barbara Rion

1	medium eggplant, peeled and cubed	1	small bell pepper, chopped
5	tablespoons melted butter, divided	1	small onion, chopped
			Salt and pepper to taste
3	tablespoons flour	1	tablespoon brown sugar
2	(15-ounce) can tomatoes, chopped		Breadcrumbs
			Parmesan cheese

Preheat oven to 350 degrees. In a saucepan, cook eggplant in lightly salted water about 10 minutes; drain. Place eggplant in a greased 8x8-inch casserole dish. Pour three tablespoons butter over eggplant and stir. Sift flour over top and mix well. In a saucepan, combine tomatoes and next four ingredients, cook 5 minutes. Pour over eggplant mixture, blend well. Sprinkle with breadcrumbs and top with remaining butter and cheese. Bake at 350 degrees for 40 minutes. Yield: 4 to 6 servings.

Oven Fried Eggplant or Squash
Phyllis Sheeley

1/3	cup fine dry breadcrumbs		Eggplant, peeled, 1/4-inch slices or squash, sliced thin
2	tablespoons Parmesan cheese		
1/4	teaspoon salt	1/4	cup mayonnaise or Miracle Whip
1/4	teaspoon black pepper		Basil

Preheat oven to 400 degrees. Combine first four ingredients in a flat pan or shallow dish. Spread both sides of eggplant or squash with mayonnaise or dressing. Dredge in breadcrumb mixture. Place on a lightly greased baking sheet. Bake, uncovered, at 400 degrees for 10 to 12 minutes or until browned. Garnish with basil, if desired. Yield: 4 to 6 servings.

Crock Pot Macaroni and Cheese

Shirley Crowley

1 (8-ounce) box macaroni
4 cups grated sharp Cheddar
   cheese, divided
1 (12-ounce) can evaporated
   milk

1 1/2 cups 2% milk
1 stick margarine, melted
2 eggs, slightly beaten
   Salt and pepper to taste

Cook macaroni according to package directions; drain. In a large bowl, mix together all ingredients reserving one cup of cheese. Pour into a greased crock pot and sprinkle with reserved cheese. Cook for three hours on low heat. Let stand about 30 minutes before serving. Yield: 10 to 12 servings.

MeMe's Macaroni and Cheese

Julie Wilhelm

1 (8-ounce) package macaroni
1 1/2 cups milk
2 1/2 cups grated Cheddar cheese

2 eggs
   Salt and pepper to taste

Preheat oven to 350 degrees. Cook macaroni according to package directions; drain. In a large bowl, combine milk, cheese, eggs, salt, and pepper. Pour pasta in a greased 1 1/2-quart casserole dish and pour milk mixture over top. May top with additional cheese if desired. Bake at 350 degrees for 45 minutes. Yield: 6 servings.

French Onion Pie

Rose Marie Newsom

1 (9-inch) pie crust, unbaked
2 (2.8-ounce) cans French fried
   onions
3 eggs

1 1/2 cups milk
1 1/4 teaspoons salt
   Dash cayenne pepper
1 1/2 cups grated Cheddar cheese

Preheat oven to 425 degrees. Spread onions in pie crust. In a small bowl, beat egg, milk, salt, and pepper. Pour egg mixture over onions. Sprinkle cheese over top. Bake at 425 degrees for 15 minutes. Reduce heat to 350 degrees and bake about 20 minutes longer, or until custard sets. Serve with fresh or hot spiced fruit. Yield: 6 to 8 servings.

Onion Casserole

Jeanne Wilhelm

12 medium onions, thinly sliced
1 (13 3/4-ounce) bag potato
   chips, crushed
1/2 pound grated Wisconsin mild
   cheese

2 (10 3/4-ounce) cans cream of
   mushroom soup
1/2 cup milk
1/8 teaspoon cayenne pepper

Preheat oven to 350 degrees. In a 9x13-inch buttered casserole dish alternate layers of onion, potato chips, and cheese. In a small bowl, combine soup and milk; mix well. Pour over top of onion mixture. Sprinkle cayenne pepper over the top. Bake at 350 degrees for 1 hour. Yield: 12 servings.

Note: Good with barbeque.

Tee's (Not Too) Spicy Onion Rings

Tee and Lizabeth Thompson

1 (5-pound) bag Vidalia onions,
   any others won't do
1 (32-ounce) bottle Texas Pete
   hot sauce
1 (5-pound) bag flour

1 (2-pound) bag cornmeal
1 (8-ounce) box Lawry's
   seasoned salt
2 gallons vegetable oil

Peel and slice onions into one-eighth to one-fourth inch slices. Place onions in a large bowl and pour hot sauce over top. Let soak 30 minutes to 1 hour. Mix dry ingredients in a large paper bag. In a extra large deep fryer or a gas fish cooker, heat oil to 350 to 375 degrees. Remove onions from hot sauce, place in bag and shake until evenly coated. Drop onion rings into cooker and fry until golden brown. Yield: 6 to 12 servings.

Note: These are a favorite among Alex's beach friends!

Company Potatoes
Dell Gandy

6 medium-large red potatoes, thinly sliced
1 (10¾-ounce) can cream of mushroom soup
1 (10¾-ounce) can cream of chicken soup
1 cup sour cream
1 cup shredded Cheddar cheese, divided
1/4-1/2 cup margarine

Preheat oven to 350 degrees. Arrange potatoes in a greased 9x11-inch baking dish. In a medium bowl, combine soups, sour cream, one-half cup cheese, and butter. Mix well. Pour over potatoes, mixing thoroughly. Cover with aluminum foil. Bake at 350 degrees for 1 hour or until potatoes are soft when pierced with a fork. Remove from oven and sprinkle with remaining cheese. Cover with foil and let sit for a few minutes or until cheese melts. Yield: 6 to 8 servings.

Baked Hash Brown Potatoes
Vickie Ferguson

1 stick margarine
1 onion, chopped
1 (3-ounce) package cream cheese, softened
1 (10¾-ounce) can cream mushroom soup
3 tablespoons sour cream
1 (10¾-ounce) can cream of Cheddar cheese soup
1 (4½-ounce) jar sliced mushrooms, drained
1 (32-ounce) bag frozen southern hash brown potatoes
   Paprika

Preheat oven to 350 degrees. Melt butter in a saucepan and sauté onion over low heat. Blend in cream cheese and next four ingredients. Add potatoes and mix well. Pour into a lightly greased 2-quart casserole dish. Bake at 350 degrees for 45 minutes. Sprinkle with paprika. Yield: 6 to 8 servings.

Everybody's Favorite Potatoes

Jane Jones

1   (32-ounce) bag hash brown
    potatoes, thawed
1   stick margarine, melted
1/2 cup chopped onion
    (optional)
11/2 teaspoons salt
11/4 teaspoons black pepper

1   (103/4-ounce) can cream of
    chicken soup
2   cups sour cream
2   cups grated extra sharp
    Cheddar cheese
    Corn flakes, crushed

Preheat oven to 350 degrees. In a large bowl, combine all ingredients except corn flakes. Spoon into a greased 9x13-inch casserole dish. In a small bowl, toss corn flakes with a little melted butter. Top casserole with corn flakes. Bake at 350 degrees for 45 minutes. Yield: 8 to 12 servings.

Note: May substitute corn flakes for cheese.

Hash Brown Casserole

Cathy Kelley

1   (32-ounce) package lightly
    thawed hash brown potatoes
1   (2.8-ounce) can French fried
    onion rings
1   (103/4-ounce) can cream of
    chicken soup

1   stick melted butter
1   teaspoon salt
1   (8-ounce) container cream
    cheese
1   (12-ounce) package grated
    sharp Cheddar cheese

Preheat oven to 350 degrees. Spray a 9x13-inch baking dish with nonstick cooking spray. Spread potatoes in dish. Reserve one-half can of onions and set aside. In a large bowl, combine remaining ingredients and mix well. Press mixture into potatoes. Bake at 350 degrees for 50 minutes. Remove from oven and sprinkle remainder of onions over top. Bake another 10 minutes. Yield: 10 to 12 servings.

Potato Casserole
Denise Walden

1	(32-ounce) bag frozen hash brown potatoes	1	small onion, diced
1	(16-ounce) container sour cream	12	ounces Cheddar cheese, grated
2	(103/4-ounce) cans cream of chicken soup		Salt and pepper to taste

Preheat oven to 350 degrees. Grease a 9x13-inch baking dish. In a large bowl, combine all ingredients and mix well. Pour into prepared dish. Bake at 350 degrees for 1 hour. Yield: 10 servings.

Twice Baked Potatoes
Danielle Hall

4	large baking potatoes	1	cup shredded Cheddar cheese
1/4	cup milk	1	tablespoon fresh chives, chopped
1/4	cup margarine, softened		Sour cream
1/4	teaspoon salt		Bacon bits
	Dash black pepper		

Preheat oven to 400 degrees. Wash potatoes and prick each potato several times with a fork. Place in oven and bake for 1 hour or until tender; cool. Cut potatoes lengthwise in half. With a teaspoon, scoop out inside, leaving a thin shell. In a medium bowl, mash potatoes until no lumps remain. Add milk in small amounts, beating after each addition. Potatoes should be smooth and fluffy. Add a little more milk if needed. Add margarine, salt, and pepper; beat vigorously until potatoes are light and fluffy. Add cheese and chives. Fill potato shells with potato mixture. Place on a ungreased baking sheet and bake at 400 degrees for 20 minutes or until hot. Top with sour cream and bacon bits. Yield: 8 servings.

Tillie's Potatoes and Onions
Kathy Boyd

4   cups mashed potatoes
1/4 cup butter
11/2 teaspoons salt, divided
1/2 teaspoon black pepper
1   (2.8-ounce) can French fried
     onions, divided

1   cup heavy cream, whipped
2/3 cups grated sharp Cheddar
     cheese, divided
11/2 teaspoons parsley flakes

Preheat oven to 325 degrees. Grease a 11/2-quart casserole dish. In a large bowl, combine potatoes, butter, one teaspoon salt, and pepper. Whip with a fork until fluffy. Reserve one-half cup of onions and set aside. Stir remaining onions into potatoes and mix well. Lightly spoon potato mixture into prepared dish. Do not mash them down. In a small bowl, combine one-third cup of cheese, whipped cream, and remaining salt. Stir well. Spread cheese mixture lightly over potatoes. Sprinkle with remaining cheese and onions. Bake at 325 degrees for 25 to 30 minutes or until lightly browned. Let stand 2 to 3 minutes before serving. Yield: 10 servings.

Note: This is one of my family's favorite recipes. Delicious with rib-eye roast or steaks.

Potatoes Deluxe
Jo Ann Smith

2   sticks margarine, divided
1   (32-ounce) package hash
     brown potatoes, thawed
1/2 cup chopped onions
1   cup sour cream

2   cups grated sharp Cheddar
     cheese
1   (103/4-ounce) can cream of
     chicken soup
2   cups crushed corn flakes

Preheat oven to 350 degrees. Melt one-half cup of margarine in a 9x13-inch baking dish. Combine potatoes and next four ingredients in dish and mix well Bake at 350 degrees for 30 minutes. Meanwhile, in a small bowl, mix corn flakes and remaining butter. Top casserole with corn flakes and bake 15 more minutes. Yield: 10 to 12 servings.

Bar-B-Que Potatoes

Betty Taylor

6 slices bacon	1/2 cup water
1 onion, chopped	1/2 cup sugar
1 3/4 tablespoons flour	5 potatoes, peeled, sliced, and
1/2 cup vinegar	boiled

Preheat oven to 375 degrees. In a skillet, cook bacon until browned; set aside. In same skillet, sauté onion in bacon drippings. In a saucepan, combine flour, vinegar, water, and sugar. Cook over moderate heat, stirring with a whisk, until flour and sugar are dissolved. Place potatoes and onion in a 9x13-inch baking dish. Crumble bacon over potatoes. Pour flour mixture over top. Bake at 375 degrees for 15 minutes. Yield: 4 servings.

Stewed Red Potatoes

Geri Jernigan

5-6 medium red potatoes sliced 1/4-inch thick	Squeeze margarine
1 large onion, thinly sliced	Parsley flakes
Salt and pepper to taste	Water

Place potatoes in a skillet. Arrange onion rings over top. Squeeze margarine over onion, about two to three tablespoons. Salt and pepper to taste. Sprinkle with parsley. Add water to about half of contents in skillet. Cover tightly and cook over medium heat until potatoes are tender and onion are done, about 30 minutes. Yield: 3 to 4 servings.

Candied Sweet Potatoes

Merle Baxley

6 medium sweet potatoes	1 cup brown sugar
1/3 cup melted butter or margarine	1/4 cup water
	1/2 teaspoon salt

Preheat oven to 350 degrees. Grease a 9x13-inch baking dish. Cook potatoes in a large pot of water until tender; drain. Peel and cut potatoes in halves lengthwise and arrange in prepared pan. Pour butter over potatoes. In a small saucepan, combine brown sugar and water and cook 5 minutes or until sugar dissolves. Pour sugar mixture over potatoes. Sprinkle with salt. Bake at 350 degrees for 1 hour, basting frequently. Yield: 6 servings.

Praline Sweet Potato Casserole

Shirley Crowley

Potatoes

3 cups mashed sweet potatoes	1 tablespoon vanilla extract
1/2 cup milk	1 stick butter or margarine, melted
3 eggs	
1 cup sugar	

Topping

1 cup brown sugar	1 cup chopped toasted pecans
1/2 cup all-purpose flour	1 stick butter or margarine

Preheat oven to 350 degrees. In a large bowl, combine potatoes and next five ingredients together. Beat until mixture is smooth. Pour into a 2-quart casserole dish. To prepare topping, in a medium bowl, combine sugar, flour, and pecans. Cut in butter until mixture is crumbly. Evenly sprinkle over potatoes. Bake at 350 degrees for 30 minutes. Yield: 8 to 10 servings.

Sweet Potato Delight
Debby Gaddy

First Layer
2   cups pretzels, crushed

2   sticks margarine, melted

Second Layer
1   (8-ounce) package cream
    cheese, softened
1   cup sugar

1   (8-ounce) container Cool
    Whip

Third Layer
3   cups mashed sweet potatoes
1   cup sugar
3   tablespoons cornstarch

1   egg
1   tablespoon vanilla extract
    Cinnamon to taste

Preheat oven to 350 degrees. In a large bowl, combine pretzels and margarine and spread on the bottom of a 9x13-inch baking dish. Bake at 350 degrees for about 15 minutes. Cool. For second layer, in a large bowl, combine cream cheese, sugar, and whipped topping. Mix until smooth. Spread cream cheese mixture over pretzel crust. In a saucepan, for third layer, combine potatoes, sugar and next four ingredients. Cook over low heat about 15 minutes. Spread over top of cream cheese mixture. Yield: 8 to 10 servings.

Sweet Potato-Apple Casserole
Marcia Camp

1/2 pound bulk sausage
1/2 teaspoon salt
1   tablespoon flour
2   tablespoons sugar
1/2 cup cold water

2   medium sweet potatoes,
    peeled and sliced
3   medium apples, cored and
    peeled

Preheat oven to 375 degrees. In a skillet, cook sausage until well done; crumble. Drain and reserve one tablespoon of sausage drippings. In a small bowl, combine salt, flour, and sugar. Blend with cold water. Arrange layers of potatoes, apples, and sausage in a 9x13-inch baking dish, pouring some of flour mixture over each layer. Top the dish with apples, sausage, and reserved drippings. Bake, uncovered, at 375 degrees; until apples and potatoes are tender, about 45 minutes. Yield: 6 servings.

Sweet Potato Pone

Jane Sox

2	cups sugar	1	cup milk
2	tablespoons flour	4	eggs, beaten
1	stick margarine or butter	4	cups grated raw sweet
2	teaspoons nutmeg		potatoes
2	teaspoons cinnamon	1	cup raisins (optional)
1	tablespoon vanilla	1	cup nuts (optional)

Preheat oven to 350 degrees. In a small bowl, combine sugar and flour. In a separate bowl, combine margarine and next four ingredients. Stir in sugar mixture and mix well. Add eggs. Fold in potatoes. Stir in raisins and nuts, if desired. Pour mixture into a 3-quart deep casserole dish. Bake at 350 degrees for 1 hour. Yield: 6 to 8 servings.

Sweet Potato Soufflé

Bonnie Hamilton

Potatoes

1	stick margarine, melted	1/4	teaspoon salt
2	cups mashed sweet potatoes	2	eggs
1/4	cup milk	1	teaspoon vanilla
1	cup sugar		

Topping

1/2	stick margarine	1	egg
1/2	cup sugar	1/2	cup chopped nuts
1/4	cup flour		
1	(8-ounce) can crushed pineapple		

Preheat oven to 350 degrees. In a large bowl, combine all potato ingredients and pour into a 2-quart baking dish. For topping, melt butter in a saucepan. Cream in sugar and flour. Stir in pineapple, egg, and nuts. Pour topping over potatoes. Bake at 350 degrees for 45 minutes. Yield: 6 servings.

Note: I double this a lot. Make sure to increase cooking time if you put it in a deep dish. Great with ham or turkey and holiday meals.

Spicy Rice Casserole

Jeanne Oneill

1	pound bulk sausage	2	beef bouillon cubes
1	teaspoon ground cumin	1/2	(11-ounce) can jalapeño
1/2	teaspoon garlic powder		peppers, chopped
2	medium onions, chopped	1	(6 1/2-ounce) package Uncle
2	medium bell peppers, red		Ben's Long Grain and Wild
	yellow or green, chopped		Rice- fast cook
2	cups water		

In a skillet, cook sausage with cumin and garlic; drain. Add onion and bell pepper to sausage and cook 5 minutes. Put water in a saucepan with bouillon and heat to boiling. Add jalapeño and rice, bring back to boil. Reduce heat and simmer, uncovered, about 10 minutes until water is absorbed. Stir in sausage mixture. Yield: 4 servings.

Better Than Hoppin' John

Kathy Boyd

1	(8-ounce) package frozen	1	cup chopped mushrooms
	black-eyed peas	1	tablespoon garlic powder
1	cup rice	1	teaspoon salt
1	pound hot bulk sausage	1	tablespoon black pepper
1	pound mild bulk sausage	2	bay leaves
1	large onion, chopped		
2	medium bell peppers, chopped		

Preheat oven to 300 degrees. Cook peas according to package directions; drain. Cook rice according to package directions. In a skillet, cook sausage until brown and crumbly. Drain and reserve 3 tablespoons of dripping. In same skillet, sauté onion, bell pepper, and mushrooms in reserved drippings. Add garlic and next three ingredients to onion mixture. In a 9x13-inch baking dish, combine rice, peas, and onion mixture. Mix well. Can freeze at the point. Bake, covered, at 300 degrees for 1 hour and 30 minutes. Yield: 8 servings.

Note: This is a New Year's Day tradition at our house. I serve with barbeque ribs, collards and cornbread.

Greek Rice Casserole
Beverly Whisnant

6 slices turkey bacon	1/2 cup sour cream
1 (10-ounce) package chopped spinach, thawed and dry	1 (8-ounce) can water chestnuts, sliced
2 cups cooked rice	1 (2.8-ounce) can French fried onion rings, divided
1 (103/4-ounce) can cream of mushroom soup	Greek seasonings to taste

Preheat oven to 350 degrees. Cook bacon in microwave; crumble and put in a large bowl. Add spinach and next four ingredients. Stir in one-half of the onions and seasonings, mix well. Pour mixture into a 7x11-inch baking dish. Top with remaining onions. Bake at 350 degrees for 30 minutes. Yield: 4 to 6 servings.

Mom's Brown Rice
Todd Jeffords

1 stick margarine	1 (101/2-ounce) can beef broth
1 (11/4-ounce) envelope onion soup mix	1 cup white rice
1 (101/2-ounce) can beef consommé	

Preheat oven to 350 degrees. Melt butter in a 2-quart casserole dish and stir in onion soup mix. Pour in consommé and broth. Pour in rice. Do not stir. Bake, uncovered, at 350 degrees for 1 hour. Yield: 6 servings.

Brown Rice

Winky Black

1	cup white rice	1/2	stick margarine
1	(10 1/2-ounce) can beef	1	onion, chopped
	consommé	1	(4 1/2-ounce) jar sliced
1	(10 3/4-ounce) can beef broth		mushrooms

Preheat oven to 350 degrees. Combine all ingredients in a 2-quart casserole dish and bake, covered, at 350 degrees for 1 hour. May be cooked in microwave for 15 minutes on high. Let sit in microwave 5 minutes. Cook 15 more minutes on high. Yield: 6 servings.

Okra Rice

Libba King

4-6	slices bacon	3 1/2	cups cooked rice
1	onion, chopped		Salt and pepper to taste
2-3	cups sliced okra		

Preheat oven to 325 degrees. In a skillet, cook bacon and remove from pan. Sauté onion and okra in bacon drippings. Combine okra mixture and rice in a greased 2-quart casserole dish. Crumble bacon over top. Bake, covered, at 325 degrees about 30 minutes. Yield: 6 to 8 servings.

Okra Rice

Elaine Hayes

1	pound bacon	1	cup finely chopped onion
1	quart fresh okra, sliced	3-4	cups cooked rice

In a skillet, cook bacon until crisp. Drain well on a paper towel. In bacon drippings, sauté okra and onion until okra is soft and onion are translucent. In a 2-quart casserole, combine, okra mixture, rice and crumbled bacon. Reheat in microwave. Yield: 5 to 6 servings.

Ricky's Wild Rice

Ricky Lowman

2 cups water	1 rib celery, chopped, divided
1 vegetable bouillon cube	1 tablespoon fresh cilantro,
1 teaspoon olive oil	chopped (optional)
1/3 cup wild rice	1/3 cup brown rice
1 small carrot, grated	1/3 cup white rice
1 scallion, chopped, divided	1/2 cup fresh mushrooms
1/3 cup red bell pepper, diced, divided	

Preheat oven to 350 degrees. In a saucepan, bring water to rolling boil. Add bouillon, oil, wild rice, carrot, one-half of scallion, one-half of bell pepper, and one-half of celery. Reduce heat, cover, and slow boil 30 minutes. Add remaining vegetables, cilantro if desired, brown and white rice. Uncover and cook or 10 minutes. Add mushrooms and cook 10 more minutes. Add water if needed. When done, remove from heat, pour off any excess water. Cover and let stand about 10 minutes. Yield: 4 servings.

Note: If brown rice instructions require more than 20 minutes cooking time, add earlier as needed. Brown rice cook times vary 20 to 45 minutes.

Wild Rice Casserole

Laura Crouch

1 (6-ounce) package Uncle Ben's Wild Rice mix	1 cup chopped ripe olives
	2 1/4 cups water
1 cup mushrooms, chopped	1/2 stick margarine

Preheat oven to 350 degrees. In a large bowl, combine rice, mushrooms, olives, and water. Mix well. Pour into a greased 2-quart casserole dish. Dot top with margarine slices. Bake, covered, at 350 degrees for 1 hour and 30 minutes. Yield: 6 to 8 servings.

Red Beans and Rice
Melinda Sansbury

1	(16-ounce) package dry red kidney beans		Black pepper
	Tony Chachere's Cajun Creole Seasoning	1	(16-ounce) package Hillshire Farms smoked sausage, cut into bite-sized pieces
	Red pepper flakes	2	large onions, chopped
	Salt		Cooked rice

Wash bean thoroughly, strain. Put beans in a large pot and cover with two times water, soak overnight. Pour off water. After soaking, cook beans on medium low heat 2 hours or until tender. Add seasonings; amount depends on how spicy you prefer beans to be. The longer cooked the better. Put sausage in a skillet and stir-fry until lightly browned. Remove from skillet. In drippings, sauté onion until tender. Remove onion with slotted spoon and add to beans. Stir sausage into beans. Serve over rice. Yield: 8 to 10 servings.

Note: Even better after it sits in refrigerator overnight!

Baked Acorn Squash
Frances Kelley

2	medium acorn squash	4	tablespoons packed brown sugar
4	tablespoons butter or margarine, melted		Salt and pepper to taste

Preheat oven to 400 degrees. Cut squash into halves, lengthwise; remove seeds. In a shallow baking pan, place halves cut side down. Bake at 400 degrees for 30 minutes. Turn cut side up; sprinkle with butter, sugar, salt, and pepper. Bake 30 more minutes. Yield: 4 servings.

Squash Casserole
Cindy Lowe

8-10 yellow squash, sliced	1/2 (8-ounce) package cream
2-3 large chicken breast	cheese, may use a little more
cooked, boned, cut in bite-	1 cup sour cream
sized pieces	21/2 cups Pepperidge Farm
1 (103/4-ounce) can cream of	Stuffing mix, divided
mushroom soup	1 (41/2-ounce) jar sliced
21/2 cups grated sharp Cheddar	mushrooms (optional)
cheese, divided	Salt and pepper to taste

Preheat oven to 350 degrees. Spray a 3-quart casserole dish with nonstick cooking spray. In a large saucepan, cook squash in a little water until soft; drain. Add chicken, soup and two cups of cheese to squash. Stir in cream cheese, sour cream, two cups of stuffing mix, and drained mushrooms. Salt and pepper to taste. Cook over low heat about 30 minutes. Pour mixture into prepared dish and top with remaining cheese and stuffing mix. Bake at 350 degrees for 30 minutes or until bubbly. Yield: 8 servings.

Squash Parmesan Casserole
Kathy McCall

4 medium yellow squash, sliced	1 egg, beaten
1 medium onion, sliced	1/2 cup milk
1/4 cup water	1/2 cup Parmesan cheese
2 teaspoons sugar	2 tablespoons melted margarine
3/4 teaspoon salt	

In a medium saucepan, combine squash, onion, water, sugar, and salt. Cook over medium heat until tender. Drain off excess liquid. Transfer to a medium bowl and beat until smooth. Add egg, milk, cheese, and margarine. Pour into a greased 2-quart casserole. Bake at 350 degrees for 45 minutes. Mixture will be set and top slightly browned. Yield: 6 to 8 servings.

Crisp Buttered Zucchini

Debbie Brown

4 medium zucchini squash	1/8 teaspoon black pepper
1/4 cup butter	Pinch sugar
1/2 teaspoon garlic salt	

Coarsely shred zucchini. Melt butter in a skillet, add squash and seasonings. Cover and cook over medium heat 8 to 10 minutes, stirring once. Yield: 4 servings.

Squash-Zucchini Grill

Phillip Crocker

4 squash, thinly sliced	2 cups Italian dressing
4 zucchini, thinly sliced	1/2 cup teriyaki sauce

Put squash in a large resealable bag. Pour next two ingredients over squash and marinate several hours. Grill on medium heat until browned and tender. Yield: 6 to 8 servings.

Zucchini Stuffed Tomatoes

Kathy Boyd

4 tomatoes, nicely shaped, uniform in size	1 medium onion, chopped
4 tablespoons butter or margarine	1/2 teaspoon salt
	1/2 teaspoon sugar
3 medium zucchini, diced	1/4 teaspoon basil
1/2 pound mushrooms, sliced	Black pepper
	1 cup croutons

Preheat oven to 350 degrees. Cut a thin slice from each tomato top; scoop out pulp and chop, leaving a one-fourth inch shell. In a skillet, melt butter. Add tomato pulp, zucchini and next six ingredients. Cook about 10 minutes, until most of liquid evaporates. Stir in croutons. Fill tomato shells with vegetable mixture. Bake at 350 degrees for 20 minutes. Yield: 4 servings.

Tomato Casserole

Mary Lutie Fletcher

1 (16-ounce) can stewed tomatoes	1 tablespoon grated onion
1 (8-ounce) package grated mozzarella cheese, divided	3/4 teaspoon black pepper
3 slices bread, toasted and cubed	1/2 stick butter, melted

Preheat oven to 375 degrees. Reserve some cheese and set aside to top casserole. In a large bowl, combine tomatoes, remaining cheese, and next four ingredients. Pour into a 1 1/2-quart casserole. Top with reserved cheese. Bake at 375 degrees for 20 minutes. Yield: 4 to 6 servings.

Note: Good served with beef tenderloin, wild rice and a mixed salad.

Tomato Pie

Shelia Gandy

1 (9-inch) deep dish pie crust, unbaked	5 slices bacon, cooked and crumbled
4-5 medium tomatoes, peeled and sliced	3/4 cup Miracle Whip
1 large Vidalia onion, sliced	1 1/2 cups grated sharp Cheddar cheese

Preheat oven to 350 degrees. Bake pie crust 10 minutes. Layer one-half of tomatoes, onion, remaining tomatoes, bacon, mayonnaise, and cheese. Bake at 350 degrees for 30 to 25 minutes. Yield: 6 to 8 servings.

Tomato Pie

Beth Clark

1	(9-inch) Pillsbury deep dish pie crust	1	tablespoon fresh chopped chives
2	tomatoes, peeled and sliced	1	cup Duke's mayonnaise
	Salt and pepper to taste	1	cup grated sharp Cheddar cheese
2-3	green onions, chopped		
1	tablespoon fresh chopped basil		

Cook pie crust according to package directions, cool. Preheat oven to 350 degrees. Sprinkle tomatoes with salt and let drain on paper towel 10 minutes. Layer tomatoes, onions, basil, chives, salt, and pepper in pie crust. In a medium bowl, blend mayonnaise and cheese. Spread over top of pie. Bake 30 to 40 minutes or until top is brown and bubbly. Let sit 10 to 15 minutes before serving. Yield: 6 to 8 servings.

Mary Nell's Tomato Pie

Laura Dawkins

3	medium tomatoes, peeled and sliced	1	cup Helmann's mayonnaise
2	onions, sliced	1	cup grated sharp Cheddar cheese
1	(9-inch) deep dish pie crust, unbaked		Dash of basil

Preheat oven to 350 degrees. Layer tomatoes and onion in pie crust. In a medium bowl, combine mayonnaise and cheese and mix well. Spread over top of pie. Sprinkle with basil. Bake at 350 degrees for 50 minutes. Yield: 8 servings

Tomato and Spinach Casserole

Pam Newsome

4   large tomatoes, sliced
    Olive oil
    Dried breadcrumbs
1   (16-ounce) package frozen
    chopped spinach
1   cup sliced mushrooms
1   onion, chopped
1/2 stick margarine

3   eggs, beaten
1   (8-ounce) container cottage
    cheese
1/3 cup mayonnaise
1/2 cup Parmesan cheese
1   cup grated sharp Cheddar
    cheese

Preheat oven to 350 degrees. Coat tomatoes in olive oil and cover with bread crumbs. Cook spinach in microwave according to package directions; squeeze dry. In a saucepan, sauté onion and mushrooms in margarine until tender. In a medium bowl, combine spinach, onion, and mushrooms. In a separate bowl, combine eggs and next three ingredients. Layer a 9x13-inch casserole dish with one-half of tomato, one-half spinach mixture and one-half egg mixture. Repeat layers. Top with Cheddar cheese. Bake at 350 degrees for 30 to 45 minutes. Yield: 6 to 8 servings.

Apricot Soufflé

Margaret Galloway

3   (15-ounce) cans chopped
    apricots, drained
1   sleeve Ritz crackers,
    crushed

1   cup light brown sugar
3/4 cup melted butter

Preheat oven to 325 degrees. Pour apricots in a greased 2-quart casserole dish. In a small bowl, combine crackers and sugar; mix well. Top casserole with cracker mixture and drizzle with butter. Bake at 325 degrees for 30 minutes. Yield: 8 to 10 servings.

Note: Can make ahead and heat to serve.

Apricot Delights
Vermelle King

Apricot halves
Orange marmalade

Butter
Dried garden mint

Preheat oven to 350 degrees. Drain apricots. Put in baking dish and put about 1 teaspoon marmalade in each apricot. Add a slice of butter to top and sprinkle with mint. Bake at 350 degrees until bubbly hot. Yield: 2 halves per serving.

Notes: Canned peach halves may be used instead of apricots. Good with pork or chicken.

Cranberry Casserole
Lisa Gabriel

3 cups chopped McIntosh apples
2 (16-ounce) cans Oceanspray whole cranberry sauce
1 cup sugar

1 1/2 cups oatmeal
1/2 cup brown sugar
1/3 cup flour
1/2 cup melted butter
1/2 cup chopped pecans

Preheat oven to 325 degrees. In a large bowl, combine apples, cranberry sauce, and sugar. Pour into a greased 9x13-inch casserole dish. In a separate bowl, combine oatmeal and next three ingredients, mix well. Pour oatmeal mixture over apple mixture. Top with pecans. Bake at 325 degrees for 50 minutes to 1 hour. Yield: 12 servings.

Spiced Peaches

Anne Dawkins

2 (29-ounce) cans clingstone
   peach halves
1 1/3 cups sugar

1 cup cider vinegar
4 cinnamon sticks, broken
2 teaspoons whole cloves

Drain peaches, reserving syrup. Combine peach syrup and remaining ingredients in a saucepan. Bring mixture to boil; lower heat, and simmer 10 minutes. Pour hot syrup over peach halves; let cool. Chill thoroughly before serving. Store in refrigerator. Yield: about 4 pints.

Judy's Apple and Cheese Casserole

Shirley McCutchen

2 (15-ounce) cans sliced
   apples, not pie filling
1 stick margarine
1 cup sugar

1 (8-ounce) box Velvetta,
   softened
3/4 cup self-rising flour

Preheat oven to 350 degrees. Place undrained apples in a greased 9x13-inch casserole dish. In a mixing bowl, cream together margarine, sugar, cheese, and flour. Spread and press mixture over apples. Bake at 350 degrees for 30 to 40 minutes. Yield: 8 to 10 servings.

Note: Wonderful with turkey or ham.

Apple Casserole

Judy Collins

2 (15-ounce) cans sliced apples	1 sleeve Ritz crackers
1/2 cup sugar	1 cup sharp Cheddar cheese,
5 tablespoons self-rising flour	grated
1 stick margarine, melted	

Preheat oven to 350 degrees. Grease a 2-quart casserole dish. Drain apples, reserve juice. In a medium bowl, combine sugar and flour. Pour in one-half cup of juice and mix well. Place apples in prepared dish. Pour sugar mixture over apple and sprinkle with cheese. Crumble crackers over cheese and pour butter over top. Bake at 350 degrees for 25 to 30 minutes. Yield: 6 to 8 servings.

Note: May substitute 2 (15 1/4-ounce) cans crushed pineapple for apples.

Pineapple Casserole

Sherry Phillips

1 cup sugar	2 (15 1/4-ounce) cans pineapple
6 tablespoons self-rising flour	tidbits, drained
2 cups shredded Cheddar	30 Ritz crackers, crushed
cheese	1 stick melted butter

Preheat oven to 350 degrees. In a large bowl, combine sugar, flour, and cheese. Stir pineapple into sugar mixture. Pour into a 9x12-inch greased baking dish. Sprinkle cracker crumbs over top and drizzle with melted butter. Bake at 350 degrees for 30 minutes. Yield: 6 to 8 servings.

Libby's Pineapple Casserole
Libby Bannister

3	eggs	2	sticks margarine
1/2	cup sugar	6	slices white bread, cubed with
2	tablespoons self-rising flour		an electric knife
1	(20-ounce) can crushed pineapple		

Preheat oven to 350 degrees. In a large bowl, beat egg, sugar, and flour. Add crushed pineapple. In a skillet, melt butter. Stir in bread, add pineapple mixture. Pour into a 2-quart casserole dish. Bake, uncovered, for 45 minutes. Yield: 4 to 6 servings.

Note: Great with ham or chicken. Very rich, but so-o-o good!

California Garden Pizza
Leanne Lowman

1	pizza crust	1	medium cucumber, thinly
1/2	(1-ounce) package dry salad		sliced
	mix, dressing of choice		Mushrooms, sliced
4	ounces light cream cheese,	1	medium tomato, sliced
	softened	1	avocado, sliced
	Bean sprouts of choice		Salt
	Romaine lettuce, torn in		Black pepper
	small pieces		

Use any type of pizza crust and cook according to package directions until lightly browned. Do not overcook. It will be too crispy. In a small bowl, combine dressing mix with cream cheese and mix well. Spread evenly over warm pizza crust. Cover pizza with a layer bean sprouts and next five ingredients. Add salt and pepper to taste. Yield: 1 pizza .

Marinated Vegetables
Miriam Norwood

2 (11-ounce) cans shoe peg corn
2 (15-ounce) cans LeSueur peas
1 bell pepper, diced
4 ribs celery, diced
1 (2-ounce) jar chopped pimentos

2-3 onions, sliced or chopped
1/2 cup Mazola or canola oil
1 cup white vinegar
1 cup sugar
1 tablespoon salt
1 tablespoon water
Dash black pepper

Drain all liquids. In a large container, combine corn and next five ingredients. In a medium bowl, combine oil and remaining ingredients, mix well. Pour over vegetables. Let stand 24 hours in refrigerator before serving. Yield: 10 to 12 servings.

Note: Thawed frozen vegetables may be used after draining all liquids.

Vegetable Casserole
JoFreida Kelley

1 (29-ounce) can mixed vegetables
1 (10¾-ounce) can cream of chicken soup
1 stick butter

1/2 cup mayonnaise
1 small onion, chopped
1 cup grated Cheddar cheese
1 (8-ounce) can water chestnuts
1 sleeve Ritz crackers

Drain vegetables and pour in a large bowl. Add soup and next five ingredients and mix well. Pour into a 9x13-inch casserole dish. Crumble crackers on top and bake at 350 degrees for 30 minutes. Yield: 6 servings.

Vegetable Quiche

Vicki Norment

2 (10-ounce) packages chopped frozen spinach
1/2 cup chopped green onions
1 clove garlic, minced
2 tablespoons olive oil
1 1/2 cups shredded Swiss cheese
3 eggs, slightly beaten

3/4 cup milk
1 teaspoon salt
1 teaspoon basil leaf
1/2 teaspoon celery salt
1 (9-inch) pie crust, unbaked
2-3 Roma tomatoes, thinly sliced
Parmesan cheese

Cook spinach according to package directions and drain well. In a saucepan, sauté onions and garlic in oil. Add spinach and cook until mixture is dry. In a large bowl, combine Swiss cheese, eggs, milk, and seasonings. Add spinach mixture and mix well. Pour mixture into pie crust. Arrange tomatoes in a circle around outer edge and sprinkle each slice with Parmesan cheese. Bake, uncovered, at 350 degrees for 30 minutes or until center is set. Yield: 8 servings.

Note: Mixture may be prepared at least two days ahead and then put into pie crust at last minute.

★ Sweets ★

Annie Lea Brown, D Brown,
Lauren Brown, Alex Brown 11,
Katie Dawkins
Benton Boyd and Weldon Boyd
MaMa and her great grandchildren
on her 90th birthday in 1993.

MaMa had 5 grandchildren and 6 great grandchildren. Growing up, it was a treat to go our grandparents house. Da, our grandfather, was a great big kid and he would join in with all of his grandchildren. Playing chase, being a monster, swimming or teasing, he was as loud as we were. He might have enjoyed it more than we did. MaMa was quiet and would sit back and watch. She was probably amazed at all of the commotion. The family would eat Sunday dinner at their house and the food was delicious. MaMa was a great cook. I really remember her desserts! She baked a lot and always had something wonderful.

I was in the 9th grade when my grandfather died so he didn't have the joy of watching us grow up and have families of our own. MaMa watched us grow up and she did enjoy her great grandchildren. Our children had family dinners with her just as we had when we were children. They enjoyed going to see her as much as we did.

MaMa died in March of 1995 at the age of 92 but happy family memories still live in all of us.

Be completely humble and gentle;
be patient, bearing with one another
in love.

Ephesians 4:2

Banana Fiesta Cake

Annie Lea Brown
Submitted by Kathy Boyd

1/2 cup shortening	1 cup mashed ripe bananas
2 cups cake flour	1 teaspoon vanilla
1 teaspoon baking powder	1/2 cup chopped nuts
1 teaspoon soda	2 eggs (unbeaten)
3/4 teaspoon salt	Heavy cream
1 1/3 cups sugar	Powdered sugar to taste
1/2 cup minus 2 tablespoons sour milk or buttermilk, divided	

Preheat oven to 375 degrees. In a large mixing bowl, stir shortening to soften. Add dry ingredients, one-fourth cup of milk, bananas; mix thoroughly. Add remaining ingredients and mix well. Pour batter into three greased and floured 9-inch round cake pans. Bake at 375 degrees until straw comes out clean. In a medium bowl, whip cream, add powdered sugar to taste. Frost between layers, on top and sides of cooled cake. Yield: 16 to 20 servings.

Applesauce Cake

Carol O'Day

1 cup butter	2 teaspoons cinnamon
3 1/2 cups applesauce	1 teaspoon nutmeg
4 cups all-purpose flour	1/2 teaspoon allspice
2 cups sugar	2 cups nuts
2 teaspoons salt	2 cups raisins
2 teaspoons baking soda	

Preheat oven to 350 degrees. In a large saucepan, combine butter and applesauce, stirring until butter melts. Remove from heat. In a large bowl, sift flour and next six ingredients. Blend in applesauce mixture. Stir in nuts and raisins, mix well. Pour batter into a greased and floured 9x13-inch baking dish. Bake at 350 degrees for 50 minutes. To serve, frost with sour cream or vanilla icing. Yield: 16 to 20 servings.

Gooey Butter Cake

Allison Evans

Cake

1	(18 1/4-ounce) box yellow cake mix
1	egg

1	stick melted butter or margarine

Topping

1	(8-ounce) package cream cheese, softened
2	eggs

1	(16-ounce) box powdered sugar

Preheat oven to 350 degrees. In a mixing bowl, mix all cake ingredients and press into a 9x13-inch baking dish. Beat all topping ingredients in a medium bowl and spread over cake mixture. Bake at 350 degrees for 30 minutes. Yield: 16 to 20 servings.

Fresh Apple Cake

Jane Norris

3	cups all-purpose flour		1 1/2	teaspoons baking powder
2	teaspoons baking soda		1	cup cooking oil
2	teaspoons cinnamon		2	eggs
2	cups sugar		4	cups diced sour apples
1	teaspoon salt		1	cup nuts

Preheat oven to 325 degrees. Grease and flour a 10-inch tube pan. In a large mixing bowl, combine all dry ingredients. Add oil and eggs, mix well. Stir in apples and nuts. Pour into prepared pan. Bake at 325 degrees for 1 hour. Yield: 16 to 20 servings.

Banana Split Cake
Jennie Wright

2 cups graham cracker crumbs	3-4 bananas
2 sticks butter or margarine, divided	1 (16-ounce) container Cool Whip
2 cups powdered sugar	Cherries
2 eggs	Chopped pecans
1 (20-ounce) can crushed pineapple, drained	

In a medium bowl, combine cracker crumbs and one-half stick of butter. Press into bottom of a 9x13-inch dish. In a medium bowl, mix remaining butter, sugar, and eggs. Beat with an electric mixer 15 minutes or until consistency of whipped cream. Spread over crust. Slice bananas and place over filling. Pour pineapple over bananas and spread whipped topping over all. Sprinkle generously with nuts and decorate with cherries. Yield: 12 to 16 servings.

No Bake Banana Split Cake
Kathy Lee

2 cups crushed vanilla wafers	1 (8-ounce) container Cool Whip
1 stick melted margarine	1 cup shredded coconut
4 bananas	1 cup chopped nuts
1 (14-ounce) can condensed milk	1 (6-ounce) jar maraschino cherries
1/4 cup lemon juice	
1 (20-ounce) can crushed pineapple, drained	

In a medium bowl, combine vanilla wafers and margarine. Press into bottom of a 9x13-inch dish. Slice bananas and place over crumbs. Mix condensed milk and lemon juice in a small bowl and pour over bananas. Spread pineapple over milk mixture and whipped topping over pineapple. Sprinkle with coconut, nuts, and cherries. Refrigerate overnight. Yield: 12 to 16 servings.

Cheesecake

Eleanor Cannarella

Submitted by Lucy Brown

Pastry

1 cup all-purpose flour, sifted	1 egg yolk, beaten
1/2 cup sugar	1/4 cup melted butter
1/4 teaspoon salt	1/4 teaspoon vanilla
1 teaspoon lemon zest	

Filling

21/2 pounds cream cheese	1/4 cup heavy cream
13/4 cups sugar	11/2 teaspoons orange zest
3 tablespoons flour	11/2 teaspoons lemon zest
5 eggs	1/4 teaspoon salt
2 egg yolks	

To make pastry, combine all dry ingredients and lemon zest in a large bowl and make a well in the center. Add egg yolk, butter, and vanilla. Work together quickly until well blended. Add a little cold water if necessary to hold together. Wrap in wax paper and chill thoroughly in refrigerator for about 1 hour. Roll dough out to a 1/8-inch thickness and place over bottom of a greased 9-inch springform pan. Trim off excess dough. Bake at 400 degrees for 15 to 20 minutes or until light golden brown. Cool. Grease sides of pan and place over base. Roll remaining dough to a 1/8-inch thickness and line sides of pan. Fill with filling.

For filling, in a mixing bowl, beat cream cheese with an electric mixer until smooth. Add sugar gradually. Add eggs one at the time and then add remaining ingredients in order given, blend well. Mixture should be smooth. Pour into pastry-lined pan. Bake at 550 degrees for 12 to 15 minutes and reduce heat to 200 degrees and bake 1 hour. Cool before cutting. Yield: 8 to 10 servings.

Blueberry Cream Cheesecake
Linda Stanton

Cracker Crust
2 sticks melted margarine
1 cup graham cracker crumbs
1 cup all-purpose flour
1/2 cup powdered sugar
1 cup chopped pecans

Cream Cheese Filling
1 (8-ounce) package cream cheese, softened
1 (15-ounce) can sweetened condensed milk
1/3 cup lemon juice
1 teaspoon vanilla extract

Blueberry Glaze
1 cup water
2 cups fresh blueberries, washed and drained, divided
1 cup sugar
2 tablespoons cornstarch

Preheat oven to 375 degrees. Spray a 9x13-inch baking dish with nonstick cooking spray. For crust, pour margarine in a medium bowl. In a separate bowl, combine all dry ingredients and pecans. Mix with butter and press in prepared dish. Bake at 375 degrees for 10 minutes. Cool.

For cream cheese filling, in a medium bowl, whip cream cheese until fluffy. Gradually add milk and blend until smooth. Add lemon juice and vanilla. Spread on top of crust. Chill.

For glaze, in a medium saucepan, combine one cup of blueberries and water. Bring to boil. In a small bowl, combine sugar and cornstarch. Gradually stir into blueberry mixture. Cook over medium heat stirring constantly until thickened. Cool and add remaining blueberries. Spread glaze over filling. Chill and serve. Yield: 12 to 16 servings.

Eddie Mae's Cheesecake

Eddie Mae Reynolds

1   (12-ounce) can evaporated
    milk
20 double graham crackers
1 1/4 sticks butter or margarine,
    melted
1   (3-ounce) package lemon
    jello

1   cup hot water
1   cup sugar
1   (8-ounce) package cream
    cheese

Chill milk overnight. In a large bowl, crumble crackers and add butter, mix well. Reserve a few crumbs to garnish top of cake and press the remaining in a 9x13-inch dish. In a small bowl, dissolve jello in water. Let cool but not gel. In a mixing bowl, cream sugar and cream cheese. In a separate bowl, whip milk until it peaks. Add jello, sugar and cream cheese to milk, mix well. Pour over cracker crumbs. Sprinkle with reserved crumbs. Refrigerate 2 hours before serving. Yield: 12 to 16 servings.

Easy Coconut Cake

Chrisie Raines

1   (18 1/4-ounce) box yellow cake
    mix
1 1/2 cups sugar
1   (8-ounce) container sour
    cream
1   teaspoon almond flavoring

1   (14-ounce) bag shredded
    coconut, divided
1 1/2 cups Cool Whip

Preheat oven to 350 degrees. Grease and flour two 8-inch round cake pans. Prepare cake mix according to package directions. Pour batter into prepared pans and bake at 350 degrees for 30 minutes. Cool. Cut layers in half to make four round, thin layers. In a large bowl, mix sugar, sour cream, and flavoring together. Stir in one-half bag of coconut. Do not beat. Fill between layers of cake with coconut mixture. Add whipped topping to leftover mixture and blend together. Frost top and sides of cake. Sprinkle with remaining coconut. Yield: 10 to 12 servings.

Date Cake with Broiled Icing

Joan Hutto

Cake

1	cup boiling water	1	egg
1	cup chopped dates	1 1/2	cups all-purpose flour, sifted
1	teaspoon soda	1	teaspoon salt
1/2	cup shortening	1	teaspoon vanilla
1	cup sugar		

Icing

4	tablespoons butter or margarine, melted	2	tablespoons milk
1/2	cup brown sugar	1	cup shredded coconut or chopped nuts

Preheat oven to 350 degrees. Grease and flour a 9x13-inch baking dish. In a small bowl, pour boiling water over dates and soda and set aside. In a mixing bowl, cream shortening and sugar. Add egg and beat. Mix flour and salt; add alternately with date mixture to creamed mixture and blend. Stir in vanilla. Pour into prepared pan. Bake at 350 degrees for 25 minutes or until done.

For icing, immediately after cake is baked, combine all ingredients in a medium bowl. Spread evenly over cake and place under broiler until lightly browned. Yield: 12 to 16 servings.

Favorite Layer Cake

Eddie Mae Reynolds

2	sticks butter	3	cups self-rising flour
2	cups sugar	1	cup milk
5	eggs	1	teaspoon vanilla flavoring

Preheat oven 350 degrees. In a mixing bowl, cream butter and sugar until light and fluffy. Add eggs one at the time, beating well after each addition. Sift flour and add alternately with milk. Stir in vanilla and blend well. Pour batter into three greased and floured 9-inch round cake pans. Bake at 350 degrees for about 30 minutes. For six thin layers, cool cake and cut each layer in half. Frost with your favorite frosting! Yield: 16 to 20 servings.

Mom's Pineapple Cake
Karen Jeffords

Cake

1   stick margarine, softened
1   (18 1/4-ounce) bow yellow
    cake mix
2   eggs

1   cup milk
1   teaspoon vanilla

Topping

1   (20-ounce) can crushed
    unsweetened pineapple
1   (8-ounce) can crushed
    unsweetened pineapple

3   tablespoons cornstarch
1 1/2 cups sugar

Preheat oven 350 degrees. Grease and flour four 9-inch cake pans. In a mixing bowl, cream butter and add cake mix, eggs, milk, and vanilla. Beat well. Pour batter into prepared pans.

For topping, place all ingredients in a saucepan. Boil until slightly thickened. Remove from heat and refrigerate at least 30 minutes. Spread topping between layers and on sides and top of cake. Yield: 16 to 20 servings.

Doris' Pecan Cake
Doris Atkinson

4   sticks butter
2   cups sugar
6   eggs, beaten
4   cups all-purpose flour,
    divided
1/4 teaspoon salt

1/2 pound candied cherries
1/2 pound candied pineapple
1   pound pecans, chopped
2   teaspoon vanilla

Preheat oven to 250 degrees. Grease and flour a 10-inch tube pan. In a mixing bowl, cream butter and sugar, add eggs. Add three cups of sifted flour, blend well. In a medium bowl, mix remaining flour with cherries, pineapple, and nuts. Stir mixture into batter, add vanilla. Pour batter into prepared pan. Bake at 250 degrees for 3 hours. Allow to cool in pan. Yield: 16 to 20 servings.

Nut Cake

Brenda Barfield

1	(9-ounce) box white raisins	2	sticks butter
4	cups pecans, chopped	2	cups sugar
3	cups self-rising flour	5	eggs

Preheat oven 325 degrees. Grease and flour a 10-inch tube pan. Put raisins in a saucepan and cover with water, bring to a boil. Strain. Add nuts. In a medium bowl, combine flour with raisins and nuts. Add butter, sugar, and eggs; mix well. Pour batter into prepared pan. Bake at 325 degrees for 1 hour and 30 minutes. Yield: 16 to 20 servings.

Peter Paul Mound Cake

Anna Laura McElveen

Cake

1	(18 1/4-ounce) box devil's food cake mix	1	teaspoon vanilla
3	teaspoons baking powder	3	eggs
1 1/4	cups buttermilk		

Filling

1 1/4	cups sugar	25	large marshmallows
1	(12-ounce) can evaporated milk	2	cups shredded coconut

Preheat oven to 350 degrees. Grease and flour three or four 10-inch round cake pans. In a large bowl mix all cake ingredients together. Pour batter into prepared pans. Bake at 350 degrees for 25 minutes.

For filling, in a saucepan, bring milk and sugar to boil and turn heat down to low. Add marshmallows, stirring to dissolve. Add coconut and mix well. Spread on layers. Keep refrigerated. Yield: 20 servings.

Fudge Sauce Pudding Cake

Debra Sellers

First Mixture

1   cup self-rising flour
2   tablespoons cocoa
3/4 cup sugar

1/2 cup milk
2   teaspoons cooking oil

Second Mixture

1   cup sugar
2   tablespoons cocoa

1/4 teaspoon salt
1 3/4 cups boiling water

Preheat oven to 350 degrees. For first mixture, combine all ingredients and mix well. Pour into a 9-inch square baking dish. For second mixture, combine sugar, cocoa, and salt in a sifter and sift over first mixture. Pour water over top. Bake at 350 degrees for 45 minutes. Yield: 6 to 8 servings.

Note: A thick sauce will form on bottom of cake. Great with vanilla ice cream!

Chocolate Pound Cake

Jane Sowell

2   sticks butter or margarine
1/2 cup Crisco
3   cups sugar, divided
5   eggs
3   cups all-purpose flour

1/2 cup cocoa
1/2 teaspoon salt
1   cup milk
1   teaspoon vanilla

Preheat oven 325 degrees. Grease and flour a 10-inch tube pan. In a mixing bowl, cream butter and shortening. Add one and one-half cups of sugar, beating until thoroughly mixed. Add remaining sugar. Beat well. Add eggs one at the time, mixing well after each addition. Sift together flour, cocoa, and salt. Reserve one-fourth cup of flour. Set aside. Add remaining flour in three parts alternating with milk, mix well. Add vanilla. Mix in the reserved flour and beat well. Pour batter into prepared pan. Bake at 325 degrees for 1 hour and 25 minutes. Yield: 16 to 20 servings.

Esther's Pound Cake

Diane Fedorchuk

3	cups sugar	1/2	teaspoon baking powder
1/2	cup Crisco	1	cup milk
2	sticks butter	1	teaspoon vanilla extract
5	eggs	1	teaspoon lemon or almond
3	cups cake flour		flavoring (optional)

Preheat oven 325 degrees. Grease and flour a 10-inch tube pan. In a mixing bowl, mix sugar, shortening and butter until creamy. Add eggs one at the time, mixing well after each addition. Sift together flour and baking powder. Alternately add flour and milk, mix well. Stir in vanilla and flavoring. Pour batter into prepared pan. Bake at 325 degrees for 1 hour and 15 minutes. Yield: 16 to 20 servings.

Mama's Pound Cake

Nancy Bell

2	sticks butter	1	teaspoon lemon extract
3	cups sugar	3	cups all-purpose flour
6	eggs, room temperature	1/2	pint whipping cream
1	teaspoon vanilla extract		

Grease and flour a 10-inch tube pan. In a mixing bowl, cream butter and sugar with an electric mixer. Add eggs one at the time, mixing well after each addition until mixture is creamy. Add vanilla and lemon extract. Alternately add flour and cream. Mix well. Pour batter into prepared pan and put in a cold oven. Turn oven to 325 degrees and bake for 1 hour and 30 minutes or until wooden pick comes out clean. Cool 20 minutes before removing from pan. Yield: 16 to 20 servings.

Pound Cake

Evelyn Cromer

3   sticks butter
3   cups sugar
3   cups all-purpose flour
1   teaspoon baking powder

Pinch of salt
1   cup whole canned milk
1   teaspoon vanilla extract
1   teaspoon lemon extract

Preheat oven 300 degrees. Grease and flour a 10-inch tube pan. In a mixing bowl, cream butter and sugar. Add eggs one at the time, beating well after each addition. Sift together flour, baking powder, and salt. Alternately add flour and milk to mixture; beat thoroughly. Stir in vanilla and lemon. Pour batter into prepared pan. Bake at 300 degrees for 1 hour and 30 minutes. Cool in pan 10 minutes and remove. Yield: 16 to 20 servings.

Sour Cream Pound Cake

Lisa Fagan

3   sticks Land o Lakes sweet
    cream butter
3   cups sugar
6   eggs
1   tablespoon vanilla extract

1   teaspoon lemon extract
3   cups all-purpose flour
1/4   teaspoon baking soda
1   heaping cup sour cream

Preheat oven to 325 degrees. Grease and flour a 10-inch tube pan. In a mixing bowl, cream butter and sugar. Add eggs one at the time, mixing well after each addition until mixture is creamy. Add vanilla and lemon. Sift together flour and baking soda. Alternately add one cup of flour at a time with sour cream. Mix well. Pour batter into prepared pan. Bake at 325 degrees for 1 hour and 15 minutes. Yield: 20 servings.

Pumpkin Cake

Diana Skinner
Submitted by Janie Campbell

1 1/2 sticks butter
    Mazola oil
3   cups all-purpose flour
2   teaspoons baking powder
2   teaspoons baking soda

2   teaspoons cinnamon
4   eggs, separated
2   cups sugar
2   cups mashed pumpkin

Preheat oven to 350 degrees. In a saucepan, melt butter and pour in a 2 cup measuring cup. Add oil until it reaches one and one-fourth cups. Sift flour, baking powder, soda, and cinnamon together. In a large bowl, beat egg yolks until lemon yellow. Beat in sugar and oil. Add pumpkin and beat well. Add dry ingredients a little at the time, beating well after each addition. In a separate bowl, beat egg whites until stiff and fold in mixture. Pour batter into a 10-inch greased and floured tube pan. Bake at 350 degrees for 1 hour. Yield: 16 to 20 servings.

Punch Bowl Cake

Shirley McCutchen

1   prepared angel food cake
1   (16-ounce) container Cool Whip
1   (16-ounce) container sour cream
1   (16-ounce) box powdered sugar

1   (5-ounce) can evaporated milk
1   pint chopped strawberries or 1 (16-ounce) package frozen
1   (16-ounce) package strawberry glaze

Tear cake into bite-sized pieces and place in a punch bowl. In a large bowl, combine next four ingredients. Pour mixture over cake and blend together with cake. In a medium bowl, combine strawberries and glaze. Add a little sugar if not sweet enough. Pour mixture over cake. Refrigerate overnight. Yield: 15 to 20 servings.

Tropical Delight Cake
Susan Crowder

Cake

2   cups cake flour
1/2   teaspoon salt
2   teaspoons baking soda
2   eggs, beaten
1/2   cup honey
3/4   cup chopped walnuts

21/2   cups unsweetened crushed
      pineapple with juice
1   cup chopped dates
1/2   cup shredded coconut
1/4   cup dry milk powder
      (optional)
1/4   cup wheat germ

Frosting

1   (8-ounce) package cream
    cheese, softened
1   stick butter
2-4 tablespoons honey

1   teaspoon vanilla extract
1/2   cup chopped nuts (optional)

Preheat oven to 350 degrees. Grease and flour a 10-inch tube pan. In a large bowl, combine flour, salt, and soda. Combine all remaining ingredients and mix well. Pour batter into prepared pan. Bake at 350 degrees for 35 to 40 minutes. For the frosting, in a medium bowl, beat cream cheese and butter until fluffy. Beat in honey to taste. Add vanilla. Stir in nuts. Keep refrigerated. Yield: 16 to 20 servings.

Seven Minute White Icing
Kathy Boyd

11/2 cups sugar
2   egg whites
1/3 cup water

1/4   teaspoon cream of tartar
1   tablespoon light corn syrup
1   teaspoon vanilla

Combine ingredients in the top of a double boiler. Beat for 1 minute. Place over boiling water and cook constantly about 7 minutes or until mixture will form and hold stiff peaks. Remove from heat and stir in vanilla. Yield: Icing for a 2 layer cake.

Note: Mama made this icing when we were growing up. It is still one of our favorites with devil's food cake.

Chocolate Icing

Hazel Puyet

1 cup sugar	1 teaspoon vanilla extract
1/3 cup evaporated milk	1/2 cup pecans or walnuts
1/2 stick butter	(optional)
1 cup semisweet chocolate chips	

In a saucepan, combine sugar and milk and boil 2 minutes at rolling boil while stirring. Remove from heat. Stir in chocolate chips until they melt. Add vanilla. Pour while hot onto warm or cold cake layers, sweet muffins or sheet cake. Add nuts if desired. Yield: Icing for two 2 layer cakes or one 11x14-inch sheet cake.

Quick Fudge Icing

Eddie Mae Reynolds

1 cup sugar	1/2 cup milk
1/4 cup cocoa	1/8 teaspoon salt
1/2 stick margarine	1 1/2-2 cups powdered sugar
2 tablespoons white corn syrup	1 teaspoon vanilla

In a saucepan, combine sugar and next five ingredients. Stir and bring to full rolling boil. Cook about 3 minutes. Mixture must become thick and coat the spoon so be sure mixture boils hard. Cool. Beat in sugar and vanilla. Let stand until icing is of spreading consistency. Yield: Icing for a 3 layer cake.

German Chocolate Cake Frosting

Pat Hewitt

2 sticks butter	3 egg yolks
1 (12-ounce) can evaporated milk	Shredded coconut
	Chopped nuts
1 cup sugar	

In a medium bowl, melt butter in microwave. Add milk, sugar and eggs. Microwave on high for 4-5 minutes. Add desired amount of coconut and nuts. Yield: Icing for a 3 or 4 layer cake.

Grandmother's Caramel Icing
Joan Coker

4 1/2 cups light brown sugar
1 1/2 cups white sugar
2 1/4 cups whole milk

2 1/2 tablespoons light Karo syrup
1 1/2 sticks butter

Mix all ingredients and put in a heavy saucepan. Cook on high until icing comes to boil then reduce heat to low. Continue cooking until icing comes to soft boil (240 degrees on thermometer), stirring to keep from burning. Remove from heat, set aside, and let cool (without stirring) to 120 degrees. When cool, beat icing with a hand mixer until creamy and cool. If icing gets a little stiff, add Carnation or Pet milk. Yield: Icing for a 2 layer cake.

Almond Chocolate Torte
Mildred Sullivan

2/3 cups sliced almonds, toasted
8 (1-ounce) squares semisweet chocolate
2 (8-ounce) packages cream cheese, softened

1 cup sugar
1 (1/4-ounce) envelope unflavored gelatin
1/4 cup cold water
2 cups heavy cream, whipped

Set aside one tablespoon of almonds for garnish. Chop remaining almonds and sprinkle into a greased 9-inch springform pan. Melt chocolate in microwave or a heavy saucepan, stir until smooth. Cool slightly. In a mixing bowl, beat cream cheese and sugar. In a small saucepan, sprinkle gelatin over cold water; let stand one minute. Cook and stir over low heat until dissolved. Beat into cream cheese mixture. Add chocolate; beat until blended. Fold in whipped cream. Pour into prepared pan. Sprinkle with reserved almonds. Cover and refrigerate at least 3 hours. Yield: 10 to 12 servings.

Chocolate Strawberry Buttercream Torte

Kathy Varn

2   sticks plus 6 tablespoons
     unsalted butter, divided
2   cups powdered sugar, sifted
1/2 cup fresh strawberries,
     puréed
3   tablespoons strawberry
     preserves
2   (12.9-ounce) boxes brownie
     mix

3 1/2 cups pecans, finely ground
3   ounces semisweet chocolate
1/2 cup water
3   tablespoons safflower oil
3/4 cup unsweetened cocoa
     powder
3/4 cup granulated sugar
     Strawberries to garnish

Up to 1 day ahead, make buttercream. In a mixing bowl, cream two sticks of butter and powdered sugar until light and fluffy; mix in strawberries and preserves. Cover and refrigerate until set. At least eight hours before serving, make cake by preparing brownie mix according to package directions. Stir in pecans. Bake in two 9-inch cake pans as directed for cake-like brownies; cool. Cut layers in half horizontally. Spread buttercream over all layers except top. Refrigerate 6 hours. In the top part of a double boiler, combine chocolate, water, oil, and remaining butter. Heat over hot water until melted. Remove from heat; add cocoa and granulated sugar. Stir until smooth. Cool slightly. Pour over top and sides of cake. Arrange fresh strawberries on top. Remove from refrigerator 1 hour before serving. Yield: 10 to 12 servings.

Blueberry Torte

Lillian Galloway

Crust

2   cups graham cracker crumbs
3   tablespoons melted butter or
    margarine

1   teaspoon cinnamon

Cheese Filling

1   (8-ounce) package cream
    cheese
1/2 cup sugar

2   eggs
1   teaspoon vanilla flavoring

Blueberry Filling

1   (21-ounce) can blueberries
1/2 cup sugar
2 1/2 tablespoons lemon juice

2 1/2 tablespoons cornstarch
1   teaspoon vanilla flavoring

Topping

1   (12-ounce) container Cool
    Whip

1   cup powdered sugar
1   teaspoon vanilla flavoring

Preheat oven to 325 degrees. In a medium bowl, combine all ingredients for crust and mix well. Press into bottom of a 9-inch pie plate. For cheese filling combine all ingredients in a medium bowl and beat until smooth. Pour into crust. Bake at 325 degrees for 20 minutes. Combine all ingredients for blueberry filling in a saucepan. Cook over medium heat until thickened, cool. Spread over cheese layer. In a medium bowl, combine whipped topping, sugar, and vanilla; whip together. Spread topping over torte. Yield: 10 to 12 servings.

Angel Pie
Frances Hupfer

Crust

4 egg whites	1/2 teaspoon vanilla
1/2 teaspoon cream of tartar	1 cup sugar
1/8 teaspoon salt	

Filling

4 egg yolks	Dash salt
1 tablespoon lemon juice	1/2 cup whipped cream
1/2 cup crushed pineapple	1/2 cup grated coconut
1/2 cup sugar	

Preheat oven to 275 degrees. Generously grease a 9-inch pie plate. For pie crust, combine first four ingredients in a medium bowl and beat with an electric mixer until stiff. Very gradually add sugar and constantly beat until very stiff. Spread into prepared pie plate. Bake at 275 degrees for 1 hour or until delicate brown. It will fall in center when cooled for filling. In a saucepan, combine egg yolks and next four ingredients. Cook until fairly thick. Cool. Spread over meringue crust. Top with whipped cream and coconut. Yield: 6 to 8 servings.

Quick Chocolate Crunch Pie
Ammie Crocker

2 (3 1/2-ounce) Nestle's Crunch chocolate candy bars	2 cups Cool Whip
1/3 cup water	1 (9-inch) graham cracker crust
Dash of salt	

Combine candy, water and salt in a heavy saucepan. Stir over low heat until melted and smooth. Cool to room temperature. Fold in whipped topping. Spoon into crust. Chill for several hours before serving. Yield: 6 to 8 servings.

Chocolate Angel Pie

Louise DeLoach

Crust

3 egg whites	3/4 cup finely chopped nuts
1/8 teaspoon cream of tartar	1 teaspoon vanilla
Pinch of salt	4 ounces sweet chocolate
3/4 cup sifted sugar	

Filling

4 ounces sweet chocolate	1 teaspoon vanilla
3 tablespoons water	1 cup heavy cream

Preheat oven to 225 degrees. Generously grease a 9-inch pie plate. For pie crust, beat egg whites until foamy. Add cream of tartar and salt. Beat until whites stand in peaks. Add sugar gradually and beat very stiff. Fold in pecans and vanilla. Turn into prepared pie plate, building up the sides above the edge of the plate. Bake at 225 degrees for 50 minutes. Cool. For filling, melt chocolate with water in a saucepan over low heat. Cool. Stir in vanilla. Whip cream; fold in chocolate. Pour into meringue pie crust. Chill. Yield: 6 to 8 servings.

Hershey Pie

Gail Funderburk

7 ounce Hershey chocolate bar with almonds	1 (9-inch) graham cracker crust
1 (12-ounce) container Cool Whip	Slivered almonds (optional)

In a medium bowl, melt candy bar in microwave about 2 minutes. Fold in whipped topping, mix well. Pour into pie crust and top with almonds if desired; freeze overnight. Thaw slightly before serving. Yield: 6 to 8 servings.

Chocolate Cream Pie

Margie Spires

1 cup sugar	1 tablespoon butter
3 tablespoons cornstarch	1 1/2 teaspoons vanilla
1/2 teaspoon salt	1 (9-inch) baked pie crust
1/3 cup cocoa	Whipped topping (optional)
3 cups milk	
3 egg yolks, slightly beaten	

Combine sugar and next three ingredients in a heavy saucepan over medium heat stirring constantly. Gradually stir in milk and cook until mixture thickens and boils. Boil 1 minute. Remove from heat. Place egg yolks in a medium bowl and gradually stir in at least half of the chocolate mixture. Blend egg mixture in saucepan with remaining chocolate. Boil 1 minute more, stirring constantly. Remove from heat and blend in butter and vanilla. Pour into pie crust. Top with whipped topping, if desired. Yield: 6 to 8 servings.

Chocolate Chess Pie

Howard Brown

1 1/2 cups sugar	2 eggs
3 1/2 tablespoons cocoa	1 (5-ounce) can evaporated milk
1/2 stick melted butter	1 (9-inch) unbaked pie crust
1 1/2 teaspoons vanilla	

Preheat oven to 350 degrees. In a medium bowl, mix sugar and next five ingredients. Blend well. Pour into pie crust. Bake at 350 degrees for 45 minutes. Yield: 6 to 8 servings.

Chess Pie
Howard Brown

1/2 stick butter or margarine	2 tablespoons all-purpose flour
2 cups sugar	1/4 cup milk
4 eggs, lightly beaten	1/4 cup lemon juice
2 tablespoons cornmeal	1 (9-inch) unbaked pie crust

Preheat oven to 350 degrees. In a mixing bowl, cream butter and sugar, add eggs. In a small bowl, mix cornmeal and flour into milk. Add to creamed mixture and mix well. Stir in lemon juice. Pour into pie crust. Bake at 350 degrees or until set. Yield: 6 to 8 servings.

Heavenly Pie
Robin Prehoda

1 (8-ounce) container Cool Whip	1 (6-ounce) jar cherries, cut up
1 (14-ounce) can Eagle Brand condensed milk	1 1/2 cups chopped nuts
2 (8 1/4-ounce) cans crushed pineapple, drained	3-4 tablespoons lemon juice
	2 (9-inch) graham cracker pie crust

In a large bowl, combine all ingredients and mix well. Pour into 2 pie crusts. Chill. Yield: 12 to 16 servings.

Dump Pie
Sloan Brittain

1 stick butter	1 (15-ounce) can sweetened cherries, blueberries or other fruit
1/2 cup flour	
1/2 cup milk	
1 teaspoon baking powder	

Preheat oven to 350 degrees. Melt butter in a 9-inch pie plate. In a small bowl, combine flour, milk, and baking powder. Pour into butter. Do not stir. Dump fruit in middle of dish. Bake at 350 degrees for 30 minutes. Yield: 6 to 8 servings.

Hospitality Pie
Vada Gore

Pie
1   *(8-ounce) package cream cheese*
1   *(14-ounce) can Eagle Brand condensed milk*
1   *(16-ounce) container Cool Whip*

3   *(9-inch) graham cracker pie crust*

Topping
1   *(7-ounce) can shredded coconut*
1 1/2 *cups chopped nuts*
1   *stick butter*

1   *(12-ounce) jar butterscotch topping*

In a large bowl, combine cream cheese, milk, and whipped topping. Mix until smooth. Pour one-third of mixture in each pie crust. In a baking dish, toast coconut and pecans in butter. Spread one-third of mixture on top of each pie and drizzle with butterscotch topping. Yield: 18 to 24 servings.

Lemon Pie
Angela Jordan

2   *eggs, separated*
1/4 *cup lemon juice*
    Zest from 1/2 lemon or
    1/2 teaspoon lemon extract

1   *(14-ounce) can Eagle Brand condensed milk*
1   *(9-inch) baked pie crust*
4   *tablespoons sugar*

Preheat oven to 400 degrees. In a medium bowl, mix egg yolks, lemon juice and zest. Beat well. Add milk and mix. Pour into pie crust. In a separate bowl, beat egg whites at high speed with an electric mixer until foamy. Add 1 tablespoon of sugar at a time, beating until soft peaks form. Spread over pie. Bake at 400 degrees until meringue browned. Refrigerate until ready to serve. Yield: 6 to 8 servings.

Key Lime Pie

Elaine Nichols

Crust

1 1/4 cups graham cracker crumbs

1/4 cup firmly packed light brown sugar

1/3 cup butter or margarine, melted

Filling

2 (14-ounce) cans sweetened condensed milk

1 cup Nellie and Joe fresh key lime juice

2 egg whites

1/4 teaspoon cream of tartar

2 tablespoons sugar

Lime slices

Preheat oven to 350 degrees. In a medium bowl, combine first three ingredients. Press into a 9-inch pie plate. Bake at 350 degrees for 10 minutes. Cool. Turn oven down to 325 degrees. In a bowl, stir together milk and lime juice until blended. Pour into crust. In a medium bowl, beat egg whites and cream of tartar at high speed with an electric mixer until foamy. Add sugar, one tablespoon at the time, until soft peaks form and sugar dissolves. About 4 minutes. Spread meringue over filling. Bake at 325 degrees for 25 to 28 minutes or until meringue browned. Yield: 6 to 8 servings.

Lite Lemon Pie

Betty Gunnells

Sharon Brunson

1 (14-ounce) can Eagle Brand condensed milk

1 (6-ounce) frozen lemonade

1 (8-ounce) container Cool Whip

2 (9-inch) graham cracker pie crust

In a medium bowl, combine milk and lemonade and whipped topping. Blend well. Pour into pie crust. Refrigerate. Yield: 12 to 16 servings.

Note: Can make one pie instead of two. Substitute limeade for lemonade and chocolate pie crust for graham cracker crust.

Mom's Jackson Pie

Laura Dawkins

1/2 cup butter	1/2 teaspoon vanilla
1 3/4 cups sugar	1/2 cup buttermilk
3 eggs	2 cups chopped pecans
1/2 teaspoon mace	(optional)
1 tablespoon flour	1 (9-inch) unbaked pie crust

Cream butter and sugar in a mixing bowl with an electric mixer. Add eggs one at a time. Stir in flour and mace. Add milk and vanilla, mix well. Stir in pecans if desired. Pour into pie crust. Bake at 400 degrees for 10 minutes, then lower temperature to 300 degrees and bake 30 additional minutes. Yield: 6 to 8 servings.

Note: If you add nuts, it makes two pies. This was a favorite in my childhood.

Nannie's Pecan Pie

Debby Norwood

3 eggs	1/4 cup melted butter
1/2 cup light Karo syrup	1 cup chopped pecans
1 cup sugar	1 (9-inch) unbaked pie crust

Preheat oven to 350 degrees. In a medium bowl, mix first four ingredients together with a wire whisk. Stir in nuts. Pour in pie crust. Bake at 350 degrees until lightly browned, then reduce heat to 275 degrees and continue baking about 40 minutes. Yield: 8 servings.

Chocolate Pecan Pie
Debbie Talbert

3	tablespoons cocoa	1	cup sugar
1	stick margarine, melted	1	teaspoon vanilla
2	eggs, beaten	1	cup chopped pecans
1/4	cup flour	1	(9-inch) unbaked pie crust

Preheat oven to 325 degrees. In a mixing bowl, stir cocoa in with margarine. Add eggs, flour, sugar, and vanilla. Blend well. Stir in pecans. Pour into pie crust. Bake at 325 degrees for 30 to 35 minutes. Yield: 6 to 8 servings.

Peach Pie
Linda Kelley

1/2	cup cornstarch	4	cups peaches, peeled and sliced
1 1/2	cups sugar		
2	cups water	2	(9-inch) baked pie crusts
1	(3-ounce) package peach jello		Whipped topping

In a saucepan, combine cornstarch, sugar and water and cook over medium heat; stir constantly. When mixture nears boiling point add peach jello. Boil about 3 minutes. When mixture begins to thicken, remove from heat and let cool a few minutes. Fold in peaches. Pour one-half of mixture in each pie crust. Refrigerate until pies jell. Top with whipped topping. Yield: 12 to 16 servings.

French Crunch Peach Pie

Belva Prozzi

1 (9-inch) unbaked deep dish pie crust	1 (16-ounce) can sliced peaches, drained
2 eggs	1 cup finely crushed vanilla wafers (22 wafers)
1 tablespoon lemon juice	
1/3 cup sugar	1/2 cup chopped toasted almonds
1 (29-ounce) can sliced peaches, drained	1/4 cup butter, melted

Preheat oven to 450 degrees. Bake pie crust 5 minutes. Remove and set aside. Turn oven down to 375 degrees. In a mixing bowl, beat eggs and lemon juice until blended. Stir in sugar. Fold in peaches. Turn into pie crust. In a small bowl, combine vanilla wafers, almonds, and butter. Sprinkle over peach mixture. To prevent over browning, cover edge of pie crust with aluminum foil. Bake at 375 degrees for 20 minutes. Remove foil; bake until filling is set in center, about 25 minutes. Cool on rack. Cover and chill. Serve with vanilla ice cream or Cheddar cheese triangles. Yield: 6 to 8 servings.

Japanese Fruit Pie

Sarah G. Brown

2 eggs	1/2 cup pecans
1 stick margarine, melted	1/2 cup raisins or chocolate chips
1/2 cup sugar	1 tablespoon vinegar
1/2 cup shredded coconut	1 (9-inch) unbaked pie crust

Preheat oven to 300 degrees. In a mixing bowl, combine eggs and next six ingredients. Blend well. Pour into pie crust. Bake at 300 degrees for about 40 minutes. Yield: 6 to 8 servings.

Peanut Butter Cream Cheese Pie

Ruby Wofford

1 (8-ounce) package cream cheese, softened	1 (16-ounce) container Cool Whip
1 (12-ounce) jar crunchy or smooth peanut butter	2 (9-inch) chocolate cracker crumb pie crusts
2 cups powdered sugar	Hershey's chocolate syrup
1 cup milk	

Using an electric mixer with a large mixing bowl, mix cream cheese, peanut butter, sugar, and milk. Fold in whipped topping. Pour one-half of mixture into each pie crust. Freeze. Serve frozen with chocolate syrup drizzled over top. Yield: 12 to 16 servings.

Peanut Butter Pie

Daphne Arthur

1 cup peanut butter, creamy or crunchy	1/2 cup milk
1 (8-ounce) package cream cheese	1 (8-ounce) container Cool Whip
1/2 cup powdered sugar	1 (9-inch) chocolate or graham cracker crust

In a medium bowl, cream peanut butter and cream cheese. Add milk and sugar. Stir until well blended. Fold in one-half of whipped topping. Pour into pie crust. Top with remaining whipped topping. Refrigerate several hours before serving. Yield: 6 to 8 servings.

Strawberry Meringue Pie

Renee Peavy

2-3 egg whites
1/2 teaspoon baking powder
3/4-1 cup sugar
10 (2-inch) square saltines, rolled fine

1/2 cups chopped pecans
1 quart fresh strawberries
Whipped cream

Preheat oven to 300 degrees. In a medium bowl, beat egg whites and baking powder until mixture is stiff. Gradually beat in sugar. Fold in saltine crumbs and pecans. Spread mixture in a well greased 9-inch pie plate. Bake for 30 minutes at 300 degrees. Fill with strawberries. Cover top with whipped topping. Garnish with whole strawberries. Chill for several hours. Yield: 6 to 8 servings.

Easy Strawberry Pie

Debra Galloway

2 cups strawberries, washed and halved
1 (9-inch) baked pie crust or graham cracker crust
3/4 cup sugar
2 tablespoons cornstarch

Pinch of salt
1 cup water
1 (3-ounce) package straw-berry jello
1 (8-ounce) container Cool Whip

Place fruit in pie crust. In a saucepan, mix sugar, cornstarch, water and salt. Bring to a boil. Add jello. Blend well. Pour jello mixture over fruit. Refrigerate several hours or overnight. Top with whipped topping before serving. Yield: 6 to 8 servings.

Anne's Shortbread Cookies

Anne Dawkins

1 cup butter, not margarine	2 cups flour
1/2 cup powdered sugar	

Preheat oven to 325 degrees. In a mixing bowl, cream butter, add sugar gradually and cream well. Add flour one-half cup at the time. Cream well. Knead 5 minutes. Form into walnut-size balls and put on ungreased baking sheet. Press down with a fork. To keep fork from sticking to dough, dip fork in water. Bake at 325 degrees for about 20 minutes or until light golden brown. Yield: 64 cookies.

Christmas Cookies

Annie Lea Brown
Submitted by Kathy Boyd

1 egg	1 1/2 cups ground pecans
2 sticks butter	All-purpose flour
2 cups brown sugar	

Preheat oven to 400 degrees. In a large mixing bowl, beat egg, butter and sugar. Add nuts. Beat well. Add flour needed to make a soft dough. Roll dough out to a 1/8-inch thickness. Cut with cutters and decorate with colored sugars. Bake at 400 degrees until edges are light brown.

Note: Daddy and Aunt Anne made these cookies when they were little children.

Cookie Jar Special
"Especially For Alex"

Anne Dawkins

1 cup butter	1/2 teaspoon ginger
1 cup sugar	2 teaspoon cinnamon
1 egg	1/2 teaspoon ground cloves
1/4 cup molasses	2 teaspoons baking powder
1/4 teaspoon salt	3 1/2 cups all-purpose flour

Preheat oven to 375 degrees. In a large mixing bowl, mix all ingredients well. Put in a covered bowl and chill overnight. For cookies, make dough into small one inch balls and roll in sugar. Place on a baking sheet and press flat with the bottom of a smooth glass that has been dipped in sugar. Bake at 375 degrees about 10 minutes. For gingerbread men, roll out dough into a 1/8-inch thickness on a floured surface. Cut out gingerbread men with cutter and place on a baking sheet. Decorate with raisins and/or candies. Bake at 375 degrees about 10 minutes. Do not overbake.

Note: When the Brown's celebrate Christmas, I always make gingerbread men for the children. The joke is that the adults enjoy them as much as the children - especially Alex! This will bring out the child in you!

MaMa's Potato Chip Cookies

Annie Lea Brown

Submitted by Kathy Boyd

1 cup margarine	1/2 cup potato chips, crushed
1/2 cup sugar	1/2 cup nuts, finely chopped
1 teaspoon vanilla	2 cups all-purpose flour

Preheat oven to 350 degrees. In a large mixing bowl, mix all of the ingredients. Roll dough into marble-sized balls and place on baking sheet. Flatten each ball with the bottom of a glass that has been dipped in sugar. Bake at 350 degrees for 16 to 18 minutes or until golden brown.

Chocolate Surprise Cookies

Lori Wenstrup

2 1/4 cups flour
3/4 cup unsweetened cocoa powder
1/2 teaspoon baking powder
1/2 teaspoon baking soda
1 cup butter, softened
1 1/2 cups packed light brown sugar

1/2 cup plus 1 tablespoon sugar, divided
2 eggs
1 teaspoon vanilla
1 cup chopped pecans, divided
1 (13-ounce) package Rolos
3 ounces white chocolate

Preheat oven to 375 degrees. In a medium bowl, combine flour, cocoa, baking powder, and baking soda. Set aside. In a mixing bowl, beat butter, brown sugar, and one-half cup sugar with an electric mixer at medium speed until light and fluffy. Beat in eggs and vanilla. Gradually add flour mixture and one-half cup pecans; beat well. Cover dough, refrigerate until firm - the longer the better. Place remaining pecans and tablespoon of sugar in a shallow dish. Roll tablespoon of dough around a Rolo, covering completely. Press one side into nut mixture. Place nut side up on a ungreased baking sheet. Place cookies three inches apart. Bake at 375 degrees for 10 to 12 minutes or until slightly cracked. Let stand on baking sheet 2 minutes and then transfer to cooling rack. Cool completely. In a saucepan, melt white chocolate and drizzle over top of cookies. Yield: 4 to 5 dozen.

Chocolate Chip Cookies

Lori Douglas

4	sticks margarine	2	teaspoons vanilla
2	cups sugar	5	cups all-purpose flour
2	cups packed brown sugar	1	(12-ounce) package
4	eggs		chocolate chips
2	teaspoons baking soda	1	cup chopped nuts
2	teaspoons salt		

Preheat oven to 350 degrees. In a mixing bowl, cream margarine and sugars, add eggs. Beat well. Stir in baking soda, salt, and vanilla. Add flour and mix well. Stir in chocolate chips and nuts. Drop by tablespoonful on ungreased baking sheet. Bake at 350 degrees for 12 to 15 minutes. Yield: 6 to 8 dozen.

Note: Cookie dough may be refrigerated and used later.

Brandi's Brownies

Brandi Wheeler

Brownies

1/4	cup cocoa	2	cups sugar
1	cup hot water	2	eggs, slightly beaten
3/4	cup butter	1/2	cup buttermilk
1	teaspoon baking soda	1	teaspoon vanilla
1/2	teaspoon salt	1	cup chopped nuts
2 1/2	cups flour		

Icing

1/4	cup cocoa	1/4	teaspoon hot water
1/4	cup powdered sugar	2	tablespoons softened butter

Preheat oven to 375 degrees. For brownies, in a mixing bowl, mix cocoa and water. Stir in butter. Cool. In a separate bowl, stir dry ingredients together. Add to cocoa mixture. Add eggs. Beat in buttermilk and vanilla. Stir in pecans. Spread in a greased 10x15-inch jelly roll pan. Bake at 375 degrees for 20 minutes. For icing, mix all ingredients. Blend well. If too thick add a little more water for spreading consistency. Yield: 4 dozen.

Neiman Marcus Cookies

Jeane Knight
Margie Hall

5	cups blended oatmeal	4	eggs
4	cups flour	2	teaspoons vanilla
1	teaspoon salt	1	(8-ounce) Hershey chocolate
2	teaspoons baking powder		candy bar, grated
2	teaspoons baking soda	1	(24-ounce) bag chocolate
2	cups butter		chips
2	cups brown sugar	3	cups chopped nuts
2	cups sugar		

Preheat oven to 375 degrees. Grind oatmeal in blender until a fine powder. Mix oatmeal with flour and next three ingredients. Set aside. In a large mixing bowl, cream butter and sugars. Add eggs and vanilla. Mix well. Stir in the flour mixture. Add candy bar, chocolate chips, and nuts. Roll into balls and place two inches apart on a ungreased baking sheet. Bake at 375 degrees for 10 minutes. Yield: 112 cookies.

"Mmm, What's In Them?" Cookies

Danielle Hall

2	cups all-purpose flour	1	egg
1	(6-ounce) package butter-	1/2	cup canned pumpkin
	scotch chips	1	cup quick-cooking oats,
1	teaspoon baking soda		uncooked
3/4	cup butter or margarine,	1	(6-ounce) white chocolate
	softened		baking bar, chopped
2/3	cup sugar	2/3	cup walnuts
2/3	cup firmly packed brown		
	sugar		

Preheat oven to 350 degrees. Position knife blade in food processor bowl; add flour and butterscotch. Process 30 seconds or until butterscotch chips are finely ground. Add soda, mix well. Set aside. In a mixing bowl, beat butter at medium speed with an electric mixer until creamy. Gradually add sugars, beating well. Add egg and pumpkin. Beat well. Beat in flour mixture. Stir in oats, chocolate, and walnuts. Drop by heaping teaspoons onto a lightly greased baking sheet. Bake at 350 degrees for 12 minutes. Remove to wire racks and let cool completely. Yield: 6 dozen cookies.

Easter Story Cookies

Janie Campbell

1	cup whole pecans		Pinch salt
1	teaspoon vinegar	1	cup sugar
3	egg whites		

These cookies are to be made the evening before Easter.

Preheat oven to 300 degrees.

Place pecans in a resealable bag. Let children beat them with a wooden spoon to break into small pieces. Explain that after Jesus was arrested, He was beaten by the Roman soldiers. Read John 19:1-3.

Let each child smell the vinegar. Put vinegar into a mixing bowl. Explain that when Jesus was thirsty on the cross He was given vinegar to drink. Read John 19:28-30.

Add egg whites to vinegar. Eggs represent life. Explain that Jesus gave His life to give us life. Read John 10:10-11.

Sprinkle a little salt into each child's hand. Let them taste it and brush the rest in the bowl. Explain that this represents the salty tears shed by Jesus' followers, and the bitterness of our own sin. Read Luke 23:27

So far the ingredients are not very appetizing. Add sugar. Explain the sweetest part of the story is that Jesus died because he loves us. He wants us to know and belong to Him. Read Psalms 34:8 and John 3:16.

Beat with a mixer on high speed 12 to 15 minutes until stiff peaks are formed. Explain that the color white represents the purity in God's eyes of those whose sins have been cleansed by Jesus. Read Isaiah 1:18 and John 3:1-3.

Fold in broken nuts. Drop by teaspoonfuls onto waxed paper covered baking sheet. Explain the each mound represents the rocky tomb where Jesus' body was laid. Read Matthew 27:57-60.

Put baking sheet in oven, close door and turn oven off.

Give each child a piece of tape and seal the oven door. Explain that Jesus' tomb was sealed. Read Matthew 27:65-66.

Go to Bed! Explain that they may feel sad to leave the cookies in the oven overnight. Jesus' followers were in despair when the tomb was sealed. Read John 16:20 and 22.

On Easter morning, open the oven and give everyone a cookie. Notice the cracked surface and take a bite. The cookies are hollow! On the first Easter Jesus' followers were amazed to find the tomb open and empty. Read Matthew 28:1-9.

Humdingers

Mary Lathan Steele

1 stick margarine	1 cup crushed pecans
1 cup sugar	1 cup Rice Krispies
1 cup chopped dates	1 teaspoon vanilla
5 tablespoons evaporated milk	Powdered sugar

In a saucepan, melt margarine. Add sugar, dates and milk. Bring to a boil and cook 5 minutes, stirring frequently. Remove from heat, add pecans, Rice Krispies, and vanilla. Cool until able to handle. Using a teaspoon for measurement, shape into balls and roll in powdered sugar. Yield: 2 to 3 dozen balls.

Nutty Fingers

Nancy Wilhelm

1 stick butter, softened	1 teaspoon vanilla
2 tablespoons powdered sugar	1 cup chopped nuts
1 egg	Powdered sugar
1 cup flour	

Preheat oven to 300 degrees. In a mixing bowl, blend and cream first three ingredients. Slowly add flour and nuts. Mix well. Roll into finger shaped cookies. Place on a ungreased baking sheet. Bake at 300 degrees for 45 minutes. Cool. Roll in powdered sugar. Yield: 2 dozen.

Mother's Fudge Bars

Marsha Oates

1 stick butter	3 squares baking chocolate,
2 cups sugar	melted
1 cup all-purpose flour, sifted	1 cup chopped nuts
Pinch salt	

Preheat oven to 325 degrees. In a mixing bowl, beat butter and sugar. Add eggs. Add flour, salt, chocolate, and nuts. Mix well. Do not over beat. Pour batter into a 7x11-inch baking dish. Bake at 325 degrees for 40 to 45 minutes. Will have a crust on top. Let sit about 15 minutes before cutting. Cut into squares. Yield: 20 squares.

Mrs. Huff's Pecan Bars

Vivian Kelly

1	cup butter	1	egg, separated
1	cup sugar	1	teaspoon vanilla
2	cups all-purpose flour	2	cups chopped nuts

Preheat oven to 300 degrees. In a mixing bowl, combine butter, sugar, flour, egg yolk, and vanilla. Mix together to form dough. Press dough out on a 12x18-inch ungreased pan. Spread egg white evenly over dough. Spread nuts over top of egg white. Press nuts into dough with hands so they won't be loose. Bake at 300 degrees until golden brown. Cut into squares while hot and let squares cool in pan. Yield: 48 bars.

Caramel Bars

Patricia Hughes

2	sticks butter or margarine	2	eggs, beaten
1	cup light brown sugar	2	teaspoons vanilla
1	cup granulated sugar	1	cup chopped nuts
2	cups sifted self-rising flour		

Preheat oven to 325 degrees. In a saucepan, over low heat, melt butter. Add sugars, stir occasionally until smooth. Add flour and remaining ingredients. Pour into a ungreased 9x13-inch baking dish. Bake at 325 degrees 20 to 25 minutes or until edges are slightly darker and leave edge of pan. Cool in pan. Cut when cool. Store tightly covered. Yield: 30 to 35 bars.

Frosted Banana Bars

Carla Dunton

Bars

1/2 cup butter or margarine
1 1/2 cups sugar
2 eggs
1 (8-ounce) container sour
 cream
1 teaspoon vanilla

2 cups all-purpose flour
1 teaspoon baking soda
1/4 teaspoon salt
2 medium ripe bananas, mashed

Frosting

1/2 cup butter or margarine,
 softened
1 (8-ounce) package cream
 cheese, softened

2 teaspoons vanilla
3 3/4 cups powdered sugar

Preheat oven to 350 degrees. In a mixing bowl, cream butter and sugar. Beat in eggs, sour cream, and vanilla. In a separate bowl, combine flour, baking soda, and salt. Gradually add to creamed mixture. Stir in bananas. Pour into a greased 15x10-inch baking pan. Bake at 350 degrees for 20 to 25 minutes. Cool. For frosting, cream butter and cream cheese in a medium bowl. Add vanilla. Gradually add powdered sugar. May need to a little more to achieve desired consistency. Spread over top. Cut into bars. Yield: 3 to 4 dozen bars.

Chinese Chews

Teresa Hendrix

2 sticks butter
1 (16-ounce) box brown sugar
3 eggs
2 cups self-rising flour

1 teaspoon vanilla extract
1/2 teaspoon almond extract
2 cups chopped nuts

Preheat oven to 350 degrees. Combine all ingredients in a large bowl and mix well. Pour into a greased and floured 9x11-inch baking dish. Bake at 350 degrees for 25 minutes. Yield: 30 to 35 bars.

Peri's Lemon Squares
Kitty Jackson

Shortbread

1/2 cup butter	1/4 cup powdered sugar
1 cup all-purpose flour	Pinch of salt

Topping

2 eggs	Juice and zest of 1 lemon
1 cup sugar	1/4 cup flour
1/4 teaspoon salt	1/2 teaspoon baking powder

Preheat oven to 350 degrees. For shortbread, process all ingredients in a food processor until they form a ball. Press with fingers into bottom of a lightly buttered 8-inch baking dish. Bake at 350 degrees for 20 minutes.

For topping, reduce oven to 325 degrees. In a medium bowl, beat eggs well. Gradually add sugar. Continue to beat, slowly adding remaining ingredients. Pour topping over hot shortbread. Return to oven at once. Bake at 325 degrees for 30 to 35 minutes until top is light gold. Remove pan from oven and run a knife around edge. Cool 20 minutes. Sprinkle with powdered sugar. Cut into squares. Yield: 9 squares.

Easy Fruit Cobbler
Mickie Garland

2 cups fruit, peaches, apples, pears or berries	1 cup self-rising flour
Sugar	1 stick butter, partially melted
	1 egg

Preheat oven to 350 degrees. Place fruit in a 2-quart shallow baking dish. Cover with sugar. Use less sugar with peaches and more with tart fruit. For apples or pears, sprinkle lightly with apple pie spice mix. In a small bowl, mix flour, butter and egg. Spoon over fruit. Bake at 350 degrees for about 1 hour or until golden brown. Yield: 8 servings.

Blueberry Crisp
Lee Hicks

4 cups blueberries	1/2 cup flour
1 teaspoon lemon zest	1/4 teaspoon cinnamon
3/4 cup packed brown sugar	1/4 cup butter, softened

Preheat oven to 375 degrees. Place blueberries in a 2-quart shallow baking dish. Sprinkle with lemon zest. In a small bowl, blend remaining ingredients and spread over berries. Bake at 375 degrees for 25 minutes. Serve warm. Top with whipped topping or vanilla ice cream. Yield: 6 servings.

Strawberry Dessert
Sandra Gaskins

1 prepared angel food cake	2 cups milk
1 pint of fresh strawberries or frozen, chopped	1 (8-ounce) container Cool Whip
1 (3-ounce) package instant vanilla pudding mix	

Break cake up in the bottom of a punch bowl. Cover with strawberries. In a small bowl, combine pudding mix, milk, and whipped topping; mix well. Spread over top of strawberries. Refrigerate until ready to serve. Yield: 12 servings.

Snowball Dessert
Marsha Oates

1 1/2 (1/4-ounce) envelopes unflavored gelatin	1 1/2 cups fresh orange juice Juice of 2-3 lemons
1/4 cup cold water	1 prepared angel food cake
1/2 cup boiling water	2 cups heavy cream, divided
2 cups sugar	Shredded coconut

In a medium bowl, soften gelatin in cold and hot water. Add sugar, orange juice and lemon juice. Set aside. Trim crust off of cake and break cake into bite-sized pieces. Place in a 3-quart greased dish. In a small bowl, whip one cup of cream and fold into gelatin mixture. Pour over cake. Refrigerate overnight. Top with remaining cup of whipped cream. Sprinkle with coconut if desired. Yield: 20 to 24 pieces.

Frozen Fruit Slush
Becky Elliott

1	cup sugar	1	(20-ounce) can crushed
1	cup boiling water		pineapple
1	(16-ounce) can frozen orange	5	bananas cut into small pieces
	juice	1	(6-ounce) jar maraschino
1	can of water		cherries, drained
1	(16-ounce) package frozen		
	strawberries, sliced		

Prepare simple syrup by dissolving sugar in boiling water. Cool to room temperature. Pour into a large clear bowl and add all other ingredients. Freeze overnight. Remove from freezer and thaw to slushy consistency before serving. Yield: 15 servings.

Note: Perfect to take to a cookout. It can thaw while other food is being prepared and eaten.

Rainbow Sherbet Dessert
Ann Rhodes

2	cups heavy cream	2 1/2	cups raspberry sherbet,
3	tablespoons powdered sugar		softened
1	teaspoon vanilla	2 1/2	cups lime sherbet, softened
12	coconut macaroons, crumbled	2 1/2	cups orange sherbet, softened
	and toasted		Strawberries
3/4	cup chopped nuts		

In a medium bowl, whip cream, add sugar and vanilla. Beat until soft peaks form. Fold in macaroons and pecans. Spread one-half of mixture into a 9-inch springform pan; freeze. Spread a layer of sherbet over whipped cream mixture, allowing each layer to freeze before adding next one. Top with remaining whipped cream mixture. Cover and freeze. Remove from pan and place on a serving plate. Garnish with strawberries. Yield: 12 servings.

Ice Cream Sandwich Dessert
Kathy Boyd

19 ice cream sandwiches
1 (12-ounce) container Cool
    Whip

1 (11¾-ounce) jar hot fudge
    ice cream topping
1 cup salted nuts, divided

Arrange ice cream sandwiches in bottom of a 9x13-inch pan. Will have to cut some in half to fit. Spread with one-half of the whipped topping. Spoon fudge topping by teaspoonfuls onto whipped topping. Sprinkle with one-half of nuts. Repeat layer with remaining ice cream sandwiches, whipped topping and nuts. Cover and freeze. Remove from freezer 20 minutes before serving. Yield: 12 to 16 servings.

Boiled Custard
Cathy Hines

5 eggs
1 cup sugar
1/4 teaspoon salt

1 quart milk, whole or 2 percent
2 teaspoons vanilla

In the top of a double boiler, beat eggs. Gradually add sugar and salt. Pour in scalded milk. Place over boiling water. Cook, stirring constantly, until mixture coats spoon. Do not overcook. Stir in vanilla. Yield: 6 to 8 servings.

Banana Pudding
Donna Crocker

1 cup milk
1 (3-ounce) package instant
    banana cream pudding mix
1/2 cup sour cream

1 (8-ounce) container Cool
    Whip
    Vanilla wafers
3-4 bananas, sliced

In a medium bowl, combine milk, pudding mix, sour cream and one-half of the whipped topping. Beat 2 minutes. In a 2-quart casserole dish, layer vanilla wafers, bananas, one-half of the pudding mix. Repeat layers. Top with remaining whipped topping. Keep refrigerated. Yield: 8 servings.

Chocolate Delight
Vanessa Wilhelm

First layer

1   cup pecans, chopped
1/2 cup margarine, softened

1   cup all-purpose flour

Second Layer

1   cup Cool Whip
1   cup powdered sugar

1   (8-ounce) package cream
    cheese, softened

Third Layer

2   (3.9-ounce) packages instant
    chocolate pudding mix

3   cups milk

Preheat oven to 325 degrees. To prepare first layer, combine pecans, margarine, and flour in a medium bowl. Blend well. Press into the bottom of a 13x9-inch baking dish. Bake at 325 degrees for 15 minutes. Cool.

To prepare second layer, combine whipped topping, sugar, and cream cheese in medium bowl and mix until smooth. Spread over crust.

To prepare third layer, in a medium bowl, beat pudding mix and milk until thickened. Spread over cream cheese mixture. Top with remaining whipped topping. If desired, garnish with chocolate shavings or coconut. Yield: 12 servings.

Aunt Sudie's Chocolate Roll
Kathy Boyd

Cake

4	eggs, separated
1	cup powdered sugar
1/4	cup unsweetened cocoa

2	tablespoons sifted flour
1 1/2	teaspoons vanilla extract

Filling

1/2 pint heavy cream   1/4 cup sifted powdered sugar

Frosting

1/2	stick butter
1 3/4	cups sifted powdered sugar
3	tablespoons cocoa

1/2	teaspoon vanilla
3	tablespoons hot coffee

Have eggs at room temperature. Preheat oven to 350 degrees. Grease bottom of a 15x10-inch jelly roll pan. Line with waxed paper. In a large bowl, beat egg yolks until thick and lemon-colored. Beat in sugar. Sift cocoa and flour together and beat into mixture. Add vanilla. Place egg whites in a large bowl. Beat until stiff, but not dry. With a wire whisk, fold egg whites into mixture. Pour into prepared pan. Bake at 350 degrees for 12 to 15 minutes or until surface springs back when touched lightly. Place a damp dish towel down on counter top with a dry one over it. Turn cake onto towel. Peel off waxed paper. Begin at long end, roll cake up jelly roll fashion and let cool.

For filling, beat cream until stiff. With spatula gently fold in sugar. Carefully unroll cake and remove towel. Spread filling and re-roll. Place seam side down on a piece of cardboard covered with aluminum foil.

For frosting, in a mixing bowl, cream butter and sugar. Add cocoa, vanilla and coffee gradually until frosting is the right consistency to spread. Frost roll, being sure to cover ends. Chill until serving time. Yield: 10 servings.

Note: When I was a little girl, Aunt Sudie would make these for my family. They have been a long time favorite of the Browns. We still enjoy them. Especially at Christmas!

Sin
Wilma Casstevens

1 1/4 cups famous chocolate wafer crumbs

1/2 stick melted margarine

1/2 gallon vanilla ice cream

6 (1 1/8-ounce) Heath candy bars, crushed

1 (6-ounce) package semi-sweet chocolate chips

1 (12-ounce) can evaporated milk

2 cups powdered sugar

In a medium bowl, mix chocolate wafer crumbs and margarine. Press in the bottom of a 2-quart shallow dish and chill. Place ice cream in a medium bowl and fold candy bars into ice cream. Spread over crumbs. In a saucepan, combine chocolate chips, milk, and sugar. Cook over medium heat until thickened. Let cool completely. Spread over top of ice cream and freeze. Yield: 18 servings.

Lemon Bisque
Suzanne Bogardus

1 (3-ounce) package lemon gelatin

1 cup boiling water

1/3 cup honey

3 tablespoons lemon juice

Zest of 1 lemon

1 (14 1/2-ounce) can evaporated milk, chilled and whipped

3 cups vanilla wafer cookie crumbs, divided

In a large bowl, dissolve gelatin in water. Add honey, lemon juice and zest. When slightly congealed, add milk. In the bottom of a 9x13-inch pan, spread one-half of the crumbs. Pour gelatin mixture over crumbs. Top with remaining crumbs. Refrigerate 3 hours. Yield: 16 servings.

Lemon Delight

Edith Cook

First layer

1/2 cup pecans, chopped
1 cup all-purpose flour

1 stick margarine, melted

Second Layer

1/2 (12-ounce) container Cool
Whip
1 cup powdered sugar

1 (8-ounce) package cream
cheese, softened

Third Layer

2 (3.9-ounce) packages instant
lemon pudding mix

2 3/4 cups milk

Preheat oven to 325 degrees. To prepare first layer, combine pecans, margarine, and flour in a medium bowl. Blend well. Press into the bottom of a 12x8-inch baking dish. Bake at 325 degrees for 15 minutes. Cool.

To prepare second layer, combine one-half container of whipped topping, sugar, and cream cheese in medium bowl and mix until smooth. Spread over crust.

To prepare third layer, in a medium bowl, beat pudding mix and milk until thickened. Spread over cream cheese mixture. Top with remaining whipped topping. Yield: 12 to 16 servings.

Pineapple Trifle

Barbara McElveen

1 (6-ounce) box instant vanilla pudding mix
1 (12-ounce) container Cool Whip

1 prepared angel food cake
1 (20-ounce) can pineapple tidbits, reserve juice

Mix pudding according to directions on package. Add some whipped topping to pudding, saving enough for top of trifle. Break cake up into bite-sized pieces. In a large glass bowl, layer cake, pour a little juice from pineapple over cake, pineapple tidbits and pudding mixture. Repeat layers until all ingredients are used. Top with remaining whipped topping. Refrigerate overnight before serving. Yield: 12 servings.

Pumpkin Log

Margaret Theisman

Cake

3 eggs
2/3 cup Libby's canned pumpkin
1 cup sugar
1 teaspoon baking soda

1/2 teaspoon cinnamon
3/4 cup flour
Chopped pecan (optional)

Filling

1 (8-ounce) package cream cheese, softened

3/4 teaspoon vanilla
1 1/4 cups powdered sugar

Preheat oven to 350 degrees. Grease bottom of a 15x10-inch jelly roll pan. Line with waxed paper. In a medium bowl, combine all ingredients for cake; mix well. Pour into prepared pan and bake at 350 degrees for 12 to 15 minutes or until toothpick comes out clean. Lay a dish towel down flat on counter top and cover with powdered sugar. Immediately after cake is done, turn onto towel. Let sit about 3 minutes and peel off waxed paper. Beginning at long end, roll cake up in towel jelly roll fashion. Put on a wire rack and let cool.

For filling, combine cream cheese, vanilla and sugar in a medium bowl. Mix well. When cake is cool, carefully unroll cake and remove towel. Spread filling almost to edges of cake and re-roll. Wrap in plastic wrap and refrigerate. Before serving, sprinkle with sifted powdered sugar. Yield: 10 to 12 servings.

French Crêpes

Jean Puyet

1 cup all-purpose flour	2 tablespoons butter, melted
1/2 teaspoon salt	3 teaspoons pure vanilla extract
5 eggs	3 tablespoons cognac
5 level tablespoons sugar	(optional)
2 cups whole milk	

In a large bowl, mix the salt with the flour. Mix eggs into the flour until it makes a smooth dough. Add sugar and stir in well. Add milk, a little at the time, mixing well after each addition. Add butter and vanilla. Add cognac if desired. Mix well. Let sit in refrigerator at least 30 minutes. Heat a 6 to 8- inch teflon pan on top of the stove. Rub it with butter for first crêpe only. Dip about two to three tablespoons of pastry into the pan and tilt to make sure pastry covers the entire bottom. Cook until light brown on the underside. Carefully turn and brown the other side. Place on plate. The crêpes should be very thin, about the thickness of two pieces of paper together. Yield: 50 crêpes.

Serve plain. Sprinkle with a little sugar or with strawberries and cream inside. For crêpes flambé, pour a little alcoholic beverage, a sprinkle of sugar and one teaspoon of butter to flavor each crêpe. Place the crêpes in this sauce, light the sauce with a match. Spoon sauce over crêpes. Roll each of crêpes to serve.

There are a variety of ways to use these. Without the sugar inside the pastry, they can be used with spinach and cheese or seasoned meats or whatever you choose to place inside the rolled crêpes.

This pastry can be prepared ahead and used within two days if kept refrigerated. If cooked, they keep well in the refrigerator if covered for at least five days.

Divinity
Laura Hancock

2 egg whites	1 teaspoon vanilla
2 2/3 cups sugar	1 teaspoon baking soda
2/3 cup light corn syrup	1 cup chopped pecans
2/3 cup water	

In a medium bowl, beat egg whites until stiff peaks form. In a 2-quart saucepan, combine first three ingredients and cook until temperature reaches 251 to 258 degrees on a candy thermometer. Pour mixture into egg whites. Add vanilla and baking soda. Beat until thickens, about 5 minutes. Add pecans and drop by spoonfuls onto waxed paper. Yield: 25 pieces.

Reese Cups
Cindy McArthur

1 (16-ounce) box powdered sugar	1 cup peanut butter, plain or crunchy
1 cup graham cracker crumbs	1 (16-ounce) package chocolate chips
2 sticks margarine, softened	

In a large bowl, combine sugar and crumbs. In a separate bowl combine butter and peanut butter. Add to sugar mixture. May knead with hands or use electric mixer. Shape into quarter size balls and press into mini muffin tins. In a saucepan, melt chocolate chips over low heat. Spoon about 1 teaspoonful over each ball. Chill until firm.

Chocolate Grabs
Danielle Hall

1 (12-ounce) package peanut butter chips	1 1/2 cups pecans, chopped or halved
1 (4-ounce) package sweet baking chocolate	1/2 cup flaked coconut (optional)

In a heavy saucepan, cook peanut butter chips and chocolate over medium heat until melted, stirring occasionally. Stir in pecan and coconut. Drop by rounded teaspoonfuls onto waxed paper. Let cool completely. Yield: 1 1/4 pounds.

English Toffee

Yvette Sanders

1 cup butter, not margarine	1 1/2 cups chopped walnuts,
1 tablespoon Karo syrup	divided
1 1/3 cups sugar	1 (6-ounce) package chocolate
3 tablespoons water	chips, melted

In a saucepan, combine butter, syrup, sugar, and water. Cook over medium heat, stirring occasionally, until temperature reaches 300 degrees on a candy thermometer. Remove from heat. Stir in one cup of nuts. Spread in a thin layer on a greased 15x10-inch jelly roll pan. Cool. Spread top with melted chocolate. Sprinkle with remaining nuts. Cool. Yield: 3 to 4 dozen pieces.

Grace's Toffee Candy

Cindy McArthur

1 cup slivered almonds	1 tablespoon light Karo syrup
1 tablespoon water	4 (1.55-ounce) Hershey milk
2 sticks margarine	chocolate candy bars
1 cup sugar	

In a saucepan, over medium-high heat, combine almonds and next four ingredients, stirring constantly. Cook until mixture turns shade darker than light brown sugar. The darker, the more intensified the flavor, and the texture gets crispier. Be careful not to scorch. Work very quickly and spread mixture 3/8- 1/4-inch thick onto a 15x10-inch cookie sheet with sides. Break candy bars over top and let melt a few minutes. Spread over toffee with a knife. Cool and break into pieces. Yield: 3 to 4 dozen pieces.

★Sauces★Preserves★
Pickles

My family
October 1997

Edwin's sister Beth was married at our house and we decided to have the photographer take a family picture after the wedding. This was our last family picture with all of us together, and I cherish it. Love your family. Life is short and our biggest challenge in life is to love unconditionally. Accept each other as Christ accepted you. If love is sincere, there will be compassion, kindness, humility, gentleness and patience. Don't harbor ill feelings in your heart. Be mindful of the words you speak to one another. Say things that are encouraging. God ask that we love one another.

Live in harmony with one another, be sympathetic,
love as brothers, be compassionate and humble.
Do not repay evil with evil or insult with insult,
but with blessings, because to this you were called
so that you may inherit a blessing.

1 Peter 3:8-9

Henry's Barbecue Sauce for Chicken

Frances Kelley

1	quart white vinegar	1	cup sugar
1	pint corn oil	1/2	cup salt
4 1/2	ounces mustard	1	(8-ounce) bottle ketchup
1/4	bottle onion salt	2	heaping teaspoons black
2 1/2	ounces Worcestershire sauce		pepper

In a large container, thoroughly mix all ingredients. No cooking or refrigeration necessary. This recipe is enough to barbeque 100 chicken halves. Yield: 1/2 gallon.

Note: Sauce can be saved and used throughout outdoor cooking season. It can be used on other meats too.

Tut's Barbeque Sauce

Howard Brown

1	pint vinegar	1	tablespoon black pepper
1	(6-ounce) jar mustard	1	tablespoon sugar
3	tablespoons salt		Ketchup

In a quart jar, combine vinegar, mustard, salt, pepper and sugar. Finish filling jar with ketchup. Yield: 1 quart.

Note: This is a barbeque sauce that my grandmother had. Daddy makes this sauce and it is delicious!

Williamsburg Barbeque Sauce

Anna Williams

1	gallon cider vinegar	2	ounces black pepper
2	ounces cayenne pepper	1	(2-ounce) bottle Tabasco
2	ounces crushed red pepper		Salt to taste

In a Dutch oven, combine vinegar and next 5 ingredients. Heat to boil, then turn heat down. Simmer for 1 hour. Yield: 1 gallon.

Note: Pour into pretty bottles for gifts.

My Mother's Chili Sauce

Jacqueline Segars

25	large ripe tomatoes	4	tablespoons salt
5	large onions	1	teaspoon cloves
8	large bell pepper	1	teaspoon cinnamon
1 1/2	cups sugar	1	quart vinegar

Dice all ingredients and put in a Dutch oven. Bring to a boil then turn to low and cook for 1 hour and 30 minutes. Put in canning jars and seal.

Hot Fudge Sauce

Mickie Garland

2	cups sugar	1/2	cup butter or margarine
4	tablespoons cocoa	1	teaspoon vanilla
4	tablespoons all-purpose flour		
1	(14-ounce) can evaporated milk		

Combine sugar, cocoa and flour in a heavy saucepan. Mix well until no lumps. Add milk and margarine. Bring mixture to a slow boil over medium heat, stirring with a wire whisk. Cool slightly. Add vanilla. Can add milk to thin if needed.

Salmon Sauce
Cynthia Roberson

1 stick butter	2 tablespoons mustard
1 clove garlic, minced	1/2 cup ketchup
4 tablespoons soy sauce	Dash Worcestershire sauce

Combine all ingredients in a saucepan; heat. Cool. Use as a basting sauce while grilling or broiling salmon. Use remaining sauce as garnish on cooked salmon.

Tartar Sauce
Kathy Boyd

2 cups mayonnaise	1 cup pickle relish
1/2 cup onion, finely chopped	

Combine all ingredients in a small bowl. Stir until thoroughly mixed. Cover and chill before serving. Yield: 3 cups .

Hot Mustard
Kathy Boyd

1 cup white vinegar	1 cup sugar
1 cup dry mustard	1/8 teaspoon salt
2 eggs, well beaten	

In a medium bowl, mix vinegar and mustard and let stand overnight. Stir in eggs, sugar and salt. Pour into a saucepan. Bring to a slow boil over medium heat, stirring constantly. Cook until mixture coats the spoon. Cool and refrigerate. Yield: About 2 cups.

Pesto Sauce

Susan Crowder

1	cup fresh basil leaves	2	cloves garlic
1/2	cup fresh parsley leaves	1/4	teaspoon salt
1/2	cup grated Parmesan cheese	1/2	cup olive oil
1/4	cups pine nuts or walnuts		

Blend all ingredients, except oil, in food processor. Slowly add oil.

Mama's Spaghetti Sauce

Jimmy Atkins

2	pounds ground chuck	1	bell pepper, chopped
1	(8-ounce) package Hillshire sausage, cut into pieces (optional)	2	(10 3/4-ounce) cans tomato soup
1	large onion, chopped	1	(14-ounce) bottle ketchup
		1	soup can water

In a 8-quart saucepan, brown ground chuck and sausage, if desired. Drain grease. Add onions and bell pepper. Stir. Pour in tomato soup and ketchup. Add water. Cook, covered, for 1 hour on low to medium heat. Yield: 10 to 12 servings.

My Favorite Spaghetti Sauce

Angelyn Bateman

1 1/2	pounds lean ground beef	2	teaspoons salt
2	cups chopped onions	1	teaspoon black pepper
1	cup chopped bell pepper	1	teaspoon basil leaves
2	cups chopped celery	1	teaspoon garlic salt
1	(28-ounce) can Italian Plum tomatoes	1	tablespoon Worcestershire sauce
1	(6-ounce) can tomato paste	2-3	bay leaves

In a large saucepan, brown ground beef and drain. Add celery and onions. Add remaining ingredients. Cover and simmer for 2 hours. Yield: 8 servings.

Peach Honey

Rose Marie Newsom

2   cups soft peaches   2   teaspoons Fruit Fresh
4   cups sugar

Combine all ingredients and blend in a blender until mixed well. Pour into a saucepan, bring to a boil and cook over medium heat for 30 minutes. Put in sterilized jars and seal.

Peach Marmalade

Jane Sox

5   cups crushed peaches   7   cups sugar
1   (20-ounce) can crushed   1   (6-ounce) package orange or
    pineapple   peach jello

Blend peaches in a blender. In a large canning pot, combine peaches, pine apple and sugar. Cook 15 minutes. When mixture comes to a rolling boil, start counting time. After 10 minutes into the boil, add jello. Cook until dissolves. Pour into 8-ounce jars and seal.

Note: Can use blueberries with blueberry jello or fresh pears with strawberry jello. Put pears through blender. Before cooking prepare jars. Fill with hot water. Place jar lids in a small pot of hot water and keep hot. This makes a good seal.

Brandied Cranberries

Lilyanne Inabinet

1	pound fresh cranberries	1/2-3/4	cups brandy
2	cups sugar		

Preheat oven to 350 degrees. Spread cranberries in a single layer over a 10x15-inch baking pan. Sprinkle sugar over top of the cranberries. Cover tightly with aluminum foil. Bake at 350 degrees for 1 hour. Remove from oven. Add brandy to cranberries. Immediately transfer to container or ladle into hot sterile jars leaving one-fourth inch head space. Wipe jar rims, cover at once with metal lids and screw on bands. Process in boiling water bath 10 minutes. Yield: 61/2 pints.

Note: Serve with turkey, chicken or my favorite, over ice cream.

Cranberry and Orange Relish

Ginger Holland

1	pound fresh cranberries	1/2	lemon
1/2	cup water	1/2	teaspoon allspice (optional)
1	cup sugar, may need a little more	1/2	teaspoon cinnamon (optional)
1	orange		

Place cranberries in a saucepan with water and sugar and cook over medium heat until cranberries burst. Remove seeds from unpeeled orange and lemon. Put in blender and chop fine. Pour orange mixture in saucepan with cranberries and cook 1 minute. Yield: 8 to 10 servings.

Bread and Butter Pickles
Kathy Boyd

12	cucumbers, sliced thin	5	cups sugar
6	medium onions, sliced thin	3	cups cider vinegar
2	bell peppers, chopped	1 1/2	teaspoons tumeric
3	cloves garlic, minced	1 1/2	teaspoons celery seed
1/3	cup salt	2	teaspoons mustard seed

Combine first four ingredients in a large canning pot. Mix in salt and cover with ice cubes. Let stand for 3 hours. Drain well. In a large bowl, mix sugar, vinegar and seasonings. Pour over cucumber mixture and heat just to a boil. Seal in jars. Yield: 8 pints.

Note: I made these pickles with cucumbers and bell peppers from Daddy's garden. They are delicious!

Watermelon Rind Pickles
Lee Hicks

10	pounds peeled rind, 2 small watermelons	40	drops oil of cinnamon
		12	pounds sugar
40	drops oil of clove	1	quart white vinegar

Cut rind into cubes or strips. In a large canning pot, cover in cold water for 24 hours. Wash and drain well. Cover with cold water. Bring to a boil and simmer for 10 minutes. Wash again in cold water. Drain well. Mix clove and cinnamon in with sugar and vinegar. Stir and pour over rind. Stir mixture often until clear and let stand for 24 hours. Bring to a hard boil and boil 7 to 10 minutes. Put in a large crock and let stand for 5 days. Can cold. Yield: 14 pints.

Katherine Farless' Cucumber Pickles

Paula Bowen

7 1/2 pounds cucumbers, sliced thin
1 (Number 40) bottle Lilly's lime
1 cup salt
1 (1 1/4-ounce) package alum

7 1/2 pounds sugar
2 quarts vinegar
1/2 box pickling spices, remove red peppers before using

Soak cucumbers overnight in lime, diluted in 1 gallon of water. After 12 hours, wash in clear water. Drain; soak 2 hours in salt, diluted with 1 gallon of water. Wash; drain. Soak 4 hours in clear water. Drain cucumbers. Prepare for final steps. Boil alum in 1 gallon of water. Drop cucumbers into alum water and let come to a boil. Drain and wash in hot water. Boil sugar and vinegar with pickling spice tied in a cloth bag. When mixture boils, drop cucumbers in and boil 20 minutes. Pack in hot jars and seal.

Sunrise
November 22, 1999

Aunt Judy took this picture the morning of Mama's death at Ocean Isle Beach. I called her from the hospital in Winston Salem to tell her that Mama was not doing well. Surrounded by her family and an angel that found us at the hospital, Sister Eileen Dennis, Mama peacefully drifted off to sleep.

After my phone call, Judy looked out at the sunrise from her balcony and took pictures. She gave me this picture during Christmas of that year and it brought me such peace. It looks as if the sky opens up and Mama's soul is flying to heaven. If we only take the time to stop and look at our world, I believe that God does talk to us and helps us find inner peace and strength.

Let your gentleness be evident to all.
The Lord is near. Do not be anxious about anything
but in everything, by prayer and petition,
with thanksgiving, present your requests to God.
And the peace of God, which transcends all understanding,
will guard your hearts and your minds in Christ Jesus.

Philippians 4: 5-7

INDEX

C

★Cauliflower★

★Cheese★

Index

★Chicken★ (See Poultry)

★Chili★

★Chocolate★

★Coconut★

★Corn★

Index

Index

★Poultry★

★Preserves★

Q

★Quiche★

R

★Sandwiches★

★Sauces★

★Seafood-Crab★

Index

★ Index

★NeNa's Garden★
Order Forms

Faith Publishing
154 Erwin Road
Hartsville, South Carolina 29550
E-mail: kathy@www.nenasgardencookbook.com

Please send me _____ copies of NeNa's Garden cookbook @ $19.95 each plus
$3.50 per book for shipping and handling. South Carolina residents add 6% sales tax.
Enclosed is a check or money order for _____ made payable to NeNa's Garden
Cookbook.
You may also order from our web page: www.nenasgardencookbook.com

Name _____

Address _____

City _____ State _____ Zip _____

Allow 2-3 weeks for delivery

★★★

★NeNa's Garden★
Order Forms

Faith Publishing
154 Erwin Road
Hartsville, South Carolina 29550
E-mail: kathy@www.nenasgardencookbook.com

Please send me _____ copies of NeNa's Garden cookbook @ $19.95 each plus
$3.50 per book for shipping and handling. South Carolina residents add 6% sales tax.
Enclosed is a check or money order for _____ made payable to NeNa's Garden
Cookbook.
You may also order from our web page: www.nenasgardencookbook.com

Name _____

Address _____

City _____ State _____ Zip _____

Allow 2-3 weeks for delivery

Names and addresses of book stores, gift shops, etc. in your area would be appreciated.

★★★
Names and addresses of book stores, gift shops, etc. in your area would be appreciated.

★NeNa's Garden★
Order Forms

Faith Publishing
154 Erwin Road
Hartsville, South Carolina 29550
E-mail: kathy@www.nenasgardencookbook.com

Please send me _____ copies of NeNa's Garden cookbook @ $19.95 each plus
$3.50 per book for shipping and handling. South Carolina residents add 6% sales tax.
Enclosed is a check or money order for _____ made payable to NeNa's Garden
Cookbook.
You may also order from our web page: www.nenasgardencookbook.com

Name _____

Address _____

City _____ State _____ Zip _____

Allow 2-3 weeks for delivery

★★

★NeNa's Garden★
Order Forms

Faith Publishing
154 Erwin Road
Hartsville, South Carolina 29550
E-mail: kathy@www.nenasgardencookbook.com

Please send me _____ copies of NeNa's Garden cookbook @ $19.95 each plus
$3.50 per book for shipping and handling. South Carolina residents add 6% sales tax.
Enclosed is a check or money order for _____ made payable to NeNa's Garden
Cookbook.
You may also order from our web page: www.nenasgardencookbook.com

Name _____

Address _____

City _____ State _____ Zip _____

Allow 2-3 weeks for delivery

Names and addresses of book stores, gift shops, etc. in your area would be appreciated.

★★★
Names and addresses of book stores, gift shops, etc. in your area would be appreciated.